casebook
of a ufo
investigator

BOOKS BY RAYMOND E. FOWLER

The Andreasson Affair
UFOs: Interplanetary Visitors
Casebook of a UFO Investigator

CASEBOOK OF A UFO INVESTIGATOR

a personal memoir

Raymond E. Fowler

Prentice-Hall, Inc., Englewood Cliffs, New Jersey

This book is dedicated to the late Dr. James E. McDonald: a friend, a dedicated UFO investigator, and a scientist who believed that UFOs are *The Greatest Scientific Problem of Our Times.*

Casebook of a UFO Investigator, by Raymond E. Fowler
Copyright © 1981 by Raymond E. Fowler

Printed in the United States of America
Prentice-Hall International, Inc., London/Prentice-Hall of Australia, Pty. Ltd., Sydney/
Prentice-Hall of Canada, Ltd., Toronto/Prentice-Hall of India Private Ltd., New Delhi/
Prentice-Hall of Japan, Inc., Tokyo/Prentice-Hall of Southeast Asia Pt. Ltd., Singapore/
Whitehall Books Limited, Wellington, New Zealand
10 9 8 7 6 5 4 3 2 1
Library of Congress Cataloging in Publication Data

Fowler, Raymond E   date
    Casebook of a UFO investigator.

    Bibliography: p.
    Includes index.
    1. Unidentified flying objects.   I. Title.
TL789.F637   001.9′42   80-24369
ISBN 0-13-117432-0
ISBN 0-13-117424-X (pbk.)

contents

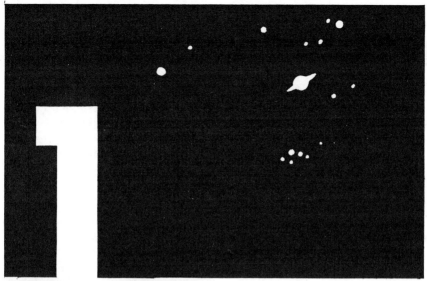

1947 - AND BEFORE

On June 24, 1947, Kenneth Arnold, a Boise businessman and licensed air-rescue pilot, was flying his plane from Chehalis to Yakima, Washington. Startled to see nine flat, shiny objects flying in line near Mount Rainier, he estimated their speed as being over 1,700 mph. They flew with a peculiar up-and-down motion like a saucer skipping over the water, and newspaper reporters covering the story coined the term "flying saucer."

In July of 1947 I was fourteen years of age. Because of my interest in experimental aircraft, I had cut out a number of newspaper clippings about these strange objects. Earlier that month, for example, a local newspaper had sported banner headlines about discs sighted over two adjoining towns.

"FLYING SAUCERS" REPORTED SEEN IN BEVERLY, WENHAM

Two Mysterious Discs, Similar to Sky Objects Which Have Entire Country in State of Wonderment, Sped Thru Evening Sky in Wenham; Single Speeding Disc Was Seen in Broad Daylight at Beverly.[1]

Even though the Army Air Force officially disclaimed the flying objects, my opinion at the time was that people were probably observing tests of secret aircraft. I can remember sorting flying-saucer news clips on the piano bench. Dad came by, glanced over my shoulder, and casually remarked that the discs were spacecraft visiting the earth! I laughed scornfully. Such an idea was incredible in those days.

Years later, when lecture audiences and friends asked, "Have you ever seen a UFO?" I would give a true, yet misleading, answer: "I have never seen a UFO at close range. I have seen several objects which I could not identify. Such objects were only observed a short time, and there were no other supporting witnesses to what I was observing. Therefore, were I to investigate myself, I would conclude that there was insufficient data for evaluation." Nonetheless, it took more than a childhood hobby to cause me to sacrifice a good part of my life to investigating UFO reports. I can no longer hide the fact that there are UFOs in the family closet!

One day in July of 1947, my calloused hands were pressed palm down into the hot, dusty soil. I crawled wearily astride a row of young parsnip seedlings, one of the hundreds of rows in the plowed fields of Wrest Farm in my hometown of Danvers, Massachusetts. Thirst had prodded me ahead of perhaps a dozen fellow workers. A reward for the completion of each row was a drink of the tepid, soiled water from the common jug that served our crew. The sky was blue, with just a few clouds. It was hot and dry, with hardly a breath of wind. Then a movement in the sky caught my attention.

I glanced upward at a strange aerial object that was descending with a slight swaying motion. It looked like a white parachute canopy, but there were no shroud lines or parachutist attached. I had no idea of its real diameter, but its apparent size was about a quarter that of a full moon. Realizing that I was observing something unusual, I jumped to my feet and yelled back to the others. I tried unsuccessfully to point it out as it descended out of sight behind distant trees. My impression was that it must have landed about a mile or so from us.

For the next few days I checked local newspapers to see if anyone else had reported it, but no one had. Had I witnessed one of the strange flying discs being reported by the press? I did not know then that the falling-leaf motion of the descending object would prove to be a common characteristic of what someday would be called UFOs.

In actuality, of course, flying-object reports had already occurred. My mother too had seen something extraordinary in the sky.

In 1917 Bar Harbor, Maine, was a second home for some of the wealthiest people in the United States. Mansions, yachts, and horse-drawn carriages reflected the riches of the Rockefellers, Pulitzers, Astors, Morgans, and McLeans. My grandparents and their neighbors lived apart from such splendor in their simple wood-frame houses. They formed the year-round native constituency.

One cool, crisp autumn evening, my mother and her sister—both in their teens—were returning home with friends from a church club meeting. The group was anxious to get home, so they took a familiar short-cut across a field. Then—it came so fast that no one saw it arrive, it was just *there.* Bright-colored lights flashed down upon them. A huge, ominously silent object was hovering directly over their heads. Hues of reds, blues, greens, and yellows reflected off their frightened faces. "It was overhead," my mother later told me, "stationary . . . I was very excited. . . . One of the girls started crying." Then the terrified girls scattered in all directions for the safety of their homes. "We ran home and told our parents, but were not given any encouragement to talk about it."

A special young man soon came to live at Bar Harbor with a contingent of the United States Navy, and became her husband—my father. He was to report personal psychic experiences during the years that followed: out-of-the-body events, precognitive dreams, and visions of people who had passed on.

On June 14, 1931, my mother was very ill in bed after having given premature birth to a baby girl who died on June 17. On June 18, during the late hours of the night, my mother was awakened out of a sound sleep by a weird vibrating noise resounding all about them. Dad got up and looked for the source of the strange disturbance. It seemed to be coming from out-side, so he went out to investigate; the sound still seemed to be all around him. He could not pinpoint its source before it stopped. Years later, my first UFO investigation would involve witnesses who described the identical sound. They were able to trace its source—a UFO hovering over the power lines behind their home!

During World War II, small silver discs and globes paced Allied and enemy aircraft in broad daylight. Strange, sharply defined balls of light were sighted on nighttime missions. Our pilots nicknamed them foo fighters, an enigmatic term derived from the French word for fire (*feu*) and a statement often made by Smoky Stover, the comic-strip fireman: "Where there's foo, there's fire!"

Toward the war's end, my mother observed a flying disc-shaped object: "In approximately 1945–6, I was riding a bicycle on Route 128 in Danvers. An oval gray object came out of a cloud and then entered it again in a matter of seconds."

In 1946 over two thousand reports of cigar- and disc-shaped objects alarmed many witnesses in Norway, Sweden, and Denmark. These unknown objects were christened "ghost rockets." But the general American populace was completely unaware of these earlier UFO-report waves until worldwide media publication of Kenneth Arnold's experience.

The initial sightings, concentrated over Scandinavian countries, indicated that objects were Russian in origin. Army Air Force Intelligence teams were dispatched all over the United States to investigate sightings of similar objects in this country. Responsibility for this task fell upon the Air Material Command (AMC) at Wright-Patterson Air Force Base near Dayton, Ohio. General Doolittle headed an investigation team sent to Sweden, Norway, and Denmark. The government of Greece commissioned its most distinguished scientist, Dr. Paul Santorini, to investigate the flying objects.

Santorini was to Greece as Einstein was to the United States, yet most ufologists are completely unaware of his qualifications. He wrote me that the Greek army had supplied him with a team of engineers to ascertain whether the objects flying over Greece were Russian missiles.

We soon established that they were not missiles. But before we could do any more, the Army, after conferring with foreign officials, ordered the investigation stopped. Foreign scientists flew to Greece for secret talks with me.[2]

This indicates that selected foreign scientists and officials were thoroughly conversant with the UFO problem as early as 1947. Twenty years later, Santorini stated quite unequivocally that there is a "world blanket of secrecy" concerning UFO activity because authorities were unwilling to admit a force against which earth had "no possibility of defense." He added that his studies indicated that for the time being, aliens were probably "visiting earth to collect plant and animal specimens," but that their future purposes—if any—are entirely unknown to us."[3]

Documents now declassified by the Freedom of Information Act indicate our own government's early conclusions. By the fall of 1947, AMC analysts relayed the results of their investigation to the commanding general of the Army Air Force:

The phenomenon reported is something real and not visionary or fictitious. . . . The description is [of objects that are] metallic . . . circular or elliptical in shape, flat on bottom and domed on top.[4]

On December 30, 1947, the general initiated a *secret* UFO project dubbed Project Sign, with a 2A security classification. The Air Force now had become a separate service branch; the project came under the jurisdiction of the new Air Technical Intelligence Center (ATIC). By August of 1948, ATIC prepared a top secret estimate of the situation, which—according to the former chief of the Air Force UFO project, Edward J. Ruppelt—concluded that the objects were interplanetary.[5] This startling report proceeded up the chain of command to Air Force Chief of Staff General Hoyt S. Vandenberg, who allegedly rejected it for lack of proof and ordered it declassified and burned. Then on December 27, 1948, the Air Force announced to a most curious public (and a most dejected group at ATIC) that UFOs did not exist. Project Sign was to be terminated!

The Air Force has discontinued its special project of investigation and evaluating reported flying saucers. The reports are the result of misinterpretation of various conventional objects, a mild form of mass hysteria, and hoaxes. Continuance of the project is unwarranted.[6]

A far cry from the report sent to General Vandenberg! Neither the public nor the lower military echelon was aware of ATIC's real conclusions, of course. And the Air Force hadn't really closed its UFO project, which continued secretly as Project Grudge, a new code name that probably reflected the Air Force's conflicting opinions concerning UFOs. Other strange things happened: Air Force officials rejected Project Sign's recommendations to greatly strengthen UFO investigation teams. Those who had concluded that UFOs were interplanetary were dropped from the staff of the new Project Grudge; its members were told to treat UFO reports as misidentifications, hoaxes, or hallucinations.

My own opinion is that Project Sign had really discovered something of vast implications that had to be squelched—both within the lower military and government echelons and the civilian populace. Under the cover of Project Grudge, I believe, the real investigation had been secretly shifted to a select intelligence-gathering group.

Responsible people, including trained airline pilots, continued to report strange flying objects while the Air Force continued to explain them away. Tension and curiosity grew. Then came the publication of a well-documented article by retired USMC Major Donald E. Keyhoe in the December 1949 issue of *True* magazine.

A graduate of the U. S. Naval Academy, Major Keyhoe served as a Marine Corps pilot until he was injured in a night crash at Guam. Afterward, he became chief of information, Civil Aeronautics, Department of Commerce, and was assigned as manager of the North Pole Plane U. S. tour with Floyd Bennett, Admiral Byrd's copilot; he was later assigned as aide to Colonel Lindbergh on his nationwide flying tour. Keyhoe later became a freelance writer and lecturer, author of *Flying With Lindbergh, M-Day,* and a number of articles for leading magazines. During World War II he returned to active service and served as an executive officer of a Naval Aviation Training Section. In late 1949 *True* commissioned him to write a documented article on the mysterious flying saucers. He began as a skeptic, but as he documented report after report by highly trained observers, became convinced that the objects were real. UFO historian Dr. David Michael Jacobs states that "the January 1950 issue of *True* was the most widely sold and read in the magazine's history."[7] (Later, USAF UFO Project Chief Edward J. Ruppelt would also admit that it was probably one of the most widely read and discussed magazine articles in history.)[8]

No other person has so influenced public opinion on UFOs. Major Keyhoe presented a logical case for the interplanetary origin of UFOs, and hinted that our government was hiding information from the public. This article, although lacking proof, was convincing. Major Keyhoe suddenly found himself the leading civilian UFO expert in the United States.

An Annapolis graduate, Keyhoe had many military contacts, and his recognition as a UFO spokesman prompted them to leak UFO-related data to him. In fact, soon after, *True* published a follow-up article by Navy Commander R. B. McLaughlin, the head of a team of missile experts who had seen, tracked, and photographed UFOs from the secret White Sands, New Mexico, installation. One oval object was tracked at an altitude of 56 miles, moving at the incredible speed of 25,000 mph. McLaughlin went on record with Keyhoe that the flying discs were "spaceships from another planet."[9]

For his efforts, the good commander was shipped out to sea, but the Air Force's attempts to play down such revelations were futile. Keyhoe soon expanded his thesis into a best-selling book, *The Flying Saucers Are Real*. This blockbuster presented documented evidence that, contrary to official statements, the Air Force was convinced that the unknown objects were physically real. *The Flying Saucers Are Real* revolutionized my thinking about the origin of the mysterious flying objects and the government's handling of the whole issue.

A four-year hitch with the Air Force further confirmed my suspicions that UFOs were serious business for the military. In a transient barracks at Lockborne AFB in Columbus, a reliable photo technician told me that he had seen classified gun-camera photographs of UFOs made by pilots sent to intercept them. I was then transferred to Keesler AFB in Biloxi, Mississippi. After completing ground and airborne radio-operator training, I was assigned to another school for training in electronic espionage. Eventually I served overseas as a member of the top secret USAF Security Service. Our group carried out covert radio intercept and other specialized spying operations for the National Security Agency. One of our squadron's charters was to teletype encrypted top secret data between the United States and its foreign operations. UFO information fell into this category. This further reinforced my belief that our government was treating UFOs as a threat to national security.

In 1953, while viewing the coronation of Queen Elizabeth II, I met a very special English girl named Margaret. We were married in June 1955, and I returned to America in December. Margaret followed in February. In 1956 I enrolled at Gordon College in Wenham, and after graduation, spent one semester at a seminary before leaving and joining the ranks of GTE Sylvania. Over were the days of exams and the struggle to make ends meet. With more free time on my hands, I decided to become an associate member of the National Investigations Committee on Aerial Phenomena (NICAP) directed by my boyhood hero, Major Donald Keyhoe.

On July 20, 1956, a number of private citizens had met to discuss plans to organize a civilian UFO study group. On October 24, 1956, Thomas Townsend Brown, a researcher into electric space propulsion, became its first short-lived director. He resigned in January of 1957 and Major Keyhoe assumed NICAP's directorship.

With Keyhoe's help, this small group added to NICAP's board of governors some very prominent men: retired Rear Admiral Delmar S.

Fahrney, former head of the Navy's guided missile program, and Vice-Admiral R. H. Hillenkoetter, first director of the CIA. Admiral Fahrney held a press conference to state that neither Russia nor the United States was responsible for the strange devices. He stated that they flew in a manner indicating intelligent control because of "the way they change position in formations and override each other."[10] Admiral Hillenkoetter echoes Fahrney's position: "I know that neither Russia nor this country has anything approaching such speed and maneuvers. . . . High-ranking officers are . . . concerned . . . but through official secrecy and ridicule, citizens are led to believe the unknown flying objects are nonsense."[11] The Pentagon was jolted when the Associated Press carried these statements nationwide. Dr. Jacobs notes that: "The Air Force looked upon the establishment of NICAP with Keyhoe at its head as an ominous development. The influential people on the board of governors did nothing to ease the Air Force's anxiety. It was distressed especially over Keyhoe's efforts to obtain congressional hearings."[12] Air Force Intelligence immediately ordered a study of NICAP. Its investigative report stated that "Captain Ruppelt . . . is now affiliated with NICAP," and concluded that Ruppelt and Keyhoe "represent a formidable team from which plenty of trouble can be expected."[13]

Courageous Edward J. Ruppelt helped produce serious inquiries into the Air Force's handling of UFO information. After his discharge from the Air Force, Ruppelt wrote *The Report on Unidentified Flying Objects,* now considered one of the classics of UFO research. In its foreword he wrote:

This . . . is the first time that anyone, either military or civilian, has brought together in one document all the facts about this fascinating subject. With the exception of the style, this report is written exactly the way I would have written it had I been officially asked to do so while I was chief of the Air Force's project for investigating UFO reports—Project Bluebook.

Edward Ruppelt was part of a group within the Air Force who believed that the public should be privy to factual data on UFOs. He wrote Major Keyhoe that "I wouldn't do a book unless I told the truth exactly as it happened, and believe me, this would not follow the Air Force party line."[14]

In his book he recounted the inner workings of the Air Force's misleading public-information program. He described fascinating official Air Force UFO encounters, including radar-visual cases, and even one incident in which an Air Force interceptor fired upon a fleeing UFO! Ruppelt proceeded to appear with Major Keyhoe on national television. He also agreed to serve on NICAP's board of governors in the continuing fight against official secrecy on UFOs.

Then rumors began circulating that the Air Force was pressuring Ruppelt through his new civilian employer, a top aerospace firm. Ruppelt denied this, but just when progress was in the offing for congressional UFO hearings, Ruppelt reversed his agreement to join the NICAP board.[15] Later, new rumors surfaced that Ruppelt, under tremendous pressure, would revise the ending of his 1956 book, *The Report on Unidentified Flying Objects*. The rumors proved true, and the revised book was published in 1959. I personally found it difficult to believe that the same man had written the three new chapters. To put it in the words of national news commentator Frank Edwards, "It's absolutely incredible. Now he sneers at people he formerly labeled expert witnesses. He plays up the wildest contact stories— completely backs the Air Force line . . . and he takes sarcastic cracks at serious investigators, especially NICAP."[16]

In the fall of 1959, shortly after the revised book was published, Ruppelt died of a heart attack. Keyhoe voiced what many others were thinking:

Adding three chapters at the end, Ruppelt reversed all he had disclosed, rejecting all his strong evidence and ridiculing expert witnesses—some of whom had become personal friends. Now, he said, he knew that the UFO sightings were only illusions, mistakes and hoaxes— the standard AF line.

I knew Ed Ruppelt well. He was also a sensitive man, and when the revised book appeared there were sharp attacks on his integrity, some even by former friends who should have guessed the truth. Like several others, I have always believed that the enforced retraction and bitter criticism were partly the cause of his premature death from a heart attack.[17]

NICAP several times came very close to obtaining *open* congressional hearings on Air Force handling of the UFO problem, but was blocked each time by Air Force pressure. Many sympathetic congressmen such as William H. Ayres (R., Ohio) responded that:

Congressional investigations have been held, and are still being held on the problem of unidentified flying objects. . . . Since most of the material is classified, the hearings are never printed. When conclusions are reached, they will be released if possible.[18]

Most, however, were at a loss to implement open hearings because UFO information was being withheld from most congressmen. For example, Joseph E. Karth (D., Minn.) stated that:

As a member of the House Committee on Science and Astronautics, I, of course, have had contact with high Air Force officers and have had opportunity to hear their comments on and off the record on the subject of unidentified flying objects. Despite being confronted with seemingly unimpeachable evidence that such phenomena exist, these officers give little credence to the many reports on the matter. When pressed on specific details, the experts refuse to answer on grounds that *they are involved in the nation's security and cannot be discussed publicly* [italics mine]. . . . I will continue to seek a definite answer to this most important question.[19]

NICAP's weapon against such secrecy was a bimonthly UFO report bulletin, *The UFO Investigator,* to keep members abreast of UFO sightings in America and abroad. Keyhoe's friends within governmental and military circles kept him informed about top UFO reports and Air Force cover-up incidents. NICAP duly printed up such information and fed it to subscribers, the news media, and Congress.

The battle lines were drawn between civilian researchers and the Air Force.

CHAPTER NOTES

1. "Headlines," *Salem Evening News,* Salem, MA, July 7, 1947.
2. Personal correspondence dated August 6, 1973.
3. *Ibid.*
4. E. U. Condon, director, *Scientific Study of Unidentified Flying Objects* (New York: E.P. Dutton & Co., Inc., 1969), p. 894.
5. E. J. Ruppelt, *The Report on Unidentified Flying Objects* (New York: Doubleday & Co., Inc., 1956), p. 41.
6. Personal files (Official USAF Release).
7. D. M. Jacobs, *The UFO Controversy* (Indiana: Indiana University Press, 1975), p. 57.
8. Ruppelt, *op. cit.,* p. 64.
9. R. B. McLaughlin, "How Scientists Traced a Flying Saucer," *True* (March 1950), p. 28.
10. NICAP files.
11. *Ibid.*
12. Jacobs, op. cit., p. 149.
13. Colonel L. T. Glaser, Memorandum of Commander, ATIC, "UFO Program," 17 December 1958 (MAFB) and Major Dougher, Draft . . . to all Major Commands, 16 December 1958 (MAFB).
14. NICAP files.
15. Donald E. Keyhoe, *Flying Saucers: Top Secret* (New York: G. P. Putnam's Sons, 1960), p. 97.
16. *Ibid,* p. 260.
17. Donald E. Keyhoe, *Aliens from Space* (New York: Doubleday & Co., Inc., 1973), pp. 90, 91.
18. NICAP files.
19. *Ibid.*

CONTACTEES AND CRITICS

In 1950, Frank Scully, a columnist for *Variety* magazine, published *Behind the Flying Saucers,* based upon a lecture Scully had heard by Silas Newton, a self-proclaimed millionaire and Texas oil man who stated that a personal scientist friend of his had been involved with an Air Force investigation of three crashed UFOs. He claimed that the government had retrieved sixteen, four-feet-tall dead occupants from the crashed spacecraft.

Scully's sensational book was probably the catalyst for yet another group that claimed to have been contacted by UFO occupants and taken aboard the flying saucers. Some typical examples:

George W. Van Tassal, one of the earliest contactees, was an aircraft mechanic and flight test engineer. At age forty-two he published a book with the misleading title of *I Rode in a Flying Saucer.*[1] The book makes no mention of such a ride. Instead, it recounts personal telepathic messages, received in trance and through automatic writing, warning earth scientists against exploding atomic bombs.

Orfeo Angelucci, also an aircraft plant technician and an amateur scientific experimenter, had been in poor health from childhood. His book claimed that extraterrestrial beings had chosen him for the first earth contact because of his "higher vibrational perception."[2] A voice began to communicate religious messages to Angelucci, saying that life on earth was endangered and that the spacemen had come to help mankind. Later, Angelucci claimed that on July 23, 1952, he was actually taken aboard a spaceship and transported to another world, where he was given a new healthy body. There he met beautiful space people, including Jesus Christ Himself, who instructed him to preach the Gospel because His second coming was very near.

These contactees appeared during a major wave of UFO sightings. During these summer months of 1952, newspaper stories about UFOs were at an all-time peak. Former Air Force UFO Project Chief E. J. Ruppelt commented later that during this period, the Air Force was receiving up to twenty reports per day from all over the world. But during the same period, the United States and Russia were deeply involved in the cold war, and this era's tensions and fears were obviously reflected in the new contactee movement. The aliens' general message to these selected earthmen was antiwar in nature—in effect, a warning to do away with atomic weapons and adopt a peaceful philosophy. Obviously, this huge surge of UFO reports also provided a context for the contactees to work out their psychological problems.

Not all contactees brought warnings and messages of salvation. Daniel Fry became an orphan at age nine and was raised by his maternal grandmother. At age eighteen he was forced to strike out on his own. Most of his advanced education was self-taught. During 1949 and 1950 Fry was employed as a rocket-motor technician for Aerojet General Corporation at White Sands, New Mexico. On July 4, 1950, Fry claims, a UFO picked him up while he was walking in the desert and flew him to New York City and back. A voice told him that he was chosen because of his open mind concerning scientific concepts and revealed that the space visitors hoped to be of some assistance to our scientific progress. Fry published two science-fictionish books, the first concerning his original experience,[3] the second containing purported scientific information allegedly given him by the spacemen.[4]

Still another type of message was received by Truman Bethurum, who claimed to have gone for a flying saucer ride just four days after Orfeo Angelucci's reported trip! Truman, the son of divorced parents, was moved from home to home and from school to school. During World War II, he acquired on-the-job training in equipment repair and maintenance. At age fifty-six, Truman published *Aboard a Flying Saucer.*[5] In it, he relates his twelve contacts with Aura Rhanes, the female captain of an all-male crew. The UFO, which he nicknamed the "admiral's scow," supposedly landed in the Nevada desert. Speaking to Truman in rhymes, the beautiful alien captain told him that their race lived on a planet on the other side of the moon! Her race was visiting earth for education, relaxation, and replenishment of needed supplies.

Bethurum's book mentions being visited by a Professor Adamski. Significantly, Adamski tape-recorded Bethurum's account and showed great interest in his claims. A Polish immigrant with little formal education, George Adamski had been a teacher of Eastern religion and metaphysics in the 1930s. When UFOs became top news in 1952, Adamski generated more influence upon the contactee movement than any other person. It is obvious that Adamski, in turn, was greatly influenced by contactees such as Truman Bethurum.

At age sixty-one he claimed that on November 20, 1952, he had communicated with a Venusian on the California desert near Parker, Arizona. No stranger to the bizarre, Adamski had simply reexpressed his previous philosophical beliefs within the context of the new phenomenon. His lectures, claims of UFO sightings, dubious photographs, and alleged governmental requests for his help in UFO investigation all received wide coverage in the early 1950s. With the help of ghostwriters, Adamski published two major books chronicling his adventures with the space people and soon became a celebrity. His story was in contant demand on radio and TV talk shows. Adamski traveled all over the world telling audiences (including royalty!) about his contacts with extraterrestrials. A foundation was organized to sell literature containing the metaphysical teachings the spacemen had given Adamski for mankind.

It's a remarkable coincidence that these space people adhered to the same metaphysical beliefs that Adamski had been teaching for twenty-five years prior to their visit! But he secured a large following from the occult community. Others emulated him, and the contactee cults began to bloom.

It soon became obvious that the first contactee reports were not able to stand up to the rigors of serious investigation. Serious UFO researchers denounced the entire contactee movement, and the CIA could not have done a better job in poisoning the UFO well. Adamski and his cohorts caused the whole subject of UFOs to become the butt of jokes and ridicule. If there were any real contacts during this period, such nonsense drowned out their voices.

Richard Hall, a veteran UFO researcher and former assistant director of NICAP, has written a character profile of many of these early contactees. Hall served in the Air Force during the Korean conflict. He received his degree in philosophy with a minor in mathematics from Tulane University, where he published an excellent UFO newsletter entitled *Satellite*. Further course work in logic and the scientific method was directly applicable to his studies of UFO evidence and related problems. His outstanding contribution was editing a 200,000-word NICAP report entitled *The UFO Evidence*.

In his fine analysis of the general personality of the typical contactee, Hall states (somewhat tongue in cheek) that:

We obtain this general picture of the type of earthman sought out for the urgent mission of setting the world straight: a technician-tinkerer, typically male, 40 to 60 years old, from a troubled or disrupted childhood, poorly educated and needing a ghost writer for his book. The typical early contactee claimed he was chosen for contact because of some special quality he possessed.[6]

Hall makes other pertinent observations regarding this strange movement.

Since the claims of the early contactees preceded the United States and Soviet space programs, assertions made about space [by contactees] could not be checked at the time. Nor could predictions about coming events. Now many of them can be checked, and we find the supposedly higher intelligences stuck with *inoperative* statements.

The spacemen told *Van Tassal* that explosion of the hydrogen bomb would "extinguish life on the planet," that they were going to eliminate such projects, and that we were about to see atomic weapons used in warfare again.

Angelucci was told that atomic warfare with Russia was imminent, that the spacemen were helping medical research and that we would see "success in the fight against cancer," and that Christ would appear "soon."

Fry described heavy strain on his internal organs *during* weightlessness while landing. This was totally out of accord with the astronauts' experiences.

Bethurum was told that the planet Clarion was on the other side of the moon, invisible from earth (and, apparently, also invisible to our astronauts). He and *Adamski* were told that human forms were common to all the planets and Adamski "saw" elaborate life on the moon.[7]

Hall also discusses the possible motivations and effects of this fascinating group of people.

The early contactees came across as would-be social reformers, using spaceman parables to provide *solutions* for the earth's problems. They are reacting to real fears and concerns of the 1950's, including the potential for a devastating war inherent in the ideological Cold War. The threat of atomic destruction (thesis) and the penetration into our consciousness of the possibility of extraterrestrial visitors (antithesis) were two powerful ideas first unleashed in the 1950's. The solution (synthesis) offered by the contactees is that Space Brothers with their superior wisdom will, by example and guidance, save us from ourselves.

Just as dramatists, painters and other creative artists interpret and symbolize life and death themes of human experience, the contactees could be understood as crude *artists* trying to be creative, but severely limited by their lack of education and sophistication. Whatever good intentions may have been present, the net effect of their *artistry* has been to mislead people and to confuse serious issues.[8]

Some contactees deliberately misled people, and responsible UFO organizations sought to expose such frauds. Hall gives an example:

Reinhold Schmidt claimed to have met a *saucer* crew at Kearney, Nebraska. Later . . . he was convicted of tricking a widow out of thousands of dollars by claiming he had some miraculous crystals from Saturn, which would heal crippled children.[9]

Amazingly enough, the court called upon Carl Sagan to testify that Saturn could not possibly support the humanlike, air-breathing beings that Schmidt described! Sagan gives a very amusing yet pathetic account of the trial in his book *Intelligent Life in the Universe,* substituting Schmidt's name with the pseudonym of Helmut Winckler.[10]

But the contactee movement had a devastating effect on serious civilian UFO research. UFO historian Dr. Jacobs writes that:

The Air Force's increased secrecy coupled with contactee publicity fed the UFO controversy. The public was confused. On the one hand, it heard about the alleged Air Force cover-up . . . read about UFO sightings in the press and either heard about or read Keyhoe's books. In the resulting confusion it tended to equate Keyhoe with the contactees, which hindered Keyhoe's determined fight to bring respectability to a systematic study of the UFO phenomenon.[11]

Dr. Jacobs remarked that the contactees had given the Air Force "unexpected help in its public relations efforts."[12] Some think that some of this was planned; perhaps the government instigated the contactee movement! Dr. Jacques Vallee recently disclosed some thought-provoking news that George "Adamski's major supporter abroad was Major Ian Norrie, a former intelligence officer with the British Army."[13] Vallee also noted that Adamski traveled "with a passport bearing special privileges" and speculates that contactees like Adamski "could have been set up" by intelligence agencies to "propagate alleged extraterrestrial messages in many countries."

The huge flurry of UFO sightings in 1952 became the focal point of newspaper and magazine coverage all over the nation. "Have We Visitors From Space?," by Robert Ginna and H. B. Darrach, appeared in the April 7, 1952, issue of *Life.* Curiously, Air Force officers working in Project Bluebook wholeheartedly cooperated with its publication. Key UFO reports were declassified especially for *Life's* use! The writers also obtained weighty statements from well-known experts. Stated former German rocket research director Dr. Walter Reidel, "I am completely convinced that they have an out-of-world basis." Dr. Maurice A. Biot, a renowned expert in aerodymanics and physics, gave his opinion that "They have an extraterrestrial origin." *Life* concluded that the UFOs "cannot be explained by present science as natural phenomena—but solely as artificial devices created and operated by a high intelligence." As well-witnessed UFO sightings continued, letters and inquiries poured into *Life* and Project Bluebook.

The Air Force did not downgrade the story as in the past, but instead issued a press release stating that "The article is factual, but *Life's* conclusions are their own." Much of this reversal in Bluebook's policy was due to an influential group within the Air Force that felt strongly that the public should know more about the UFO problem.

During the summer months of 1952, the UFO wave rose to record-breaking proportions. For several nights, UFOs appeared and were tracked by radar over Washington, D.C.'s restricted air space. Every time armed fighters attempted to intercept the objects, they streaked out of sight at phenomenal speeds. One radar operator on duty during this period confided to me that at times the objects would drop down to low altitudes, out of the path of the fighter planes.

President Truman was kept fully abreast of the situation. Then on July 29, 1952, in direct response to what Air Force Chief of Staff General Vandenberg termed "mass hysteria," [14] the Air Force held the longest and largest press conference since World War II, headed by Major General John A. Samford, director of Air Force Intelligence. Admitting that the Air Force was investigating reports of unknown objects made by "credible observers of relatively incredible things" and that 20 percent of the total reports were really of unknown objects, the general stressed that none of the objects seemed to present a threat to national security—but he offered no explanation as to what they were.

This pivotal year of 1952 made two prominent astronomers into public figures because of their opposite views in the raging UFO controversy. Dr. Donald E. Menzel, director of Harvard Observatory, vehemently downgraded all UFO sightings to mirages, reflections, refractions, and temperature inversions. Dr. J. Allen Hynek, on the other hand, advised the Air Force UFO project that Menzel's theories were worthless. Hynek had been the Air Force's chief astronomical consultant since 1948. The 1952 UFO sightings had revised his thinking, and he presented his thoughts in a paper to the Optical Society of America in 1952, later published in its monthly *Journal* dated April 1953. He pointed out that as a scientist, he had found some truly puzzling and unexplained UFO cases.

Menzel continued as the chief scientist-debunker of UFOs until his death on December 14, 1976. Hynek continues to be the principal scientist-spokesman for the view that UFOs deserve scientific investigation. His credentials have grown steadily over the years. As an astronomer, he served as associate director of the Smithsonian Astrophysical Observatory and headed its NASA-sponsored satellite-tracking program. Later he became chairman of the Astronomy Department at Northwestern University, and directed the Lindheimer Astronomical Research Center. Now retired from Northwestern University, he is devoting practically all his time to UFO research, directing the Center for UFO Studies at Evanston, Illinois, and lecturing all over the world. In addition to authoring books and articles in the field of astronomy, he has written several books on the subject of UFOs, including *The UFO Experience, The Hynek UFO Report,* and *The Edge of Reality,* coauthored with Dr. Jacques Vallee.

The year 1952 also produced the first civilian UFO study groups. The Civilian Saucer Investigation at Los Angeles was organized by Edward

Sullivan, an employee of North American Aviation. Members included a number of scientists, including Dr. Walter Reidel, former chief designer and research director of Germany's rocket and missile program during World War II. The International Flying Saucer Bureau (IFSB) was founded by Albert K. Bender at Bridgeport, Connecticut. Both groups are now defunct. The Aerial Phenomena Research Group (APRO), also founded in 1952 by Mrs. Coral Lorenzen, is currently directed by Coral's husband, Jim, and has grown into one of the most respected groups of its kind in the world.[15] Its fine publication, *The APRO Bulletin*, is available to anyone by paid subscription. The year 1954 saw the birth of a well-read UFO newsletter edited by Leonard Stringfield, director of a data-collecting center called CRIFO (Civilian Research Interplanetary Flying Objects). CRIFO is now defunct, but Stringfield is still a key figure in civilian UFO research.

In early 1953 the CIA mistook the public's extreme curiosity for panic and felt forced to publicly debunk UFOs via the infamous Robertson Panel. Dr. H. P. Robertson was a brilliant scientist who had taught mathematics, cosmology, and relativity at Princeton and the California Institute of Technology. In 1953 he was director of the Weapons System Evaluation for the Defense Department, and a secret CIA employee. He was assigned to chair a panel of distinguished scientists convened by the CIA in response to the incredible UFO events of 1952.

The panel's purported charter was to examine the Air Force's best UFO cases and render their educated opinions on one of three verdicts: (1) All UFO reports are explainable as known objects or natural phenomena; therefore the investigation should be permanently discontinued. (2) The UFO reports do not contain enough data upon which to base a final conclusion. Project Bluebook should be continued in hopes of obtaining better data. (3) The UFOs are interplanetary spacecraft. However, the panel's real purpose and final recommendations were obscured by conflicting statements. In 1956, former Bluebook Chief Edward J. Ruppelt wrote that the CIA told him the panel had recommended the second alternative:

The panel didn't recommend that the activities be cut back, and they didn't recommend that it be dropped. They recommended that it be expanded. Too many of the reports had been made by credible witnesses . . . who should know what they're looking at. . . . The investigative force of Project Bluebook should be quadrupled in size. . . . Every effort should be made to set up instruments in locations where UFO sightings are frequent . . . and they said the American public should be told every detail of every phase of the UFO investigation.[16]

But the actual contents of the Robertson Panel's report remained classified—thus unknown to most people—for thirteen more years. Then, in the summer of 1966, *Saturday Review* science editor John Lear persuaded the

Air Force to prepare him an edited copy of this report. Significantly, it did not contain the words on the intent that Ruppelt had revealed back in 1956. Dr. Jacobs rightly comments, "If Ruppelt understood and reported correctly, it remains a mystery why the CIA gave out this false information."[17]

I believe that the Robertson Panel was in no way conducting a legitimate scientific evaluation. Some members joked openly about the subject at the meeting and had to be reprimanded by Dr. Robertson himself. As far as is known, none of the high-ranking scientists had any prior knowledge of the UFO problem. I feel this CIA-convened panel was a deliberate cover organized specifically to smooth the government's major change in policy on UFOs without the cognizance of lower-echelon authorities.

This was the beginning of a double standard regarding UFOs within the military itself. A reliable confidential source told me that concurrent with the meeting of the Robertson Panel, another agency was about to take over the real UFO study from Project Bluebook. My source would not reveal this agency's name, but the CIA was certainly involved—they had convened the panel!

Soon after the Robertson Panel's deliberation, Ruppelt and others who had fought so hard for scientific recognition of UFOs were terminated from Project Bluebook. From then until Bluebook's demise on December 17, 1969, it became principally a public-relations group. The real UFO investigation presumably worked undercover, undisturbed by the public, Congress, or lower-echelon military personnel.

In the meantime, Bluebook proceeded to debunk the whole UFO subject with a zest outstripping its predecessors! Why? One clue lay in the part of the Robertson Panel's report that the CIA censored before giving the Air Force a sanitized copy for John Lear of *Saturday Review*. Dr. James E. McDonald—yet another highly significant figure in UFO history—accidentally saw the complete, unabridged report.

Born in Duluth, Minnesota, in 1920, Jim McDonald received his B.A. in chemistry at the University of Omaha in 1942, M.S. in meteorology at the Massachusetts Institute of Technology in 1945, and his Ph.D. in physics at Iowa State University in 1951. During World War II, from 1942–45, Jim served in Naval Intelligence. From 1950–53, he was assistant professor of physics at Iowa State University; in 1953–54 he became a research physicist with the Cloud Physics Project at the University of Chicago. In 1954 he joined the staff of the University of Arizona, where he served as professor of meteorology and senior physicist at the Institute of Atmospheric Physics.

A respected scientist, McDonald held membership in the American Meteorological Society, American Geophysical Union, Royal Meteorological Society, and the American Association for the Advancement of Science. He served on the National Science Foundation's Advisory Panel on Weather Modification; the Advisory Panel for the U. S. Navy's Hurricane

Modification Project STORMFURY; the National Academy of Science's Panel on Weather and Climate Modification; and the American Meteorological Society's Publications Commission. I enjoyed working with him personally on a number of UFO investigations until his bizarre, untimely death in 1971.

Jim had financed his own personal UFO investigation program, interviewing hundreds of witnesses. While researching the unclassified files at Project Bluebook in the spring of 1967, he came across an uncensored copy of the Robertson Panel report that had accidentally been declassified. He took copious notes and was dumbfounded to read some of the panel's recommendations that had been edited out of the copy given John Lear. One that especially troubled him advised the government to launch a detailed program of public "training and debunking."[18]

The CIA-sponsored panel suggested that the government employ psychologists, Walt Disney Productions, and well-known personalities such as Arthur Godfrey to aid in a massive UFO-debunking campaign, stressing that such a program would decrease or eliminate civilian UFO reports. During UFO waves, large quantities of civilian reports completely disrupted military communications channels and prevented the orderly functions of the Air Force. I might add that most civilian reports contained little information the Air Force did not already know. What was needed was study of reports by controlled, trained observers, of which the military offered plenty. Thus, for the lower echelon of the military who would read this report, the cover story—the rationale for Project Bluebook—was that UFO reports by civilians, not UFOs themselves, represented a threat to national security!

Infuriated, McDonald reported his troubling find to the University of Arizona's Department of Meteorology, and the news services carried his accusation across the nation.

UFO'S AND THE CIA

A charge ... that the Central Intelligence Agency in 1953 requested the Air Force to adopt a policy of systematic "debunking of flying saucers" ... is made by Dr. James E. McDonald, professor of meteorology and senior physicist at the Institute of Atmospheric Physics. ... Dr. McDonald, who believes that the "least unsatisfactory hypothesis" about the origin of UFO's is that they are extraterrestrial probes, said his information on the CIA role comes from closed-door testimony from CIA officials before the Robertson Panel probing UFO reports. ... The CIA request that UFO's be debunked was followed, Dr. McDonald said, by promulgation of Air Force Regulation 200-2 which sharply reduced the number of UFO reports by forbidding release by air bases of any information on UFO sightings. All sightings were to be funneled through Project Bluebook where, according to Dr. McDonald, "they have been largely categorized as conventional objects with little attention to scientific considerations."

The strictures on UFO information were further tightened by a regulation which made any release of information on UFO sightings by any of the military services or, in some cases, commercial airlines, a crime punishable with fines up to $10,000 and imprisonment up to 10 years.[19]

Coincidentally, on the same day the McDonald story broke, the Air Force issued its own press release announcing the establishment of yet another *independent* panel (sponsored by the Air Force!) to study UFOs. (Years later, documents released through the Freedom of Information Act would reveal CIA involvement with this panel as well. Headed by prestigious scientist Dr. Edward U. Condon, the panel became known as the Condon committee. History was to repeat itself, except that this time the Air Force would be let off the hook.)

Jim McDonald severely criticized the Air Force's UFO program, attacked the CIA for the debunking policy set in motion by the Robertson Panel, and flew all over the nation lecturing to prestigious scientific and journalistic groups. Documents released through the FOIA reveal that the Air Force was extremely upset by McDonald's documented views and close contacts with the civilian scientific community. Dr. Jacobs writes that:

The Air Force feared McDonald. It saw him as a major threat to its public relations effort. When the American Society of Newspaper Editors asked the Air Force to allow Quintanilla [Bluebook director] to join McDonald and others in a symposium on UFOs, the Air Force Office of Information (SAFOI) thought long and hard about subjecting Quintanilla to McDonald's attacks. SAFOI decided to let Quintanilla appear, but he would have to be "brainwashed thoroughly" beforehand.[20]

A released telephone transcript between concerned Air Force officials made this quite clear:

Two Colonels with 30 years' experience in the information business will be holding his hands. They will work him (Quintanilla) over—ask him every leading dirty question he might get. He will be ready for them.[21]

The Air Force wanted to "fireproof" McDonald, and found an ally against him in the person of Phillip Klass, an avionics editor for *Aviation Weekly* who had rapidly taken over Dr. Menzel's position as chief anti-UFO spokesman because of Menzel's poor health. His first book, *UFOs-Identified,* attempted (unsuccessfully) to explain UFOs as floating plasmas—a type of coronal discharge energized by lightning or induced by power lines.

Interestingly enough, even scientists working on the Condon Committee confided to me that they privately referred to Klass's ideas as "Klass dismissed"! McDonald's field was atmospheric physics, and he proceeded to demonstrate the scientific implausibility of Klass's theories. (An excellent detailed critique is found in the minutes of McDonald's address to the Canadian Aeronautics and Astronautics Space Institute Symposium on March 12, 1968, Montreal, Canada.)

In retaliation, Klass unleashed a frenzy of verbal and written attacks upon McDonald's statements. According to McDonald, Klass falsely told columnist Jack Anderson that Jim had illegitimately used funds from a U. S. Navy grant to study UFOs in Australia. A painful scandal ensued. Even though Navy auditors later found Jim innocent, the incident resulted in strained relations with his employer, the University of Arizona.

Dr. McDonald also chided Dr. Hynek for sitting on scientifically interesting Air Force UFO information for years without informing the civilian scientific community of its potential importance. He honestly believed that Hynek had been scientifically dishonest, and no better than Dr. Menzel in this respect. Hynek tried to overlook this scathing indictment, and later joined forces with Jim after his termination by Project Bluebook. In the meantime, Klass continued his attacks upon them both.

In 1971, as a member of the National Academy of Science's panel on weather, McDonald was called to testify about the supersonic transport (SST) to the House Committee on Appropriations. He had spent months of study culminating in a report that demonstrated that the SST would reduce the protective layer of ozone in the atmosphere, but his address to the House committee was effectively squelched. Congressman Silvio Conte of Massachusetts took the floor and told the committee of McDonald's views on UFOs. McDonald replied that his views on UFOs were irrelevant to the discussion on hand. On the following day, Dr. Will Kellogg, prominent scientist and director of the National Center for Atmospheric Research, came to McDonald's aid, stressing to the committee that McDonald was a "very distinguished scientist." Conte, however, refused to let up on his attack, retorting:

...A man who comes here and tells me that the SST flying in the stratosphere is going to cause thousands of skin cancers has to back up his theory that there are little men flying around the sky. I think that this is important.[22]

The SST study was McDonald's last project. He had worked himself to the bone trying to convince the scientific community to study UFOs via NASA, but nothing seemed to be panning out. The Air Force continued its ridicule. McDonald's work on the SST was derided, not on its scientific merits but because of his association with UFOs. These factors plus other pressures were probably conducive to what happened next. On June 13, 1971, Jim was found dead in the desert. A note and a .38 revolver were found beside the body, and it is presumed that he took his own life. Nonetheless, his professional contributions to atmospheric physics and future UFO studies have not gone unrecognized.

CHAPTER NOTES

1. G. W. Van Tassal, *I Rode in a Flying Saucer* (Los Angeles: New Age Publishing Co., 1952).

2. O. Angelucci, *The Secret of the Saucers* (Amherst, Wisconsin: Amherst Press, 1952).

3. D. W. Fry, *The White Sands Incident* (Los Angeles: The New Age Publishing Co., 1954).

4. D. W. Fry, *Steps to the Stars* (El Monte, California: Understanding Publishing Co., 1956).

5. T. Bethurum, *Aboard a Flying Saucer* (Los Angeles: De Vors & Co., 1954).

6. Personal files.

7. *Ibid.*

8. *Ibid.*

9. *Ibid.*

10. I. S. Shklovskii & Carl Sagan, *Intelligent Life in the Universe* (San Francisco: Holden Day, Inc., 1966), pp. 13–18.

11. D. M. Jacobs, *The UFO Controversy* (Indiana: Indiana University Press, 1975), pp. 130, 131.

12. *Ibid.*, p. 149

13. J. Vallee, "The Conspiracy Theory," *EASTWEST Journal*, February 1979, p. 40.

14. *The New York Times*, August 1, 1952, p. 19.

15. APRO: 3910 E. Kleindale Road, Tucson, Arizona 85712.

16. E. J. Ruppelt, *The Report on Unidentified Flying Objects* (New York: Doubleday & Co., Inc., 1956), p. 225.

17. Jacobs, *op. cit.*, p. 97.

18. Robertson Panel (now declassified), pp. 18–24, Tab. A (As quoted in: E. U. Condon, *Scientific Study of Unidentified Flying Objects*, p. 525).

19. *Boston Herald*, April 24, 1967.

20. Jacobs, *op. cit.*, pp. 220, 221.

21. Resume of telephone conversation between Colonel Stanley, (SAFOI) and Colonel Holum, 4 April 1967, n.a. (typescript at MAFB).

22. U. S. Congress, House, Committee on Appropriations, *Hearings, Civil Supersonic Aircraft Development (SST)*, 92nd Congress, 1st Session, 1–4 March 1971, pp. 587, 592.

MY FIRST
INVESTIGATIONS

Back in the early sixties, Mom and Dad still lived in Danvers. Late one night, one of their neighbors was driving home. The neighborhood was dark. As he turned up the dead-end street, he was shocked to see what appeared to be a ball of fire directly over my parents' house. He watched dumbfounded as the glowing object moved off rapidly, to hover momentarily over a nearby hill. Then it disappeared into the night sky. But I just snickered at his report. Imagination, misidentification perhaps—but not a bonafide UFO sighting!

I was more impressed with my brother's sighting of a UFO in broad daylight. Richard, an engineer, sighted a noiseless, dark oval object flying over the research facility where he worked. He told me that it looked like a "metallic phonograph record sailing through the air." He carefully noted its elevation, angular size, and speed. It passed *under* a cloud. A check was made with the U. S. Weather Service to ascertain the height of the cloud base. Using simple mathematics, Richard estimated that the object was about twenty-five feet in diameter and flying 300 miles per hour at 2,000 feet.

One summer day in 1961, distant thunder rumbled as dark thunderclouds slowly dissipated. Margaret and I were on our way to a church youth meeting in Salem, New Hampshire. It was hot and muggy as we passed into open countryside beyond Haverhill, Massachusetts. As we drove by a large field, my wife cried "Ray! What is that thing over the field?"

Since she sometimes teased me mercilessly about flying saucers, I answered, "Just be the sun shining through the clouds. You can't fool me." She grabbed my shoulder and shouted, "Look, before you miss it! I'm not kidding."

It was too late. We had passed the field and were driving by heavy woodland. Margaret excitedly explained to me that she had seen an object hovering low over the field. I slowed, turned, and sped swiftly back to the field. My heart was pounding as we approached the area. When we got there, the object was gone. I couldn't believe how foolish I had been in missing it.

Margaret described it as having been silvery, somewhat cylindrical in shape, but fat around its midsection. She said it had been hanging motionless—close enough to the road to see clearly. Over and over again I have mentally kicked myself for missing this golden opportunity.

I submitted a brief description of what Margaret had seen to NICAP and to the Air Force's Project Bluebook. Bluebook responded with several questions, and I sent answers back in reply. My associate membership in NICAP consisted of nothing other than subscribing to their monthly bulletin, *The UFO Investigator*. For the most part, this newsletter contained rehashes of newspaper articles and intriguing anecdotal UFO accounts given to Keyhoe by friendly military contacts. Times, dates, and other essential data were often missing; but much space was devoted to attacking the Air Force for covering up information on UFO sightings. One wondered just how much real investigation was expended in preparing the pages of *The UFO Investigator*.

For years, only certain selected individuals in the military intelligence-gathering community had received any specialized training in UFO investigation. Most of the so-called UFO officers who screened incoming civilian reports to local Air Force bases had inherited their assignment grudgingly, and by default. Usually they had neither training nor interest; their instructions were limited to an Air Force regulation of several pages.[1] Those UFO reports that survived this initial sifting process were then submitted for real investigation by trained intelligence officers.

When well-publicized local sightings were satisfactorily explained, that information was sent to the Pentagon. Upon its receipt, the Air Force Office of Information would give the incident national publicity, laying great stress upon the Air Force's ability to identify the UFO. On the other hand, all Air Force base commanders were under strict orders not to publicize or discuss unexplained sightings. The public was shortchanged twice over: First, they remained ignorant concerning the reality of genuinely unidentified flying objects. Second, they received no substantial help on how to identify the various common objects and phenomena often reported as UFOs.

It became painfully apparent that if I wanted answers to the UFO problem, I had better get more personally involved with UFO witnesses. From firsthand experience, I knew that the majority of reports could be explained in terms of natural phenomena and man-made objects. The public desperately needed to know such facts in order to encourage accurate reporting, investigation, and research. I decided to document the next reasonable-sounding UFO sighting reported in the local newspapers and prepared a lengthy, eight-page questionnaire based largely upon an Air Force technical information sheet used in official UFO-sighting investigations. Then I sat back and waited for my first on-site investigation.

A news clip from a local paper alerted me to a sighting. This was the opportunity I had waited for.

The night of June 25—incidentally, my eighth wedding anniversary—was hot and sultry. The coastal town of East Weymouth, south of Boston, lay in the grip of an early summer heat wave. Enrico and Janet Gilberti finally found some relief by moving their bed close to the bedroom window, and dropped off to sleep around midnight. Scarcely an hour had passed when an ear-piercing, vibrating roar jolted the young couple out of a sound sleep.

"Enrico! Enrico! Get away from the window!" shrieked Janet as she plunged beneath the sheet in fright. But Enrico just stared. Hovering only a hundred feet above the ground and three hundred feet away was a lighted oval object as large as a ten-wheel truck. Two softly glowing orange lights affixed to its top and bottom midsection illuminated an unworldly structure. It was shaped like two gray bowls, one inverted upon the other and connected by a darker rim. Transfixed, Enrico leaned against the screened window for a full minute before the craft smoothly tilted upward and slowly flew away into the darkness.

I sat across the table from the Gilbertis and took notes as they excitedly related their bizarre experience. A striking young couple in their early twenties, they had just returned home from the beach with their little girl, and had almost forgotten my appointment with them. This guileless young couple were neither psychotics nor publicity seekers.

"We stayed awake until four-thirty just talking about it," said Janet. "I couldn't get to sleep."

"What did you do the next morning?" I asked.

"Well, after Enrico left for work, I called the South Weymouth Naval Air Station to see if they could tell me what it was. They told me that there were no aircraft in the area at that time. The man said that I would be called back for more information. But no one called."

"Did your neighbors say anything about seeing or hearing anything strange?"

Enrico looked at me sheepishly. "Both of us felt sort of funny about telling the neighbors about this. We just casually asked if they had heard anything strange during the night. Three different families told us they had been awakened by what they assumed was a low-flying jet."

Just before they had returned home from the beach, I had interviewed their next-door neighbors, who told me that the husband had just returned home from working the night shift. No sooner had he dropped off to sleep at about one o'clock, than a "loud vibrating sound" filled the house.

He told me that he had flown B-17s during World War II and in Korea. "I thought I was familiar with aircraft sounds, but this was different. It seemed to go right through you!"

Enrico and Janet had been greatly relieved to discover that others had at least *heard* the eerie intruder. When the local *Patriot Ledger* published other accounts about the UFO, Janet had phoned to tell the paper of their sighting. "I thought it would help other people who had seen something strange if they realized that they weren't alone in their experience."

I asked Enrico Gilberti to describe the lighted craft's shape in terms of some common object. "The lights were shaped like ice-cream cones," he replied, "but with their points cut off. Have you ever seen a Turkish fez? The wide base of each light was attached to the center of the top and bottom of the object. The object itself was like two hamburger buns, one on top of the other, with a sandwiched piece of meat sticking out all around."

I left the Gilberti home and gazed back over the sighting area, directly behind their house. The evening sky was punctuated by distant blinking red lights affixed to the tall chimneys of an electrical power plant across a saltwater inlet. Huge power lines crossed the Gilbertis' backyard and stretched across the vast salt marsh. The mysterious craft, either by choice or chance, had hovered directly above these same power lines. I did not know then that I would witness this identical environmental situation many times during the course of future UFO investigations.

I completed my report on the Gilberti incident and sent unsolicited copies to the Air Force Project Bluebook and to the NICAP. For sixteen years I had been reading about such reports, but always felt a nagging doubt about their authenticity. In a few instances I had talked to people who had sighted strange objects at a distance, but this sighting was startlingly different. If one took the Gilbertis' verbal description at full face value, only one explanation remained: Both had witnessed at close range an alien machinelike object, seemingly under intelligent control.

Still, this firsthand inquiry into a reported close encounter with a UFO caused great consternation on my part. How many other similar events were occurring and not being properly documented? How could scientists and researchers ever be sure of UFO data if all they had recourse to was information in a brief newspaper account? There and then I decided to continue documenting local UFO sightings as thoroughly as I could for possible use by military and civilian scientists.

How does one become a flying-saucer investigator? I had really nothing to offer except a general knowledge about UFOs and unbounded enthusiasm. But this, I reasoned, was not enough. I needed experience that could be gained only by continuing as a self-appointed on-the-job trainee. I persisted in investigating local incidents and sent unsolicited copies of my detailed reports to both NICAP and the Air Force.

In the early summer of 1964, NICAP informed me that they were interested in my becoming involved in an official investigative capacity. Apparently my reports had been of great value in supplementing other investigations being carried out locally by the NICAP Massachusetts Investigating Subcommittee, a local group that I had not known existed. It was directed by Mr. Walter Webb, lecturer in astronomy at Boston's Hayden Planetarium. NICAP was interested in having me meet with Walter soon so that he could check into my background for possible subcommittee membership. Needless to say, I was quite excited yet a bit wary. But my apprehension dissipated when this congenial, easygoing young man arrived promptly on schedule at my home in Wenham.

In 1957, after the launching of the Soviet Sputnik, Walter had been dispatched to a remote viewing site in Hawaii, located near the rim of Haleakala, the world's largest dormant volcano, where he assisted with the hasty installation of equipment at our nation's first satellite-tracking station. Walter told me he was finding it very difficult to serve NICAP in his dual capacity of astronomy advisor and subcommittee chairman. His primary interest lay in the area of astronomy. He had tried on several occasions to recruit his replacement as chairman of the local investigating group, but without success. In addition, NICAP needed more investigators.

I told him that I would be interested. Before he left, Walter told me that NICAP was very impressed with the reports I had been sending to headquarters. He couldn't promise me anything, but assured me that he would let NICAP know of my interest and that we would meet again.

One afternoon shortly thereafter, Walter phoned to say that he had received a tip concerning an alleged UFO landing near a cemetery at Lawrence, Massachusetts. Would I be willing to assist in his investigation? I excitedly agreed.

It was supper time on that hot summer evening when we arrived in Lawrence. After quite a search, we finally rounded up the witnesses—a bunch of small kids who gave us vague directions to the landing site, but would not accompany us. The entire situation didn't look very promising, and darkness was setting in as we arrived at the gate to a beautiful, well-kept cemetery. It was quiet except for the chirping of crickets. To get to the alleged landing site meant cutting through the rows of pale tombstones that jutted up through the rolling, manicured lawn. When Walter took out his flashlight, exclaimed, "Let's go," he was already walking briskly among the dead. Beginning to regret having become involved, I hesitated momentarily before taking up a wary position behind him.

We searched and searched, but never found the field the kids had described to us. Walter's flashlight beam, bobbing up and down, could easily have provided the stimulus for yet another UFO report. Later, we moved stealthily out of the cemetery onto the deserted street. What on earth was I getting into? This UFO-investigator business left much to be desired. No sooner had I slumped into the front seat of Walter's parked car than he noticed some light on in a house down the street. He suggested I ask whether anyone inside might have heard of a UFO sighting in the area! I decided that he must be testing my willingness to investigate, so off I went.

I walked briskly up to the door and knocked, trying to look like this was standard operating procedure. The door was opened and I was welcomed far more enthusiastically than I had expected. Several men and a girl sat in a circle drinking. An old man looked up at me through bloodshot eyes and offered me a drink. I politely declined and proceeded to ask the group if they had heard about a UFO landing near the cemetery across the street.

The old fellow looked at me in astonishment and, turning to his startled companions, asked, "Ish he crazy?" They all looked at me rather peculiarly. Suddenly I knew that it was time to call it a night. I backed toward the door very slowly and bade them all good evening!

A few days later, a fellow employee informed me that there had been a grave robbery, in this same cemetery, that very week, and the Lawrence police had staked it out! What would we have said if the police had caught us creeping from tombstone to tombstone? But several weeks later, Walter phoned to tell me the good news that I was now an official investigator for NICAP; my ID card was in the mail.

The title sounded quite imposing to a newcomer like myself. I expected to learn much from the experienced members of the local investigating subcommittee, but my expectations were soon squelched when I discovered that except for Walter Webb and a fellow named Bruce Kincaid, the local subcommittee was a mere handful of untrained and barely interested people. There was no formal training program. The investigators' instruction manual consisted of several mimeographed pages of basic things I had already learned on my own.

But headquarters did acknowledge my new status. I received a simple, unprofessional-appearing ID card and was surprised to see that the form I had designed was far superior to NICAP's two-page UFO-report questionnaire. Suddenly and painfully it dawned upon me that I had a lot to learn, and some of it would prove very discouraging.

A few months after I was unceremoniously dubbed a knight of Major Keyhoe's round table, UFOs made a dramatic reappearance in the Massachusetts skies. On August 25, two communities thirty miles apart reported close-encounter sightings of a similar object. But neither account received newspaper publicity, and it was a wonder I even heard about them.

On Friday, August 28, 1964, the phone rang in my office in Waltham. Paul, a research engineer and fellow employee who had heard of my interest in UFOs, was calling about a sighting in his hometown of Littleton. The incident involved multiple independent witnesses between twelve and eighteen years of age. We made arrangements to interview the boys at Paul's home on the very next day.

The following afternoon I set out for Littleton, taking along my six-year-old daughter, Sharon, for company. We arrived at Paul's, where I cross-examined the boys. Paul knew one of them very well and vouched for his integrity.

Two teenagers, Jim and John, were out driving that night. About nine-thirty they picked up Norman, who was hitchhiking. Continuing along their way, they sighted a low-flying oval object with a bright glowing rim. Fascinated, they gave chase as it descended and hovered about two hundred feet over a wide expanse known as Porter Field. They pulled over at the edge of the field and stopped. Spellbound, they watched the weird flying machine repeatedly undergo an odd fluttering motion like a falling leaf. It seemed to be about one hundred feet in diameter!

At first no one dared to leave the car, Jim cautiously honked his car horn at the object, but elicited no response. He then leaned on the horn several times—still no response. Curiosity finally got the best of them. Warily, the three left the car and slowly advanced toward the unearthly craft.

As they drew closer, they could hear a low rushing sound emanating from the object. Then, as if sensing their presence, it abruptly dimmed its lights and sped away into the darkness. The boys excitedly dashed back to the car to give chase. But it was too late—the object was no longer to be seen.

Unknown to this disquieted trio another boy whose house overlooked Porter Field had witnessed the event. Attracted by the persistent car horn, he glanced out the window and saw a lighted oval object fluttering over the field. He too watched it dim its lights and streak away at fantastic speed.

The boys told me that it looked like "a cowboy hat with a bowl on it!" I thanked them for their cooperation and headed for the Littleton police department to check the blotter for additional witnesses. When I walked in, holding Sharon, the officer in charge smiled kindly, probably thinking I was bringing in a lost child. But when I asked if anyone had reported sighting a UFO in the area, his grin fell to a rather incredulous look. He replied that no one had reported any such thing! I felt embarrassed and slunk back out the door to my car.

I arrived home to find that my brother, John, had telephoned. When I called back, he told me he'd heard a rumor at the factory where he worked of a UFO sighting. Finally he traced the story back to a good friend of the witness—who, unfortunately, refused to name the person involved. I decided to visit the factory during noon break and confront this individual personally.

John arranged the meeting, and after much persuasion, I obtained the witness's first name—Richard—and his telephone number. Armed with this data, I returned home and phoned him.

Richard was very hesitant to talk about his experience. It was apparent by the tone of his voice that he had been badly frightened by something he could not understand. During our conversation, he casually mentioned that he had sighted the flying object on August 25. His sighting had occurred only an hour after the Littleton episode! Richard had sighted the UFO in Lynn, just thirty miles northwest of Littleton. "It looked like an egg with a dome!" I gasped and assured him that a similar object had been sighted elsewhere that same night.

This bit of news broke the ice, as it were. Quite relieved to hear about the Littleton UFO, Richard agreed to meet me at the home of a friend. Since neither he nor his parents wanted any publicity, he was still reluctant to give me his last name and address. However, it was an easy task for me to locate both by scanning the telephone numbers in the Lynn telephone directory. During my interrogation at his friend's home, I assured him that NICAP would not release his story to the local press. Richard willingly filled out and signed a UFO report questionnaire.

For Richard, it had been a terrifying moment. His parents were out that evening, and it was 10:30 when he drove into the empty driveway. The weather was clear. Stars twinkled brightly above his home, nestled against a large rock-strewn hill.

He locked the car doors and turned to walk toward the house when a high-pitched whine pierced the quiet night air. Glancing up, he saw a slightly tilted, silvery, oval-shaped object was descending slowly and deliberately. It looked as if it were going to crash or land atop the hill about two hundred feet from the house. A glowing rim of iridescent white light encircled its perimeter, illuminating a central, domelike structure on top. It seemed to catch itself in flight momentarily before dropping out of sight behind the trees.

Richard ran to the house and fumbled nervously for his keys. He entered the house, relocked the door behind him, and went for his gun in a state of near hysteria. When his parents returned home, they were shocked to find Richard sitting, trembling, a loaded rifle on his lap. After he explained, they ordered him not to tell anyone about what he had seen, but Richard found it next to impossible to keep the incident bottled up inside. He shared his UFO sighting with his best friend, who in turn spread the story throughout the factory where my brother worked.

Before returning home that evening, I checked with various establishments around the sighting area of Lenox Hill. When asked if they had seen a UFO land on the hill, people looked at me as if I had lost my marbles. Someone suggested that I inquire at a small private hospital located on the other side of the hill from Richard's house, which I found to be a home for the very aged and senile.

To my gratified relief, the administrator took the whole business very seriously. She allowed me to question a number of nurses, and I found one who had been on duty during the time of Richard's sighting. On the night in question, she told me she had heard a strange high-pitched whistling coming from out back. Thinking it must have been a new siren from a fire or police vehicle on the other side of the hill, she never looked to investigate.

Another nurse told me that on the afternoon following Richard's sighting, she had noticed two boys wandering over the crest of the hill who seemed to be looking for something. This offered further support for Richard's story: He had told me that on the following day, he and his friend had scoured the hilltop for evidence that the object had landed, but hadn't found anything. After obtaining statements from the nurses, I called it a night.

As I wended my way down the darkened drive, I noticed an enclosed area off to the side with a large No Trespassing sign. Stopping the car to investigate, I saw an electrical power substation which served underground power lines. Was there an affinity between low-level flights of UFOs and electrical power sources?

Later in the week, Walter Webb and I revisited the sighting area. It was a rugged climb up the hill from Richard's backyard, where the terrain dropped off quite sharply. I took compass readings while Walter measured the distance between the hilltop and Richard's driveway. I typed up the Littleton and Lynn reports and forwarded them to NICAP and Project Bluebook.

But for a few light-in-the-sky reports, September of 1964 was uneventful. October turned out to be an exceptional month, however, with UFOs back in force.

On October 6, Bob drove slowly along the deserted outskirts of Haverhill. It was twelve-thirty in the morning, and his companion, Bill, gazed sleepily out the window at the cemeteries and fields bordering the dark road. At first he thought he was imagining things. He blinked his eyes and looked again before yelling to Bob to stop the car.

Bob instinctively slammed on the brakes and asked what the matter was. Bill pointed at a glowing mass floating motionlessly over a field back down the road. Thinking there must be a rational explanation for this sight, Bob slammed the car into reverse and sped back to the field, stopping broadside to the phenomenon. There, plain as day, was a large, domed, oval object emitting a soft, silvery glow. Later Bob told me that it "looked like a half ball on a flat plate. we both stared at it. No one else was around, and we got out of there real fast. We drove right back to the police station." The police told me that they were very impressed. Because the boys were so upset, no doubt that they had seen something very unusual. But by the time a cruiser was dispatched to the area, the object was gone.

Exceptionally good sightings continued. It seemed as if the powers behind the UFOs were putting this fledgling investigator through an accelerated course of study. The very next day a stubby, cigar-shaped object overflew one of our company's buildings at Waltham. It was tailgating an

Air Force C-119 Flying Boxcar on its landing leg to Hanscom Air Force Base, Bedford. After interviewing the witness—a company employee, and a highly reliable person—I phoned the base operations officer at Hanscom Air Force Base, who confirmed that a C-119 and a C-47 had landed at that time.

He then connected me to the base UFO officer, Major Brooks. His first question to me was "Did anyone see it drop anything?" He asked me many other questions concerning what I had found out from the witness. As usual, it was a one-way street: He would not admit that anyone in the aircraft or at the base had also seen the UFO. A check with the FAA indicated that there were no other aircraft in the area at that time.

Still another spectacular daylight sighting occurred four days later, on October 11, again involving military aircraft being chased by a UFO. At 4:00 o'clock on that Sunday afternoon, two loud sonic booms sounded over Brockton, Massachusetts. Overhead, two jet fighters streaked across the clear blue sky. Directly behind them—and closing fast—was a white, disc-shaped craft. It caught up with the apparently fleeing jets and then just came to a dead stop in midair. Amazingly, the strange craft suddenly dropped straight down like an elevator and abruptly halted before it began to slowly orbit the city below. Suddenly it emitted a blinding white flash, then accelerated straight up and out of sight in a matter of seconds. When I investigated, I found that the several known witnesses had already been questioned by the Air Force.

Also in 1964, NICAP published one of the finest and most concise reports of UFO sightings and examples of government cover-up—*The UFO Evidence,* edited by Richard A. Hall. This 185-page report, sent to every member of Congress, contained details relating to every known facet of the problem and listed over 700 UFO sightings. Over half of the witnesses were trained observers.

Just prior to its publication, as if on cue, Dr. Donald Menzel published his second book on UFOs, which of course debunked them. The Air Force endorsed his book as "the most significant literary effort to date" on UFOs![2]

Dr. J. Allen Hynek continued to ply an opposite course. He was genuinely impressed with some of the sightings he investigated for Blue-book, one of which took place on April 24, 1964, just when NICAP's *UFO Evidence* and Menzel's book were stoking controversy. The UFO could not have picked a better time to land at Socorro, New Mexico!

Police Sergeant Lonnie Zamora saw the object descend near a deserted dynamite shack. As he approached in his cruiser, he saw two child-sized, coveralled occupants beside it. The small entities appeared startled when they saw the police car winding down the dirt road. Zamora lost sight of the object while descending a hill. When he again sighted the gully in which it had landed, the little men were gone. Cautiously he approached to within fifty feet of the oval object, which stood on four stilts. Suddenly a blue flame and a roaring sound erupted from the object's bottom. Thinking the object was about to explode, Zamora turned, ran about one hundred feet, and lay down on the ground. Dumbfounded, he watched it rise and hover about fifteen feet from the ground. The roar died and was replaced by a whining sound that also faded away to complete silence. The craft then moved off with a weird up-and-down motion, leaving four depressions, several burned areas, and smoking vegetation.

Hynek spoke out boldly to the press that this was no hoax, nor an experimental aircraft. NICAP investigator Ray Stanford located a total of thirteen additional witnesses who either saw or heard the same UFO. (A complete account of his investigation was recently published in book form.[3]) Probably because of Hynek's statements, which were carried nationally, the Air Force evaluated the Socorro sighting as that of an unknown vehicle.

Dr. Jacobs describes this important period very aptly:

By the end of 1964 the UFO controversy had reached a type of stalemate. On the one side were Keyhoe, NICAP, and . . . the sightings, an ever-present source of embarrassment for the Air Force. . . . NICAP's policies, popular pressure, and the sightings created congressional interest and the threat of hearings. . . . Donald Menzel stood out as the Air Force's leading scientist ally. . . . In the middle of the warring factions stood Hynek. . . . By 1964, though, it was questionable whether he was the Air Force's ally. . . . Congress had not held hearings . . . but the Air Force had avoided them only barely. . . . The two variables that NICAP and the Air Force could not predict were Hynek and the number of sighting reports.[4]

The sudden spate of sightings did not cease. I found myself dividing my time between investigation and preparing reports for NICAP. Walter was busy too, but other subcommittee members had shown little interest in becoming involved. Then in November, I received an invitation from NICAP's board of governors to replace Walter Webb as chairman of the NICAP Massachusetts Subcommittee. Walter would remain with NICAP as a consultant in astronomy.

My first assignment was twofold: to begin reorganizing the sub-committee at once, and to represent NICAP locally on radio station WEEI with Major Donald Keyhoe. The radio show went well and provided a good shot of publicity for NICAP's local investigating arm.

Much to Major Keyhoe's dismay, I had asked Dr. Menzel to join us on the program. I felt that having both views publicly aired would provide a better-balanced program. Keyhoe stressed that the United States Air Force was withholding the frightening information that UFOs were interplane-tary spaceships. Menzel emphasized that UFOs were simply the result of misidentifications, misinterpretations, hoaxes, and hallucinations. I took the middle ground, insisting that a significant portion of UFO sightings represented truly unidentified objects. At times, both Keyhoe and Menzel became very emotional; before long, objectivity gave way to personal prejudices and name-calling. I was disappointed that specific UFO case histories were not rationally discussed, but the show had been much easier than I had first imagined it would be.

My other task proved to be much harder. The current local sub-committee was essentially defunct. Only one member, Bruce, elected to help out. Unfortunately, he was scheduled to enter the Navy upon graduation from ROTC. I found myself in the position of a captain without a crew. But how did one go about recruiting needed flying-saucer investigators?

I decided to approach a number of professional engineers within the defense industry. UFOs were a thought-provoking problem; engineers were basically highly trained problem solvers. Several accepted the challenge. The new subcommittee consisted of a number of electrical, chemical, and aeronautical engineers, a graphic arts director, Bruce, and myself. I quickly set to acquainting them with the precarious art of investigating flying saucers.

A spectacular UFO sighting, which soon became known as the incident at Exeter, occurred on September 3, 1965, during the largest UFO wave since 1952.

CHAPTER NOTES

1. Air Force Regulation (AFR) 200-2 and 80-17. (Both since rescinded).
2. Donald Menzel and Lyle G. Boyd, *The World of Flying Saucers* (New York: Doubleday & Co., Inc., 1963), pp. 142, 143.
3. Ray Stanford, *Socorro "Saucer" in a Pentagon Pantry* (Austin, Texas: Blueapple Books, P.O. Box 5694, Austin, Texas 78763, 1976).
4. D. M. Jacobs, *The UFO Controversy* (Indiana: Indiana University Press, 1975), pp. 191, 192.

INCIDENT
AT EXETER

It was September 11, shortly before six-thirty. The little town of Exeter, New Hampshire, was asleep as I drove by the small bandstand. I parked in front of the police station and switched off the headlights. It was still fairly dark, and the streets were deserted. Trying to look as official as possible, I strode into the station and plunked my battered NICAP ID on the desk of a semiconscious policeman. He looked up, rather startled.

"Good morning, Officer, my name is Raymond Fowler. I represent the National Investigations Committee on Aerial Phenomena in Washington." I then proceeded to tell him about NICAP and our interest in documenting the Exeter case.

"Oh," said another officer who had been standing unnoticed on the other side of the room. "You're with that Major Keyhoe's group."

I agreed and asked if it would be possible to talk with Officers Bertrand and Hunt.

The officer at the desk chuckled. "That's Hunt right there!"

I turned to look at Hunt, who had just turned a shade of red. "Well," I said, "can we sit down and talk about it?"

"What's there to talk about?" he replied cautiously. "It's all in the papers."

I showed him the standard eight-page Air Force questionnaire and explained that I wanted him to fill it in and sign it. It took a bit of convincing, but finally he agreed.

Officer Hunt explained that he had been called to the UFO-sighting area to assist Officer Bertrand, who had radioed the station for help. Bertrand had gone to a field earlier with a teenager, Norman Muscarello, to investigate the boy's story that a bright red-lighted flying object had chased him. While the officer was talking in the field with Norman, the UFO had suddenly risen up from behind some trees and made passes at them.

"By the time I got there," Hunt said, "the object was moving off to the tree line, performing fantastic maneuvers. It made right-angle turns and sort of floated down like a falling leaf. Then it took off toward Hampton and chased another guy in a car."

Hunt then gave me directions to Norman Muscarello's house. He said that if I returned to the station at eight o'clock, he would phone Officer Bertrand and ask him to cooperate with me. I thanked him and headed off to Muscarello's house.

The house was unlighted when I arrived and knocked on the door. Mrs. Muscarello warily opened the door just a crack, and we talked. She would not let me in, and seemed very upset about all the phone calls and publicity. She told me that Norman had left the state and would not return until September 14. She said that both Air Force and Navy officers had visited the house to question her son. Mrs. Muscarello and I made arrangements for me to talk to Norman later, and I headed back to the police station.

Many years later, I learned from a confidential source that the investigating Air Force officer left his official investigating manual on a table in the kitchen when he went into another room. According to my source, Mrs. Muscarello entered the kitchen to get some coffee and saw it. Curious, she picked it up and started thumbing through its pages. At that moment, the investigating officer entered the kitchen and snatched it away, severely reprimanding her. My source says that she saw photographs of, among other things, impressions made by landed UFOs.

Officer Hunt phoned Bertrand and persuaded him to talk to me. Hunt then went off duty and I followed his directions to Bertrand's home, which was located, believe it or not, on Pickpocket Road! Bertrand invited me in and proceeded to interrogate *me* to assure himself that I wasn't "some kind of a nut." Several days after the sighting, he told me, a man had driven into his yard in a car with a sign on it reading "UFO Investigator."

"Somehow the guy persuaded me to let him into the house. He made some real crazy remarks. He really scared my wife. He told her that perhaps the UFO operators were after me!"

"Oh, I think I know who that was," I said. "Was he a friendly looking fellow with a bald head?"

"Yeah, that's what he looked like. I got rid of him real fast. You seem to be serious about this, and I'm willing to tell you exactly what happened, but no more. If you'll drive me down to the field where I saw this thing, I'll fill out your forms and talk to you about it."

As we drove, Bertrand told me that about an hour before his own experience, he had come upon a woman parked in an automobile on Route 101. "She was real upset and told me that a red glowing object had chased her! I looked around but didn't see anything except a bright star, so I sent her home. Then about an hour later, I got a call from the station telling me to report in at once. A kid had just come into the station all shook up about some object that had chased him."

"What on earth was a kid doing out that time of night?" I asked.

"Hitchhiking between Amesbury and Exeter along Route 150. He'd been visiting a girl friend." Bertrand had gone back to the station, picked up Norman, and brought him back to the field where he had seen the UFO. "I know this kid," he said. "He's real tough, but something must have really scared him. He could hardly hold his cigarette and was as pale as a sheet. Whoops, slow down! This is the place right here."

I turned around and parked at the head of a field between the Clyde Russell and Carl Dining farms.

"Norman and I came out here and I parked right about here," Bertrand continued. "We sat for several minutes, but didn't see anything unusual. I radioed the station that there was nothing out here. They asked me to take a walk into the field for a quick look before coming back in. I felt kind of foolish walking out here on private property after midnight, looking for a flying saucer!"

So that Bertrand could show me where he and Norman had been, we got out of the car and strolled into the field toward a corral.

"We walked out about this far," he said. "I waved my flashlight back and forth, and then Norman shouted, 'Look out, here it comes!' I swung around and there was this huge, dark object as big as that barn over there, with red flashing lights on it. It barely cleared that tree, and it was moving back and forth. It seemed to tilt and come right at us. I automatically dropped on one knee and drew my service revolver, but I remember suddenly thinking that it would be unwise to fire at it. So I yelled to Norman to run for the cruiser, but he just froze in his tracks. I practically had to drag him back!"

"How close was the object to you then?" I asked.

"It seemed to be about one hundred feet up and about one hundred feet away. All I could see at that point was bright red with sort of a halo effect. I thought we'd be burned alive, but it gave off no heat, and I didn't hear any noise. I called Dave Hunt on the radio. He was already on his way out here and arrived in just a few minutes. Whatever it was must have really scared the horses in that barn. You could hear them neighing and kicking in their stalls. Even the dogs around here started howling. When Dave arrived, the three of us just stood there and watched it. It floated, wobbled, and did things that no plane could do. Then it just darted away over those trees toward Hampton."

"What did you do then?"

"Well, we all returned to the station to write up our report. We'd only been back a short while when a call came in from the Hampton telephone operator. She told us that she'd just talked to a man who was calling from a phone booth and was very upset. He said that he was being chased by a flying saucer, and that it was still out there! Before she could connect him with us, the connection was broken. We went out looking for him and even went to the hospital to see if he'd been brought in there, but we never found out who he was."*

Bertrand and I walked back toward my car to fill in forms and continue the interview. I sat there entranced, wistfully looking out over the field while he penciled in answers on the questionnaire. As he passed me the completed forms, I remarked to him, "This one will go down in UFO history!"

I spent the rest of the morning interviewing people in the general locale. Some had already been questioned by the Air Force just a week before. The Air Force team had asked Hunt and Bertrand to keep quiet about the incident so that it wouldn't get printed up in the newspapers.

"We told them that it was a bit too late for that," Bertrand told me. "A local reporter was in the station that night and tipped off the Manchester *Union Leader*. It was really funny. We were all standing there talking about what had happened when someone pointed at the front window. There was this reporter with a helmet on peering at us through the glass. We all jumped! He had motorcycled all the way up from Manchester."

I finally arrived back home just before three o'clock in the afternoon, weary and with an empty stomach. Margaret was worried when I hadn't shown up for lunch, and I had been too busy to think to call. After gobbling some warmed-up leftovers, I informed her rather hesitatingly that I had to get back to Exeter to take some photographs: I had discovered a set of power lines crossing the road about a half mile from the field where the object had been seen. It looked to me as if they might pass just behind the trees from where the object had first appeared. I wanted to walk back there, check out this aspect of the sighting, and take some photographs of the sighting area. I phoned my brother Richard to assist me, and off I went to Exeter again. I wasn't usually so callous in putting flying saucers before family, but this was an exceptional case.

We took some photos, then drove down the road where the power lines crossed Route 150. Leaving the car, we began hiking along the lines until stopped short by a swamp. Our feet were soaked as we headed back to

---

*I found out later that this man hung up the phone when the object suddenly flew away. He got back in his car and hurriedly drove home, where he phoned Pease Air Force Base. He was asked not to talk about the incident.

the car, but it was a worthwhile jaunt. The power lines did pass directly behind the field. When I arrived home bedraggled and wet, Margaret just gave me a look and shook her head.

For the next few days I worked on the initial report and managed to mail it out early Tuesday morning. On Thursday, a most encouraging response from Richard Hall, acting director of NICAP, contained news about an excellent opportunity.

Dear Ray,

Your excellent report on the September 3, New Hampshire sightings has been received. You certainly are to be commended for a prompt and thorough investigation. The information is most interesting and will be of great value. . . .

Mr. John Fuller of *Saturday Review* may be in touch with you about these sightings. He is doing a straightforward column on the recent wave of sightings. . . . We are cooperating fully. Thanks again for your hard work on our behalf.

Sincerely,
Dick Hall

"The *Saturday Review?*" I thought. I showed the letter to my not-too-sympathetic wife, who said in effect, "I'll believe it when I see it!"

She believed it several days later. John Fuller had indeed phoned to tell me that he did not want to write about the Exeter incident until he had personally reinvestigated the case to his own satisfaction. I agreed to provide him with a Xerox copy of my initial report, along with any follow-up data that might come in.

The following weekend, John arrived at our home for dinner armed with tape recorder and notebook. He explained that he had been reading with great interest about the increase in UFO sightings. Overwhelming curiosity had prompted him to track down and document at least one specific case. "To be frank," he said, "I'm very skeptical about this subject." But we all liked John. He took the time to chat with the children and my wife, and it was readily apparent that he was interested in getting to know us as people as well as a source of information about the Exeter sighting.

John left for Exeter armed with my report and copious notes. After he talked with the witnesses, local newspaper editors, and Air Force officers at Pease AFB, he phoned back to tell me that he was absolutely convinced that "these people really saw something!"

Many other strange things occurred on that very same night. Let me quote what the Exeter police told John:

Most of the people who've been reporting them are level-headed. And

I'll tell you something. I've had three different people tell me the same story *that night.* . . . This fellow from Brentwood . . . was telling me that he woke up that night, and the whole room was lit up. And he figured somebody was coming in the driveway, or down the road with a high beam. So he got up and looked out the window. And there wasn't a car in sight, no sound or nothing. And all of a sudden, the room went dark again. And then the wife of this fellow who runs the machinery over the mill—she woke up and the room was all lit up . . . right in the vicinity of the time they saw it. . . . The room was all lit and no cars or planes around, then all of a sudden it went dark again.[1]

(This brings to mind another night when my aunt was visiting my parents in November 1972. During the wee hours of the night, a brilliant light blazed through the windows of the downstairs bedroom in which she was sleeping. The curtains were drawn, yet it seemed brighter than daylight. She woke with a start and froze in terror, thinking that the house was on fire. The light lasted only a few moments, and then all was darkness again. There had been no electrical storm. Nothing outside could account for the strange phenomenon.)

John's story soon appeared in the October 2, 1965, issue of *Saturday Review*'s "Trade Winds" column. Then *Look* magazine asked John to return to Exeter to obtain additional material for an in-depth story on the incident. Soon after, *Reader's Digest* printed a summary of the *Look* article, and G. P. Putnam's Sons commissioned him to write a book on the Exeter sighting.

John soon made a return visit to us and secured from my files information relating to other sightings. He insisted that I would be given full credit. "You are going to be the hero of this book," he said.

To me, all of this seemed too good to be true. The results of my personal efforts, coupled with the support of the subcommittee, had hitherto been known and used by only a small segment of the public via NICAP's auspices. Now, in just the space of several months, my reports had become the basis of national magazine articles. However, the crowning event was yet to come.

On April 5, 1966, the House Armed Services Committee unanimously voted my entire Exeter report into the *Congressional Record* during the first open congressional hearing on UFOs! By that time my report had grown considerably, to contain a blow-by-blow description of a fight with the Pentagon, whose initial evaluation of the incident was "stars and planets twinkling"![2]

Later, I learned that when the Pentagon issued this misleading statement, the commander at Pease Air Force Base had not even sent the base's report out to Project Bluebook. The same source told me that after this press release was made, an urgent wire from Bluebook came into Pease Air Force Base, reprimanding the commander for not being more punctual in submitting the report through channels. Then—since the "twinkling star" answer was so obviously contrary to the well-publicized facts—the Pentagon tried to explain the sightings away as military aircraft.

Each of these attempts to explain the Exeter sightings was futile, and a fully documented account of my running battle with the Air Force became part of the *Congressional Record*. One of the first attempts to cover up what really happened at Exeter appeared in local newspapers on October 6.

The unidentified flying object spotted in this area by many residents has finally been identified. It's a flying billboard which contains 500 high-intensity lights that spell out an advertising message.[3]

When I saw this, I was horrified, and immediately wrote to newspapers in the area to put the matter straight:

At the time of the September 3, 1965, UFO sighting, I checked with the manager of Sky-Lite Aerial Advertising Co., and its aircraft was not flying on this night. On October 9, I went over the advertising plane's flight paths between August 1 and October 8. The plane was not even airborne between August 21 and September 10.

In all fairness to the Air Force, this explanation was apparently an overzealous newspaper reporter's attempt to explain the sighting. About two weeks after my letter was printed in the local news, however, the Pentagon issued a number of explanations for the incident, including: "a high altitude Strategic Air Command exercise" and a temperature inversion that causes "stars and planets to dance and twinkle." These explanations did come directly from Washington and were prominently displayed in the papers around the Exeter area:

PENTAGON DOESN'T BELIEVE UFO
EXETER SIGHTINGS

Washington, D.C.—The Pentagon believes that after intensive investigation, it has come up with a natural explanation of the UFO sightings. . . . The spokesman said, "We believe what the people saw that night was stars and planets in unusual formations."[4]

Some intensive investigation! This official release from Washington was all too familiar and completely frustrating. The witnesses felt that such statements jeopardized their hard-earned reputations as responsible police officers. In response to a request for further information about the Strategic Air Command aircraft exercise, Project Bluebook forwarded the following information:

Big Blast *Coco*, a SAC/NORAD training mission was flown on 2–3 September, 1965. By 03/0430Z, the operational portion of the mission was complete. . . . The town of Exeter is within the traffic pattern utilized by Air Traffic Control in the recovery of these aircraft at Pease AFB, N.H. During their approach the recovering aircraft would have been displaying standard position lights, anti-collision lights, and possibly over-wing and landing lights.[5]

Undaunted, Bertrand and Hunt drafted another letter to Project Bluebook outlining the facts of the matter. Excerpts from their letter are as follows:

. . . we have been the subject of considerable ridicule since the Pentagon released its "final evaluation" of our sighting. . . .both Ptl. Hunt and myself saw this object at close range, checked it out with each other, confirmed and reconfirmed the fact that this was not any kind of conventional aircraft. . . . Since our job depends on accuracy and an ability to tell the difference between fact and fiction, we were naturally disturbed by the Pentagon report. . . . Since one of us [Ptl. Bertrand] was in the Air Force for four years engaged in refueling operations with all kinds of military aircraft, it was impossible to mistake what we saw for any kind of military operation, regardless of altitude. . . . Immediately after the object disappeared, we did see what probably was a B-47 at high altitude, but it bore no relation at all to the object we saw. . . . Another fact is that the time of our observation was nearly an hour after 2:00 A.M., which would eliminate the Air Force Operation Big Blast. . . .[6]

In other words, Bertrand had discovered that the alleged Air Force aircraft were not even airborne during the time that he, Muscarello, and Hunt concurrently observed the object. Outflanked, Bluebook gave some ground, but not much. In regard to the earlier sightings by the woman motorist and Muscarello (when alone), the Air Force still maintained that those two had seen the aircraft!

The early sightings . . . are attributed to aircraft from operation Big Blast "Coco." The subsequent observations by Officers Bertrand and Hunt occurring after 2 A.M. are regarded as unidentified.[7]

This was typical of the Air Force's pattern of playing down and debunking reliable UFO sightings. I felt that I could not take this matter sitting down, and I drafted a long letter to the office of the secretary, department of the Air Force:

The UFO sighted by Norman Muscarello was identical to the UFO sighted later by Muscarello, Bertrand, and Hunt. Norman observed the UFO at close range during his initial sighting. There is no question in my mind that the same or similar object was involved in both . . . sightings. The number of pulsating lights, the yawing motion, the same location, etc., make this so very apparent. Since I did not interview the unnamed *woman*, I am not certain of the details . . . but according to Officer Bertrand, the object . . . was very similar to the UFO they sighted later. I might add that another witness, a male motorist, also sighted a similar object. He tried to phone the police from a pay station at nearby Hampton, N.H., but was cut off. Later he reported the incident to U.S. Air Force authorities at Pease AFB. The chances are astronomical that six people, entirely independent of each other, should report the identical description of a UFO within the span of several hours in the same general area.[8]

The Air Force never answered this letter, but probably wondered how I knew that the male motorist had reported the object to Pease AFB—because he had been strictly instructed to tell no one about the incident. I found out about this when lecturing to a management club in the area. One of the managers, a good friend of the witness, informed me.

The Exeter incident is typical of hundreds of other cases in which our government's policy forces it to deny the existence of UFOs at the expense of witnesses' reputations. In this case, public, witness, and congressional pressure forced the Air Force to back down, though this is an exception rather than the rule. The interested reader should secure a full copy of these controversial hearings. They contain statements made by persons intimately associated with the Air Force investigations of UFOs that utterly contradict documented facts in formerly classified and unclassified source material.

Why did this incident create so much fuss? In addition to its normal debunking policy, the local Air Force base may have been trying to cover up the fact that Exeter seemed to be the hub of a number of "haunted hamlets." First I, then John Fuller, found that the area abounded in UFO sightings. During the rash of sightings, the police told me that the base commanding officer and public information officer, dressed in old civilian clothes, would drive around the area at night in an old car—sometimes spending the night in the car! Their attempt at being inconspicuous was a hopeless failure—beside the local natives in the area, they stood out like sore thumbs.

One evening the commanding officer drove up to the site of the incident at Exeter, where a large crowd had gathered to watch the skies. He addressed the crowd with a megaphone and told them that the UFOs were just reflections from some powerful lights at Pease Air Force Base—and that he would demonstrate this! Picking up the microphone of his staff car's two-way radio, he ordered personnel at the base to "turn the lights on." Everybody looked and waited—and nothing happened. Frustrated, he yelled into the mike to turn on the lights. A voice replied that the lights *were* on. The very embarrassed officer slunk back into the seat of the staff car and drove off amongst the laughs and jeers of the crowd.

One of our special investigators has taken up residence in this area, to record and analyze past and continuing UFO events. The Strategic Air Command's Pease AFB and the U.S. Naval Atomic Submarine shipyard are both in Exeter's backyard, so this must cause the military much consternation.

CHAPTER NOTES

1. John G. Fuller, *Incident at Exeter* (New York: G. P. Putnam's Sons, 1966), p. 83.

2. *Haverhill Gazette,* October 27, 1965.

3. *Amesbury News,* October 6, 1965.

4. *Haverhill Gazette,* October 27, 1965.

5. House Report No. 55: *Unidentified Flying Objects Hearing* by Committee on Armed Services of the House of Representatives, 89th Congress, 2nd Session, April 5, 1966, p. 6040.

6. *Ibid.,* pp. 6039, 6040.

7. *Ibid.,* p. 6039.

8. *Ibid.,* p. 6042.

INCIDENT
AT BEVERLY

During the huge 1965 UFO wave that engulfed the whole world, there had been unprecedented, long-term media and public criticism of the Air Force's UFO information policy. In response, General E. B. LeBailly, Air Force director of information, instigated the forming of an ad hoc committee in February of 1966 to review the situation. Then UFO sightings increased in tempo.

During the UFO blitzkrieg of March 1966, police and a crowd gathered to watch one of several lighted objects that descended into a swamp at Dexter, Michigan. Public pressure soon brought the Bluebook boys in to perform their routine program of debunking and reassurance. By the time Dr. Hynek arrived with Bluebook director Major Hector Quintanilla, local media coverage had whipped the public into a frenzy. The country waited with baited breath for the latest Bluebook "explanation." Dr. Hynek stepped up to the array of microphones and stated quite matter-of-factly that some of the sightings could be attributable to swamp gas!

As usual, the public cried foul. Notables like Congressman Gerald Ford called for congressional hearings, and the media played up the "swamp gas" explanation for all it was worth.

In retrospect, the local Civil Defense director and others demonstrated that weather conditions made it nigh impossible for swamp gas to have stimulated the Dexter sightings. (Two witnesses who were familiar with the swamp ventured close enough to see what the lights were. They were affixed to a hovering oval craft with a central dome! When they approached it at close hand, it flew away rapidly with a ricocheting sound.) Hynek's statement became the butt of jokes and innumerable cartoons throughout the United States.

Several years later, in the privacy of my living room, Dr. Hynek admitted that his superiors had pressured him to come up with an answer for the press conference. What type of natural activity, he had asked himself, could occur in a swamp to produce strange lights? The answer—swamp gas—was exactly what the Air Force wanted, but Hynek had rued the day ever since. He told me that he had carefully prefaced his statement with the clarification that *some* of the reports might be attributed to such, but the media made it appear that he meant *all* sightings. Fortunately he has a good enough sense of humor to enjoy the swamp gas cartoons!

March and April 1966 were banner months for UFOs. There were hundreds of good reports and not enough investigators, so those available were forced to conduct their inquiries by setting priorities on the best sightings. The front page of the *Bangor Daily News* was typical of newspaper stories from all over the country: "REPORTS OF UFOs IN BANGOR AREA MOUNT." The mayor of Brewer, Maine, located just across the river, erected a huge billboard reading, "BREWER WELCOMES UFOs— *Landing Sites Available,* Signed Barry Ivers, Mayor"!

One of the most spectacular close-range sightings was made by John King on March 23.[1] Just before midnight King saw an object hovering low, almost touching the ground, in a swampy area off Bangor's Mt. Hope Avenue. He stopped the car, removed a .22-magnum pistol from the glove compartment, and walked cautiously toward the object. He described it as being twenty or twenty-five feet in diameter, with a bubblelike canopy on top. As he neared it, the unearthly craft suddenly began to emit a humming sound and glided across the open field toward John. It was so low that he could hear it scraping bushes as it came closer! In blind panic, John fired at it. Abruptly it turned and hovered briefly over a small body of water near the road. John fired again and heard the bullet ricochet off a metallic surface. Lights flashed from the object as it moved rapidly away. Investigating police found a scorched area where the UFO had hovered.

On that same night, twenty-five miles southeast of Bangor, my mother and a friend were returning along Route 172 to Surrey. In the sky over Newbury Neck, an orange-glowing round object as big as a full moon hovered motionlessly over the peninsula jutting into the Union River. The real moon was in its waxing crescent phase and had set long before. My mother persuaded her friend to stop the car to watch. Then another glowing object exactly like the first came sailing noiselessly along from the northeast. It headed directly for its hovering companion, and abruptly stopped in midair beside it. That was quite enough: Despite my mother's pleas to stay, her terrified friend sped the car away to the safety of her home!

On the evening of April 22, 1966, I received a phone call from the Beverly Police about the many reports they had received of a flaming green object streaking across the sky. When I arrived at the area of town where the reports had originated, the car radio announced that a huge meteor called a fireball—that is, an *identified* flying object—had been seen all along the eastern seaboard.

Disgusted, I headed home to work on a huge backlog of investigator's reports. As I drove, I noticed an orange light in the sky moving toward me. I kept glancing up, fully expecting to see the conventional running lights of an aircraft. When it drew closer, however, I saw that the whole craft seemed to be glowing. There were no identification lights. It crossed the highway very slowly, and I immediately exited onto a minor road and gave chase.

In no time at all, I got ahead of it and parked in a dark field. As it approached, I jumped out of the car and listened intently. A faint purring sound emanated from the glowing thing as it passed almost directly over my head. I signaled to it with my flashlight, to no avail. It continued on into the distance, then swung downward in a graceful arc somewhat like half a pendulum swing, and vanished behind distant trees.

It was about seven P.M. when I headed on home. In just a few hours, Beverly and Wenham would be visited by something more substantial than a distant orange-red light.

That Saturday morning, Mrs. Claire Modugno phoned to tell me that lots of people had seen three UFOs over the Beverly High School the night before. Tired of UFO reports, I started to dismiss the sighting as the fireball or perhaps the planet Jupiter. Then it dawned on me that this poor woman was trying to describe a spectacular close-encounter!

What Claire described was so fantastic I began to wonder if it were a hoax. She claimed that the Beverly police had confirmed the UFO sighting among many witnesses. I retorted that if such an incident had really happened, the police would have routinely phoned me about it. She agreed, but added that she had just phoned the police for more information, and they had denied having been involved at all! She remained unruffled when challenged, so I decided to drop everything and check out this report personally.

I immediately phoned the police, who told me that there was no UFO report on the blotter—except that of the fireball, which they had called me about. Told that the Beverly police had not been involved in any UFO incident at the Beverly High School, I was tempted to drop the whole matter, but intuition urged me to obtain the names of all officers on duty during the time frame of the UFO sighting. I then phoned each one and proceeded to ask questions about the incident as if I *knew* that the officer was personally involved.

This procedure narrowed the list down to police officers Bossie and Mahan. Both admitted they had been involved and agreed to be interviewed at the station!

On Sunday I interviewed the civilian witnesses and then proceeded to police headquarters. Again I was given a runaround, but finally convinced the officer in charge to summon in Bossie and Mahan by radio. Upon their arrival, their superior officer told them to tell me exactly what they had witnessed.

Ushered into a private room, I interrogated them and obtained signed UFO-report forms. I found that both had been confronted by a flying object resembling something out of a science fiction movie.

Shortly after nine P.M., Nancy Modugno, age eleven, lay on her bed. Her father, Angelo, was watching a TV program downstairs. Suddenly a bright, blinking light blazed through her window. Curious, she climbed to the end of her bed, glanced out, and saw a flying football-shaped object about the size of an automobile! Flashing intense blue, green, red, and soft white lights, barely clearing housetops only forty feet away, the weird craft made a whizzing, ricocheting sound as it headed toward a large field behind the Beverly High School. The lights could still be seen as the object descended behind bordering trees, as if landing!

Terrified, Nancy came tearing down the stairs. Unfortunately, her father was in no mood for flying saucers. He was more interested in trying to adjust the TV, which, inexplicably, had just lost its picture. Ordered back to bed, Nancy became hysterical and refused to budge. Her mother, Claire, was in an adjoining apartment visiting Barbara Smith and Brenda Maria.

At that very moment, Barbara and Brenda walked in to use the telephone to order pizza. Both tried unsuccessfully to comfort Nancy. Stepping outside, they could see the flashing lights near the high school. They told Nancy that they would fetch her mother, walk down to the field, and prove that it was just an airplane. Picking up Claire, they walked down Sohier Road to Herrick Street before descending an incline onto the high school field.

Reaching the field's edge, they glanced skyward. Three brilliantly lighted flying objects were responsible for the flashes. Mystified, the trio watched the objects circle, halt abruptly in midair, and resume circling again as if playing tag. Two maneuvered over distant research buildings. One was closer, directly over the high school.

Believing the lighted craft must be helicopters, the three crossed the field to get a closer look. As they drew closer to the circling craft, no sound could be heard. No fuselage or rotor blades could be seen; the object was oval-shaped! Flashing lights raced around its perimeter in rapidly changing hues of red, green, and blue. They halted dead in their tracks. Brenda, in an apparent attempt to relieve the tension, began waving her arms at the unknown vehicle, gesturing to it to come closer. Immediately, the object broke off from its circular flight pattern and silently glided across the open field. Later, Barbara stated that:

It started to come toward us. . . . I started to run. Brenda called, "Look up, it is directly over us!" I looked up and saw a round object. . . . like

the bottom of a plate. It was solid, grayish white. . . . I felt this thing was going to come down on top of me. It was like a giant mushroom. I was unable to think, and automatically found myself running away.

Barbara and Claire turned and ran up the rise onto Herrick Street. They looked back in horror to see that Brenda was still out there—all alone! Unaware that her companions had left, Brenda was staring upward at the silent machine directly over her head. Barbara and Claire watched the unknown object begin to descend and stop just twenty feet short of Brenda, who was screaming and covering her head with her hands. Later, Brenda told me that:

This object appeared larger and larger as it came closer. The lights appeared to be all around and turning. The colors were very bright. When overhead, all I could see was a blurry atmosphere and brightly lit-up lights flashing slowly around. . . . I thought it might crash on my head!

Barbara and Claire shouted and begged her to run. Suddenly realizing that she was alone, Brenda broke into a dash toward her worried companions. With a smoothly executed semicircular maneuver, the object moved back toward the school building.

The three terror-crazed women ran back to the Modugno home, where they breathlessly phoned neighbors about their frightening experience. (The sheer horror generated by this close encounter had actually induced involuntary urination on the part of one of the witnesses.)

Mrs. Theresa Scanzani was already observing one of the UFOs from her backyard. Mr. and Mrs. Bob Lessor convinced the Modugno family and others to walk down to a fence at the corner of Herrick Street and Salem Road to observe the UFOs at a safer distance.

Again, two maneuvering objects exhibiting the same changing colors could be seen in the distance. About six hundred feet away, the other object was hovering, motionless, a mere thirty feet above the high school. People inside the building observing a basketball game were totally oblivious to its presence overhead. Bob Lessor tore back up the street and phoned the Beverly police department.

Police Officers Bossie and Mahan were inside a small general store about a mile away. They had left the radio volume turned up in their parked cruiser. When the radio call came in, others in the shop heard the message and watched them drive away to investigate. Colored, sparkling lights could be seen in the distance.

In the meantime, the UFO had begun to move alternately up and down over the school. As the police cruiser pulled up, the officers jokingly inquired, "Where's the airplane?" The witnesses excitedly pointed to the starlike object now hovering at a high altitude above the school. The policeman laughed, until the object turned bright red and descended straight down toward the school building. In Police Officer Bossie's words:

It hovered and then began *gliding*. Some of the people got on the ground and were real scared! We drove down into the schoolyard.

Witnesses told me that the police were visibly shaken when the UFO dropped down to just above the school roof level. Both jumped into the cruiser and sped down Salem Road and into the parking lot behind the high school. They had just started to get out of the cruiser when the object began to move away. In his report for NICAP, Officer Mahan wrote:

I observed what seemed to be a *large plate* hovering over the school. It had three lights—red, green and blue—but no noise.... This object hovered.... The lights were flashing.... The object went over the school about two times and then went away.

"Then it moved slowly toward the reservoir," Officer Bossie added, "and made a swing around heading toward the United Shoe buildings. It picked up speed . . . and disappeared . . . behind buildings."

Later I found that the police station had immediately notified the Air Force. Shortly afterward, two airplanes and a helicopter were seen circling in the area, perhaps in response to this call. In any event, witnesses easily identified these conventional aircraft in comparison with the bizarre-looking object they had observed earlier.

During the excitement, no one had noticed how the two other distant, circling objects had disappeared. However, a concurrent sighting seems to indicate that perhaps one buzzed the campus of Gordon College in Wenham, just three miles away. Several groups of witnesses watched dumbfounded as a silent, glowing orange oval object made a pass one hundred feet above the college quadrangle before executing a perfect ninety-degree turn and streaking away.

The Beverly and Wenham sighting areas were strikingly similar. Each featured a large grassy quadrangle, a school, and adjoining reservoirs of water. Months later, a reliable source informed me that one object had briefly touched down on nearby Folly Hill in Beverly, setting the grass ablaze. The following day he saw two men with a Geiger counter examining the burned area. When he approached and asked what was going on, one man showed him FBI credentials. By the time I visited Folly Hill, the barely discernible burned patch had been mostly obliterated by new grass.

The Condon committee showed a special interest in the Beverly case. One Friday night in the spring of 1967, I came home from a busy week of work. "Any interesting mail?" I asked.

"There's something from the University of Colorado on your desk," answered Margaret. "But don't get involved. Supper's just about ready."

She was too late. I had already opened the letter from the University of Colorado study's principal investigator, David R. Saunders.

Beginning in early June, the CU UFO Study expects to have enough staff to permit the conduct of one or more on-the-scene investigations per week.... The involvement of persons like yourself is highly desirable ... because your prior familiarity with the UFO problem can facilitate preliminary screening of these events. ...

In effect, the letter invited me to serve as an early-warning coordinator for the New England area, screening reports according to specific guidelines. Although quite suspicious of Air Force's involvement in this study, I nonetheless accepted the invitation. I was given tollfree hot lines that connected me with alert teams of investigators ready to fly anywhere in the United States.

During my tenure with the Condon committee, I relayed two sighting reports to them via the early-warning system. When Drs. Roy Craig and Norman Levine arrived to conduct an inquiry into these sightings, they also conducted a reinvestigation of the Beverly affair, a report of which I had sent earlier to Project Bluebook. During their investigation of sightings in the area, they accepted an invitation to dinner at my home, where they told me that scientists at the University of Colorado were designing a new UFO questionnaire: The form I had designed was being used as a model. I was quite pleased; it was beginning to look as if my time spent in personal investigations was worthwhile.

Shortly after returning to the University of Colorado, Dr. Levine was terminated from the project by Edward Condon. I learned that Norman had helped release a memo written by the assistant project director Robert Low to *Look* magazine. The memo indicated that the project was not meant to be an objective study; in fact, Low described it as a trick on the public. Its release caused further terminations and resignations of personnel employed on the UFO study.

In the midst of this turmoil, rumors reached me that Dr. Craig was going to explain the policemen's confirmation of the UFO sighting at Beverly as a misidentification of the planet Jupiter! Upon hearing this, UFO researcher Dr. James McDonald set out to counter this absurd explanation.

Jim, a highly respected scientist, had taken a leave of absence from the University of Arizona to conduct a personal, in-depth study of the UFO phenomenon. His investigations into selected cases convinced him that the United States Air Force was entirely incompetent in dealing with the UFO problem. He found it hard to believe that the government would withhold UFO data from the public, but shortly before his death in 1971 he admitted to friends that he was wrong about this aspect: He was beginning to find evidence of an official cover-up of UFO information.

Jim took a keen interest in monitoring the efforts of the UFO study at the University of Colorado. It seems that Dr. Craig had discovered that a few persons leaving the school building in Beverly after the basketball game were told of the UFO sighting by some of the witnesses. The newcomers looked up over the high school grounds and saw Jupiter. However, this was long after the police and initial witnesses had watched the real UFO leave the area. Needless to say, the policemen were shocked to hear that they had not observed a large flying object! One remarked that he had not even been interviewed by either Craig or Levine.

Craig's paradoxical attitude amazed Dr. Levine, whom I reached at his new job by phone. He related to me that during and after the investigation, Craig had seemed very impressed with the sighting. Levine said he found the Jupiter explanation "pretty hard to understand." I wrote Craig about the matter; he replied that, "I will not speculate, here or elsewhere, as to what the women saw,"[2] so I assumed that the "Jupiter" rumor must have been true. In any event, Jim and I were forced to wait for the project to release its final results, in what has since become known as the Condon report.

In January of 1969 the outcome of Air Force Contract F44620-67-C-005 was published. Entitled the *Scientific Study of Unidentified Flying Objects,* it immediately came under fire by civilian UFO researchers. Over the years it has been called a trick, a whitewash, inadequate, etc. However, this Air Force study could not explain 30 percent of the sightings investigated by project scientists! The Beverly affair is especially noteworthy because it is the only case within the Condon report that specifically refers to an alien vehicle. Craig indeed concluded that the police officers had mistaken Jupiter for a UFO! Concerning the object seen by the child and the three women, however, he concluded:

While the current cases investigated did not yield impressive residual evidence, even in the narrative content, to support an hypothesis that an *alien vehicle* **was physically present, narratives of past events, such as the 1966 incident at Beverly, Mass., (Case 6), would fit** *no other explanation* **if the testimony of the witnesses is taken at full face value [italics mine].[3]**

Craig made no mention of the detailed follow-up analysis prepared by Dr. McDonald and myself, which clearly refuted the Jupiter hypothesis.

The Beverly affair, like the Exeter incident, became well known in civilian and military scientific circles. It too was discussed in congressional circles and was introduced as evidence during UFO hearings before the Committee on Science and Astronautics, House of Representatives. During these hearings, Dr. James E. McDonald told this committee that:

... three adult women and subsequently a total of more than a half-dozen adults (including two police officers) observed three round lighted objects hovering near a school building. . . . At one early stage of the sightings, one of the discs moved rapidly over the three women, hovering above one of them at an altitude of only a few tens of feet and terrifying the hapless woman until she bolted. *This case was thoroughly checked by Mr. Raymond E. Fowler, one of NICAP's most able investigators, who has studied numerous other UFO incidents in the New England area.*[4]

CHAPTER NOTES

1. *Bangor Daily News,* Bangor, Maine, March 26, 1966.
2. Personal correspondence dated October 16, 1968.
3. E. U. Condon, director, *Scientific Study of Unidentified Flying Objects* (New York: E. P. Dutton & Co., Inc., 1969), pp. 72, 73.
4. House Report No. 7, "Symposium on Unidentified Flying Objects," *Hearings before the Committee on Science and Astronautics,* U.S. House of Representatives, July 29, 1968, p. 58.

FLAPS AND FRUSTRATIONS

The brief open segment of the 1966 congressional hearings was a far cry from the full-blown congressional inquiry that NICAP and congressmen had demanded, but decisions made during the earlier ad hoc meetings and the hearings ultimately relieved the Air Force of being publicly accountable for civilian UFO-sighting reports. The Air Force-sponsored University of Colorado UFO study also struck nearly a death blow to NICAP and civilian UFO research in general.

Originally, the news that a civilian group of scientists would conduct a UFO investigation independent of Bluebook had met with a mixture of delight and cautious skepticism. Condon had infuriated NICAP and civilian researchers by making derogatory remarks to the press and publicly fraternizing with contactees. It seemed as if he had already made up his mind before the project even got underway. For a full description of the now infamous Condon committee, I would refer the reader to *UFOs? YES!*, Dr. David Saunders's well-documented account of this project from an insider's view.

Dr. Saunders was principal investigator for the University of Colorado UFO project. He and another scientist released to *Look* magazine a private memo written by the late Robert Low, the project's assistant director. It read, in part:

The trick would be, I think, to describe the project so that, to the public, it would appear a totally objective study but, to the scientific community would present the image of a group of non-believers trying their best to be objective but having an almost zero expectation of finding a saucer.[1]

When *Look* published Low's controversial memo, Condon called Drs. Saunders and Levine into his office and fired them both for incompetence—which caused near anarchy within the project. Condon's longtime administrative assistant resigned in disgust. Most of the other project scientists were seriously considering resigning en masse and writing their own report. Condon bent over backward to assure them that each would have a free hand in writing their particular segment of the project's final report. The resignations were thus averted, and the report written. However, Condon's personal summary and recommendations received the most publicity:

We place very little value for scientific purposes on the past accumulation of anecdotal records. . . . we have recommended against the mounting of a major effort for continuing UFO studies for scientific reasons.[2]

His former administrative assistant contradicted his assertions, writing to J. Allen Hynek that "I think that there is fairly good consensus among the team members that there is enough data in the UFO question to warrant further study."[3]

As soon as the Condon committee's true colors became apparent, NICAP withdrew its investigative support. I decided to keep my commitment as an early-warning coordinator until the project's termination. In the meantime, the Low memo and Condon's conclusion drew fire from a number of congressmen. Representative J. Edward Roush made speeches to the House on April 30 and May 1, 1968, calling for a congressional investigation of the matter. Dr. Hynek spoke out publicly against Condon's conclusions, pointing out that 30 percent of the investigated objects remained unidentified. The prestigious American Institute of Astronautics and Aeronautics (AIAA) organized its own subcommittee to examine the Condon report, and later concluded, "We find it difficult to ignore the small residue of well-documented but unexplainable cases that form the hard core of the UFO controversy."[4] When Dr. Saunders left the project, he developed his computer study of UFOs into sixty-thousand entries with the aid of the Center for UFO Studies (CUFOS) and other civilian groups. Called UFOCAT, it is available from the center to interested researchers.

The publicity over the Low memo indicated just another in a series of government whitewashes. In the meantime, UFO sightings had died down and newspapers largely ignored the few sightings still being reported. To make matters worse, the Condon report received an endorsement from the National Academy of Science. NICAP membership dropped drastically, and in the August 1968 issue of the *UFO Investigator* bulletin, Keyhoe was forced to print an emergency message to its members. It read, in part:

Dear Fellow Members:
I regret having to make this public. . . . NICAP is on the brink of disaster. We have pledged full cooperation to legislatures and scientists in what will probably lead to a momentous reversal of present UFO debunking. But now, at this important time in our history, we face an imminent shutdown.

NICAP's discouraged members barely heeded Keyhoe's pleas. NICAP continued to limp along, and by mid-1969 was on the verge of bankruptcy.

I always made certain that all copies of reports evaluated in the "unknown" category were sent to Project Bluebook. This led to my receiving and answering correspondence from Bluebook's chief astronomical consultant, Dr. J. Allen Hynek. Although we had never met personally, a mutual comradeship developed through our letters. Then in June of 1969 I received the following letter from Dr. Hynek:

Dear Mr. Fowler:
It so happens that I shall be in Boston from late June 12 to early June 14. . . . It occurs to me that it might be a good time, at long last, for us to meet and have a good chat. . . . There are a number of things I should like to ask you, for I certainly have been an admirer of your highly systematic and businesslike way of approaching the UFO problem and its investigation. . . .

I wrote immediately and made arrangements to visit him in Boston.
When I drove into town to meet Hynek, the cool air of the Boston Common underground parking lot was a temporary respite. The hot summer air welcomed me again as I climbed up the stairs from the garage and made my way to the cool lobby of the nearby Parker House, where Dr. Hynek was staying. I glanced around nervously for the face I had seen so often connected with Air Force press releases. I soon spotted the bearded scientist and, walking up behind him, extended my hand and said, "Dr. Hynek, I presume?" We wandered into the hotel restaurant for a sip of iced tea and a very interesting conversation.
Hynek shocked me when he revealed confidentially that on the basis of the Condon committee's final report, the Air Force was about to close Project Bluebook! UFO reports would be processed through Air Force Intelligence channels. Hynek's job was about to be terminated. I could not believe our government would ignore enigmatical craft that were continually violating its airspace at will. Shortly after we left the restaurant and went to his room to continue our discussion, Mrs. Hynek arrived and reminded him that they had another engagement to keep. Accompanying

me to the elevator, Hynek casually mentioned that he would be directing a civilian UFO project sometime in the future. Would I be interested in working full-time on such a project? I quickly replied in the affirmative and bade him good-bye.

On July 1, 1969, Margaret and I left New York's Kennedy Airport for England to visit Margaret's parents.

One bright, cloudless day in July, her father was driving us all to Hornsea for a day at the beach on the North Sea. I was in the front passenger seat, admiring the neatly manicured fields and woods, when my eye caught a bright reflection in the sky. I saw a sharply defined white disc-shaped object descend in a rapid arc behind trees on a distant hill, but no one wanted to deviate from our planned trip to look for it. It was very frustrating to see something so clearly, yet for such a short time.

July 29, 1969, found us winging home again over the Atlantic after a wonderful vacation. We were elated over our country's success in placing the first men on the moon, but our baby, David, fussed continually. We took turns holding him until he finally fell into a sound sleep in my arms. I hardly dared to breathe lest I awaken him. Then—and why did it have to happen *then?*—my eleven-year-old daughter, Sharon, shouted across the aisle that two square, wingless objects "like box kites" were flying under the plane. The woman sitting beside Sharon nervously confirmed my daughter's observations.

I looked at my wife and asked her if she'd mind very much if I gave her the baby to hold. Needless to say, she objected strenuously—it had taken almost an hour to get him quiet. We were interrupted by the pilot's voice over the intercom: "Ladies and gentlemen. Please return to your seats and fasten your safety belts. We are expecting strong turbulence." But as I saw the others watching and commenting on what was flying formation with us, I stamped my foot in utter dismay.

Then the objects disappeared under the plane. I strained at my window, hoping they would appear on our side of the aircraft. With camera ready, I waited and watched. Several minutes later, I spotted several white blobs reflecting sunlight far behind and below us. I took a photograph. Later, when the picture was developed, two white blobs showed up. They could have been tiny clouds. Who knows?

Interestingly enough, we never encountered the predicted turbulence. Years later, a commercial airline pilot told me that when UFOs were sighted near an aircraft, it's standard operating procedure to ask passengers to fasten their safety belts "because of possible turbulence."

Even though Bluebook's days were numbered, the elite American Association for the Advancement of Science (AAAS) made the unexpected announcement that it would conduct its first symposium on UFOs at its 134th annual meeting in Boston in December of 1969!

The AAAS symposium was organized by a committee composed of Dr. Philip Morrison of MIT; retiring AAAS president, Dr. Walter Orr Roberts; Dr. Carl Sagan of Cornell; and Dr. Thornton Page of Wesleyan University. Curiously enough, Sagan had been a member of the ad hoc UFO committee headed by General LeBailly. As if that were not a strange enough coincidence, Thornton Page had been one of the members of the infamous CIA-sponsored Robertson Panel.

The AAAS committee invited both Drs. Hynek and McDonald to present their views, along with others of an opposite persuasion. The confused press carried news of the symposium to an equally confused public—who had recently been told that UFOs weren't worthy of the Condon committee's scientific consideration! *Then,* nine days before the symposium began, the Air Force made the announcement that after twenty-two years of investigation, "The continuance of Project Bluebook cannot be justified either on the ground of national security or in the interest of science."[5]

Pro-UFO speakers found the symposium heavily weighted with speakers against the concept that UFOs were real unknown objects. Once again, hopes for serious civilian scientific recognition of UFOs were dashed to pieces. Then, almost as if on cue, strange and abrupt changes took place at NICAP.

The board of directors, headed by Colonel Joseph Bryan III, began a chain of events that led to its complete reorganization and eventual neutralization as a lobbying force against military UFO secrecy. (It has since been learned that Colonel Bryan was a former covert agent for the CIA.) John L. Acuff, a complete outsider, was suddenly elected to serve on NICAP's board. Keyhoe, director of NICAP for thirteen years, was forced to retire at age seventy-two, with painful regrets. Colonel Bryan also dismissed Assistant Director Gordon Lore, Jr., and replaced him with G. Stuart Nixon, who became acting director. Then John L. Acuff was appointed director of NICAP on May 29, 1970. Who was Acuff and where did he hail from?

John Acuff graduated from the American University with a B.S. in distributive science. His professional background included positions with Technology, Inc., of Dayton Ohio, and Flow Laboratories, of Rockville, Maryland. Now executive director of the Society of Photographic Scientists and Engineers (SPSE), he took on the NICAP presidency on a part-time basis. The SPSE had already been cooperating with NICAP informally in the area of photographic analysis. (Later, it was found that the SPSE had CIA connections.)

Acuff and Nixon proceeded to dispense with the long-standing NICAP affiliates throughout the country which had done so much over the years to promote NICAP's views. The UFO investigation subcommittees that Major Keyhoe, Richard Hall, and Gordon Lore had organized at the state level were officially disbanded. Pressure was put on the old-time Keyhoe followers to quit NICAP. Quit they did. Discouraged by these new policies, many of the faithful left to serve other UFO organizations.

NICAP then instituted a new scheme, asking certain members to become regional investigators for their area. They were discouraged from intercooperation and told to operate independently of one another. All information the regional investigators collected was declared *NICAP Proprietary,* and could not be shared with the media or other organizations without NICAP headquarters' express approval! Each regional investigator was required to sign a statement to that effect.

At the time of this internal shake-up, I was serving as chairman of the NICAP Massachusetts Investigating Subcommittee. My position was done away with, and rather reluctantly I accepted a position as a regional investigator. The rest of the subcommittee investigators automatically lost their NICAP investigator status. Some resigned in disgust; others agreed to continue with me as informal assistant investigators. Later on, in 1971, we *all* resigned, feeling that NICAP's new policies were detrimental to UFO research. Most of us joined MUFON—which, oddly enough, first appeared in the fortuitous year of 1969. MUFON was headed by Walter Andrus, an executive for the Motorola Company. I became Massachusetts state director for this fast-growing, well-organized network of investigators.

For a number of years I wondered if NICAP headquarters might have been influenced by the CIA: a civilian cover would have access to valuable civilian UFO reports and photographs not collected by Air Force intelligence. Recently, UFO researcher Todd Zechel independently suggested a similar scenario. Mr. Zechel has worked very closely with a group of researchers who have filed a suit against the CIA, forcing it to release hundreds of documents, some of which clearly indicate their involvement with UFOs up to the present. Zechel's thesis appeared in a copy of a bulletin published by Citizens Against UFO Secrecy (JUST CAUSE).

When space propulsion researcher T. Townsend Brown founded NICAP in October 1956, at least two CIA covert agents worked themselves into key positions with the organization. One, an ultra-mysterious character named Count Nicolas de Rochefort, was a Russian immigrant and employee of the CIA's Psychological Warfare Staff, where the Count wrote scripts in French and Russian for Voice of America radio broadcasts. Among other covert missions, Count de Rochefort managed to get himself appointed Vice-Chairman of NICAP in late 1956. The Count was a controversial ultra-right-winger and a leading force in the lobbying effort to prevent Red China from being recognized or admitted to the U.N. For covers (visible employment to mask his CIA involvement), he utilized professorships at Georgetown and American Universities, as well as claiming to be an escort interpreter with the State Department.

The other CIA agent was an even more mysterious... Bernard J. O. Carvalho, a native of Lisbon, Portugal. Among other missions, Carvalho had been a [go-between] for such [secretly owned CIA companies] as Fairway Corporation, a charter airline utilized by Agency executives. He managed to get himself appointed to chairman of NICAP's membership subcommittee....

Since the Air Force had been interested in Townsend Brown's propulsion theories back in the early 1950s, as Project Bluebook records attest, one might expect the CIA was interested as well.... (Additionally, because of... concern over the potential subversiveness of UFO groups, as articulated by the Robertson Panel Report in 1953, one might well expect to find covert CIA agents infiltrating a newly founded, Washington-based UFO organization.)

Obviously, since de Rochefort is dead and Carvalho hasn't been heard from in many, many years, the exact nature of the two agents' roles in NICAP may never be learned. One writer who attempted to obtain confirmation of de Rochefort's CIA employment through the Freedom of Information Act, ended up losing an expensive FOIA lawsuit when the U.S. District Judge upheld the CIA's "can neither confirm or deny" posture on covert employees.

Evidently because Keyhoe's attacks on the government excluded the CIA... he managed to induce Vice-Admiral (USN-Ret.) Roscoe Hillenkoetter, former and original Director of the CIA (1947–50), to join NICAP's Board of Governors.... Hillenkoetter told Keyhoe privately that the CIA had been interested in UFOs from the very beginning... and kept a watchful eye on the subject despite the lack of directives to do so. He also allowed himself to be quoted as saying: "The Air Force has constantly misled the American public about UFOs.... I urge Congressional action to reduce the danger from secrecy."

... By early 1962, Keyhoe was well on the way to forcing Congress to open hearings on UFOs and the Air Force's means of dealing with the subject.... But suddenly, Hillenkoetter pulled the rug out from under him by abruptly resigning from the Board, and Keyhoe's Congressional investigation collapsed faster than a three-story house of cards.

Hillenkoetter's letter of resignation said: "In my opinion, NICAP's investigation has gone as far as possible. I know UFOs are not U. S. or Soviet devices.... The Air Force cannot do any more under the circumstances... and I believe we should not continue to criticize their investigations...."

Since Hillenkoetter's letter represented an almost total reversal from his earlier positions, Keyhoe has long suspected the Admiral was pressured by the CIA and/or the Air Force to drop out of the picture and quit making troublesome statements.... CAUS has determined that Hillenkoetter was in fact pressured by the Agency at the behest of the Air Force, which communicated a number of complaints about Hillenkoetter's role in NICAP to high-level Agency officials. But, . . . another Board member who held a high-level position in the CIA apparently wasn't pressured at all and *remains on the Board to this day* [italics mine]. Col. (USAF-Ret.) Joseph Bryan, III . . . is the founder and original chief of the CIA's Psychological Warfare Staff (1947–53). . . . Very few people, including Keyhoe, knew of Bryan's CIA connections. . . . Bryan approached Keyhoe in late 1959, asking to see some of his "really hot cases." Since Bryan was ostensibly an Air Force officer, Keyhoe immediately suspected an AF plot to infiltrate his organization, and he resisted the Colonel's advances. However, Bryan soon put Keyhoe . . . at ease by allowing himself to be quoted as saying: "The UFOs are interplanetary devices systematically observing the Earth, either manned or remote-controlled, or both. Information on UFOs has been officially withheld. This policy is dangerous." . . . While admitting (in 1977) to having been a former covert official for the CIA and asking that this fact not be made public since "it might embarrass CIA," Bryan denied any association or communication with the CIA during the period he has served on the NICAP Board. . . .

Former CIA briefing officer Karl Pflock was chairman of NICAP's Washington, D.C., subcommittee during the late 1960s and early 1970s. Pflock denies the Agency ever asked him for information on UFOs or NICAP, although he kept his CIA affiliation secret from most NICAP officials. But someone close to NICAP gave the CIA information on the group, as a 1973 document recently released to Ground Saucer Watch reveals.

The undated CIA document, written by an unnamed person from an unnamed component of the Agency, indicates some familiarity with G. Stuart Nixon, at the time a top assistant to NICAP President, John L. Acuff. Interestingly, the NICAP daily activity logs from the late 1960s and early 1970s reflect that Nixon met with several past and present (then) CIA employees on a frequent basis. The CIA officials include Art Lundahl, then the Director of the CIA's National Photographic Interpretation Center, Fred Durant, author of the Robertson Panel Report and a former CIA Office of Scientific Intelligence missile expert, and Dr. Charles Sheldon, a consultant to the Agency now with the Library of Congress. . . . Curiously, however, none of the NICAP logs reflect any conversations between Nixon and Colonel Bryan, either by phone or in person, although almost every other daily occurrence is denoted in the logs. Questioned recently about this discrepency, Nixon refused to comment.

Even more curious is the fact Nixon refuses to discuss his involvement in the ouster of Keyhoe. . . . However, . . . Bryan flatly denied during a 1977 interview that he had anything to do with Keyhoe's abrupt removal. . . . Yet, NICAP files . . . clearly establish that Bryan not only was Chairman of the Board of Governors at the time, but that he wrote and distributed a memo in which he called Keyhoe "inept." Evidently, this memo . . . from the Chairman of the Board, helped convince an otherwise loyal-to-Keyhoe panel to approve his firing. . . .

Keyhoe's abrupt dismissal paved the way for Jack Acuff to be appointed the new President of NICAP. Acuff had been meeting with Stuart Nixon since mid-1968, seemingly waiting in the wings. Prior to his NICAP appointment, Acuff had been the head of the Society of Photographic Scientists and Engineers (SPSE), a Washington-based group that had been the target of frequent KGB spying attempts. Apparently, the Soviets were interested in the Society because a large number of its members were photo-analysts with Department of Defense intelligence components and *with the CIA* [italics mine].[6]

Interestingly enough, I received a mysterious unsigned letter dated December 14, 1977, addressed to a list of major embassies and important personalities. The memo was written on USAF stationery from Bolling Air Force Base, Washington, D.C. Among other alleged exposés, it mentioned Air Force Regulation (AFR) 200-23 and asked:

Why is this regulation entitled *Project NICAP?* What could possibly be so secret that its description is not even listed in the Official AFR Manual of USAF Regulations? And is it a mere coincidence that its name is identical to a civilian organization called NICAP?[7]

Upon receipt of this letter, I immediately phoned Acuff at NICAP and read this portion to him. He denied any knowledge of this Air Force regulation and hastily excused himself, saying that he was expecting an important telephone call. It was the briefest telephone call I had ever had with him. Curiously, he didn't mention his important phone call until I mentioned AFR-200-23; up to that point, he had seemed very content to chat with me.

I then called the Pentagon and talked to a number of offices concerning this AFR. The Air Force requested that I send them a copy of the unsigned memo posthaste, denying that this regulation had anything to do with UFOs, and denying that its title was *Project NICAP*. When I asked them what the real title was, they refused to tell me because both the title and the contents of AFR-200-23, Change 1, were classified!

Concerning NICAP's suspicious history, Zechel concludes his article:

One would naturally have to be suspicious of any board of governors comprised of two former CIA covert employees (Bryan and Lombard), a retired Air Force General once associated with the Foreign Technology Division (FTD), the component that took over UFO analysis, and an ultra-conservative political activist who once compiled files on millions of Americans he considered "potentially subversive" (Fisher)....

Maybe it's a coincidence that the founder of the CIA's Psychological Warfare Staff has been on the board for nearly twenty years. Maybe it's another coincidence that Charles Lombard, a former CIA covert employee (according to himself) would seek out a retired CIA executive to run the organization (i.e., after Jack Acuff was replaced by *retired* CIA agent, Alan N. Hall in 1979!)....

Or maybe we're all paranoid.... Perhaps Keyhoe deserved to be fired from the organization he built with his own sweat, blood, and sacrifice. The timing couldn't have been better, in any case. Keyhoe, after all, was beginning to focus on the CIA in 1969, instead of his tunnel-visioned attacks on the Air Force.... With Keyhoe out of the way, the laughable conclusions of Condon and his gang of merry UFO debunkers allowed the Air Force to get off the hook for good.... *if they wanted to destroy the leading anti-secrecy organization of the 1960s, they couldn't have done a better job if they'd tried.*

In the 1970s civilian UFO research was at a low ebb. The public regarded the whole subject as a past fad, but Air Force Intelligence quietly continued (without interruptions) collecting government-controlled-source UFO report information, including reports made by airline pilots.

Then a new wave of UFOs peaked during October and November 1973, leaving many new believers in its wake. MUFON membership and investigative capability increased at a spectacular rate under the leadership of its international Director Walter H. Andrus, Jr. Scientists, engineers, and professional people increasingly joined the ranks of civilian UFO researchers.

Before the end of the year, Dr. Hynek organized the Center for UFO Studies (CUFOS). Major Keyhoe, now 75, released his fifth book on UFOs.[8] John Wallace Spencer and Charles Berlitz's books on the Bermuda Triangle rode to success on the coattails of UFO interest. Erich Von Däniken's *Chariots of the Gods?,* previously popular in Europe, became a resounding hit in the United States.

By March 1974 the growing evidence for UFO reality became so great that the AIAA UFO subcommittee, directed by Dr. Joachim Keuttner, petitioned for full committee status. Kuettner, a well-known scientist with impressive credentials, directed the Environmental Research Laboratories of the National Oceanic and Atmospheric Administration at Boulder, Colorado. Major radio and TV networks began devoting prime time to serious discussions of UFOs. Talk-show hosts and hostesses interviewed old-time researchers and a number of newcomers to the field, including Stanton Friedman, a retired nuclear physicist who now lectures full-time on UFOs. Astronauts James McDivitt and Gordon Cooper publicly related their own personal UFO experiences. The Air Force released its files on

Project Bluebook to the National Archives, and gave strong support to a new TV series, *Project UFO,* directed by Jack Webb, well known for the earlier *Dragnet.*

Interestingly enough, *Project UFO* was produced by retired Air Force Colonel William Coleman, SAFOI's former chief information officer for Project Bluebook! This show attempted to dramatize actual sightings from Bluebook files, with names, dates, and places changed to protect witnesses. However, the hodgepodge of variously configured UFOs depicted each week had no resemblance to what was actually reported. Although some interesting "unexplaineds" appeared from time to time, most shows portrayed cases explainable in terms of man-made objects or natural phenomena. The plots followed almost verbatim the scripts suggested by the Robertson Panel. Suspense was built up at the beginning of each program concerning what appeared to be a real, unexplained craft. Then the Air Force sleuths—always the head of Project Bluebook and his faithful sergeant—would move in to explain the sighting. (In reality, the head of Project Bluebook hardly ever investigated UFO sightings personally.)

One theme was emphasized over and over and over again: The Air Force never covers up UFO information. Project Bluebook guys were portrayed as wearing the white hats. Civilian UFO organizations and their directors were depicted as incompetent, unscrupulous crackpots out to make a fast buck on the gullible public. No wonder the series did not last another season: It was the same old gobbledygook that Bluebook had dished out to the public for years.

CHAPTER NOTES

1. John G. Fuller, "Flying Saucer Fiasco," *Look,* May 14, 1968, p. 60.

2. E. U. Condon, director, *Scientific Study of Unidentified Flying Objects* (New York: E. P. Dutton & Co., Inc. 1969), p. 48.

3. J. Allen Hynek, *The UFO Experience* (Chicago: Henry Regnery Co., 1972), p. 250.

4. "UFOs, An Appraisal of the Problem," *Astronautics and Aeronautics,* November 1970, p. 50

5. Office of Assistant Secretary of Defense, *News Release: "Air Force to terminate Project Bluebook,"* December 17, 1969.

6. Todd Zechel, "NI-CIA-AP or NICAP?" *Just Cause,* January 1979, pp. 5–8.

7. Personal files.

8. Donald E. Keyhoe, *Aliens from Space* (New York: Doubleday & Co., Inc., 1973), pp. 90, 91.

GUIDELINES FOR AN INVESTIGATOR

Dr. Hynek has pointed out that the term "UFO" should apply only to flying objects that "remain unidentified after close scrutiny of all available evidence by persons who are technically capable of making a common sense identification, if one is possible." Thus in a very real sense it is the investigator, plus the results of an investigation, that make a UFO! The reported object itself may be intrinsically identifiable or unidentifiable. Who could know for sure, barring its physical confiscation? For the present, a UFO must remain a report.

A tremendous responsibility rests upon an investigator's shoulders, since an accurate evaluation of his report by others depends completely upon the caliber of his investigation. Hence, UFO organizations cannot be too careful in ascertaining the motivation of potential investigators. Some otherwise-qualified individuals join groups and clubs purely for prestige. The applicant should be informed at the very outset that field investigation is *work*. The position isn't necessarily glamorous or exciting; it demands a person with a proven record for stability and objectivity in other areas of life. Ample spare time is a must: When called to investigate, such a person must be willing and able.

Ideally, a UFO investigator should have a technical or scientific background. Besides engineers and scientists, other potential prospects include science and mathematics teachers, detectives, insurance or crime investigators, newspaper reporters, and former military intelligence-gathering officers—most of whom have had experience working directly with people and/or investigating certain incidents. Some good investigators have had little formal technical or scientific training, but their many years of field experience have given them a broad knowledge.

An essential period of learning and practical training can be accomplished by first becoming thoroughly familiar with the contents of a comprehensive field investigator's manual. I would recommend *The MUFON Field Investigator's Manual*[1] and *The UFO Handbook*.[2]

The *MUFON Manual* helps provide knowledge gained firsthand from those who have already been involved in UFO investigations for many years. In 1975 I became a board member of MUFON in the capacity of national director of investigations. My first assignment was to write a detailed field investigator's manual to provide uniform procedures and instructions. I was given free rein to share experience gained from over a decade of personal, on-site investigations of reported UFO sightings; and I contributed eight of its fifteen sections. They provide uniform guidelines concerning the establishment of a UFO reporting network, required equipment, investigation, and writing a report. Published in June of 1975, *The MUFON Field Investigator's Manual* was immediately adopted for use by CUFOS as well.

One lengthy and crucial section deals with how to identify a large variety of phenomena commonly reported as UFOs. A general question-naire covers simple visual sightings of an unidentified object in the sky. Other supplementary forms ask pertinent questions relating to electrical/magnetic effects, animal effects, psychological/physiological effects, landing/traces/artifacts, entity reports, and photographic and radar cases.

A period of on-the-job training with an experienced investigator is a must. One never completely graduates, learning a little bit about a number of disciplines including astronomy, aviation, biology, chemistry, meteorology, photography, physics, psychology, and sociology. You will need to acquire a broad knowledge about a lot of things to effectively separate the true UFO from the homemade hot-air balloons, stars, planets, meteors, and aircraft. You necessarily become an integral part of every UFO sighting that you personally investigate. It is you who compiles a report on the data extracted from UFO-sighting witnesses. Your prejudices, precon-ceived thoughts about UFOs; family responsibilities, social pressures, and relationship with the witnesses are all apt to color your written report. You must be objective, scrutinizing all available evidence in a dedicated effort to identify the reported object.

Before launching a full-scale investigation, ask the witness some initial questions about the alleged sighting. This can be done by telephone. First, obtain the witness's full name, address, phone number, age, edu-cational background, and place of employment. Second, ask the witness to describe briefly what was seen, including the date, time, and place of the incident. Ask the observer to compare the object's apparent size with the apparent size of a full moon. (To double check the object's estimated size, have the witness point out a familiar object with the same apparent size as the UFO. You can measure apparent size with a ruler held at arm's length.) Next, try to acquire a rough estimate of the object's *real* size, shape, color, distance, and altitude. Find out the approximate direction of the object from the observer, in what direction it was traveling, and its estimated elevation above the horizon.

Armed with such data, a trained investigator can often identify the reported object, or provide at least a probable identification. I supplied a checklist to the *National Enquirer* to alert its readers to this identification process.[3] For example, if a witness described a bright light source hovering in the western sky near the horizon at the same time that Venus was prominent and setting, that investigation need go no further! Other obvious suspects: nocturnal lights that behave like bright stars or conventional aircraft. If the reported UFO isn't readily identifiable after preliminary analysis, an on-site examination of the sighting area is in order.

By use of a compass, the investigator records the azimuth of the UFO when first and last observed. The elevation is then determined by estimation or utilization of an inclinometer. Measurements should then be made concerning the size and distance of any known objects—trees, houses, hills, towers, etc.—in front or in back of which the UFO passed. Knowledge of apparent size, elevation, and the distance of objects which the UFO passed in front of make it possible to mathematically estimate the object's real size. You may also obtain a fairly accurate estimate of the sighting's duration: Have the witness mentally reenact the experience while being timed by a watch.

While at the site, carefully check the environmental situation. The witness may have forgotten to mention the presence of power lines, railroad tracks, a river, stream, or pond. Now is the time to note the exact sighting location on a topographical map. Also make a hand-drawn map of the immediate sighting area to supplement the witness's sketch. Compass directions, location of the witness versus the UFO and its flight path should be clearly denoted, along with any other pertinent features.

If possible, photograph the sighting area, showing the horizon over which the UFO was first and last seen. This may require more than one exposure; a wide-angle lens is helpful. Place a piece of tracing paper over the photograph and have the witness draw in the UFO's flight path and draw its apparent size in relation to other details on the photograph. If photographs of the sighting area aren't taken, sketch a rough drawing of the horizon and initiate the same process.

Next, make a thorough check for additional witnesses by inquiring in adjacent houses or places of business. A number of agencies keep a blotter of incoming reports. Check with local and state police, military bases, airports, civil defense organizations, planetariums, observatories, newspapers, and radio stations.

Cases of a special nature—involving associated electromagnetic effects, animal effects, psychological and physiological effects, the documentation and handling of UFO photographs, physical traces and artifacts, and UFO incidents involving entities—are more involved. A series of additional questionnaires and detailed instructions are found in *The MUFON Field Investigator's Manual.*

After collecting pertinent data during a personal visit to the witness's home and the sighting area, the investigator's next step is to search for a known stimulus for the UFO sighting. This may require a professional analysis of photographs or suspected UFO effects and by-products. Only after all possible natural phenomena and man-made objects are eliminated does the investigator evaluate the *reported* flying object as *unidentified.* The collected data is then put into a report format and submitted to headquarters for further study and evaluation.

The investigator's report is a permanent record of a UFO experience, its contents based upon the completed questionnaires, interviews, and all other pertinent data gathered in the course of an investigation. A description of the MUFON investigator's report format (excerpted from Chapter 8 of *The MUFON Field Investigator's Manual*) is outlined below:

8.2.1 REPORT HEADING

Subject:
Type of Report:
Date of Report:
Date of Sighting:
Time of Sighting:
Place of Sighting:
Local Evaluation:

To:
From:

8.2.2 SIGHTING BACKGROUND: A description of the circumstances surrounding the receipt of the initial UFO sighting information. How and When was the information received?

8.2.3 SIGHTING ACCOUNT: A brief chronological composite or consolidation of the UFO sighting account(s). A summarization of the Personal Account from the Form 1 and additional related data uncovered during the investigation.

8.2.4 SIGHTING INVESTIGATION

8.2.4.1 *An Activity Log:* A simple chronological log by date, time and place denoting the tasks the Investigator carried out during the investigation.

8.2.4.2   *The Interview and Interrogation:* **A** description of the interview and interrogation including the Investigator's personal impressions of the primary witness and his or her home environment, interests, etc.

8.2.4.3   *Additional Witness Check:* The circumstances surrounding how, when, and where additional witnesses were located and any subsequent interviews and interrogations including the Investigator's personal impressions of the witnesses and their home environment, interests, etc.

8.2.4.4   *Natural Phenomena Check:* A list of what natural phenomena were checked in an effort to identify the stimulus for the reported UFO. The reasons for rejecting or suspecting each, as being the stimulus, should be clearly noted.

8.2.4.5   *Man-Made Object Check:* A list of what man-made objects were checked in an effort to identify the stimulus for the reported UFO. The reasons for rejecting or suspecting each, as being the stimulus, should be clearly noted.

8.2.4.6   *Other Possibilities:* A list of other possible stimuli for the UFO sighting, such as: hallucination, hoax, psychic phenomena, etc. The reasons for rejecting or suspecting each, as being the stimulus, should be clearly noted.

8.2.4.7   *Witness Background Check:* A list of the persons checked, their comments about the witness's character and their relationship to the witness. This section should include the Investigator's impressions of the witness's personality, credibility, etc.

8.2.5   *SIGHTING EVALUATION:* The result of an overall analysis of the data collected by the Investigator. If the object was identified, the identification should be noted both here and within the Report Heading of the cover letter. If the object is evaluated as unknown, grade it according to the following captions: Great significance, Significant, Ordinary, or Borderline. The evaluation should be noted here and within the Report Heading of the cover letter.

8.2.6 *DETAILED BACK-UP:* Cross-reference all back-up material by date and location of the sighting. Back-up material would consist of: Signed questionnaires, news clips, maps, photographs, recording tape, etc.

Upon arriving at the witness's home, limit investigation time to collecting data. Discussing UFOs with witnesses during an inquiry might introduce information that could color their stories. First, obtain a verbal account of the reported sighting from start to finish. The witness should not be interrupted, except for necessary prompting. The use of a tape recorder is highly desirable if the witness is agreeable. Some people don't converse freely when a recording is being made; in cases like this, take notes instead.

During a MUFON investigation, after the interview the witness fills out the first page of Form 1. That provides personal data, a sketch of the object and area, and a written sighting account. When this step is completed, an interrogation of the witness is undertaken. (This differs from the interview—this time the investigator is doing the talking.) The investigator now reviews the story with the witness, filling out page 2. Again, a tape recording of this proceeding is valuable for cross-checking and future reference. Form 1 also contains certain questions designed to alert the investigator to the need to use additional forms to record pertinent information about special events and effects that might have been associated with the UFO sighting. Forms 3–8 provide coverage for such cases; Form 2 is simply a computer input sheet.

A personal evaluation of the witness precedes a formal character reference check. To become acquainted with the witness's personality and background, especially in regard to the subject of UFOs, ask pertinent questions and note what kind of reading material is in the home. (*The MUFON Field Investigator's Manual* offers suggestions in this respect.) Names and organizations obtained from the witness during this personal evaluation are contacted later as part of a formal character-reference check, normally entailing specific inquiries to neighbors; teachers; employers; and priests, ministers, or rabbis concerning the witness's honesty, personality, interests, and capabilities.

Do these witnesses represent a particular segment of the population?

Polls taken in the United States have indicated over 51 percent of the public believe that UFOs are real. That adds up to the impressive figure of 78 million people. Commenting on his 1973 survey concerning UFOs, George H. Gallup, Jr., writes that UFO sightings are proliferating.

Currently 11 percent of American adults (18 years old and older) report having seen something they thought was a UFO. This is more than double the percentage who reported similar experiences in 1966.

Translated into numbers, an astonishing 15 million persons now say they have seen UFOs![4]

What is their educational background? Gallup states that:

The typical UFO sighter is simply an average sincere American citizen. About the same number of women report seeing UFOs as men. Education makes no difference either, for persons in the higher education bracket are just as likely to have sighted a UFO as those with high school or grade school diplomas.

... Most sightings have been in the south and midwest; 15 and 14 percent of the persons living in those regions, respectively, have seen something in the sky they couldn't explain. In the west, 11 percent have reported sightings and the lowest proportion, 5 percent, live in the east. Also, persons living in smaller towns and rural areas are more likely to have seen UFOs.[5]

Such statistics are at odds with the popular—yet unsubstantiated—notion that UFO witnesses must be irresponsible, uneducated, or mentally unbalanced. Such critics fail to realize that most witnesses just happened to be in the right place at the right time.

At precisely 12:35 A.M., January 6, 1979, the telephone beside our bed jolted me out of a sound sleep. Margaret, who has the telephone on her side of the bed, usually answers our nocturnal calls. By the time the phone is passed to me, I'm usually wide enough awake to deal with the caller.

This time it was the state police at Boston. The barracks at Sturbridge had received a number of anonymous calls on UFOs. One woman reported that a diamond-shaped object had hovered only 100 feet above her car. Another person related that UFOs had caused a minor traffic jam as cars stopped to watch. One caller did identify himself; he reported that his sister, Anmarie Emery, had been stopped by three glowing objects while en route to her parents' home at Springfield.

Later in the morning, I called Anmarie and taped my telephone interview with her as a preparatory step to a more detailed investigation. Pertinent excerpts follow:

Raymond Fowler: Are you interested in filing a report?
Anmarie: I don't know. I just saw something, three objects that were kind of triangular. I saw them flying for about twenty minutes before I actually saw them close. They were off to my left, about maybe a quarter of a mile. They were flying, like around a mountain, and then I—. Do you know the Mass Pike coming this way from Boston? There's a split-off at

the right where it goes down to Sturbridge. Well, I turned around the corner there, and there were no other cars in the area.

As Anmarie rounded the bend, three glowing red pyramidal-shaped craft were hovering over the road directly in front of her car!

Anmarie: My car came to a stop! It's a standard; I never shifted. My foot was still on the gas and it never stalled out. The engine was still running. It's not exactly a quiet car. I could hear the engine going because there was no other noise. My radio and CB went off.
Raymond Fowler: They just stopped operating with no crackling sound or anything?
Anmarie: Right. I was listening to my car radio, but I had my CB light on so that I could tell if someone was talking on the CB. That light went off, and my radio went off.
Raymond Fowler: When the car stopped, did you notice the panel lights?
Anmarie: My headlights stayed on. The panel lights stayed on.
Raymond Fowler: How about the alternator or generator light?
Anmarie: I don't remember seeing it go on.
Raymond Fowler: None of your warning lights came on?
Anmarie: Not that I can remember.
Raymond Fowler: How close were the objects to your car?
Anmarie: At this point, about ten feet in the air. They were really close.
Raymond Fowler: How big were they, compared to the size of your automobile?
Anmarie: I've got a small 1970 Ford Maverick. They were wider than my car, but not as deep—maybe ten feet wide. The objects glowed red, and each had blinking red lights on the back. Like the entire back walls were blinking and the rest of it was just a red glow. It wasn't like a red *light*; there was no center of intensity. It was kind of like just one straight color.

Each object was shaped like a four-sided pyramid. Their apexes were facing her car, and their flat sides were horizontal, parallel to the ground. They appeared to be constructed of a smooth glasslike material. The red glow seemed to be emanating from within the objects, but there was no noticeable point source; the glow was uniform all over the craft. Four brighter red, blinking portions protruded along either side of the back of the objects.

I appeared to Anmarie that each object had four red bars of light affixed to its rear. They blinked slowly about once every two seconds. The weird craft were in the same type of formation that she had noted earlier when they were flying in the distance. The closest was only twenty feet away and ten feet above the road. The second hovered to its right, but about forty feet away. The third hovered to the first object's left, about sixty feet away.

Anmarie: There was this very funny smell, almost like a skunk, but like a sweet skunk, you know? It was really weird but . . .

Raymond Fowler: Have you ever played with an electric train and smelled the odor? For your information, I think that was ozone. . . . Did you press down on the accelerator to try to make the car go?

Anmarie: No, I was just frozen. As I approached them, my car slowed down and came to a stop. They never approached me. My foot was still on the gas. My engine was still running. It wasn't racing like if I had it in neutral. It was still running at the pace when I was driving.

Raymond Fowler: You heard nothing and you felt no heat?

Anmarie: Yeah, I felt my face getting very, very hot; and when I came back to my parents' home my face was like sunburned.

Raymond Fowler: Did it flake at all?

Anmarie: Ah, above my eyebrows it did, but that's all.

Raymond Fowler: And it's disappeared now, has it?

Anmarie: I don't know. I haven't looked in a mirror yet. I just got up.

Raymond Fowler: Did you have a watch on? Is it keeping good time?

Anmarie: My watch is keeping the right time.

Raymond Fowler: OK, are both your car radio and the CB okay? No problems since?

Anmarie: They came back on. You know, I was listening to WHYN on the way in. When the objects left, the CB just lit up, and then the needle went shooting over to the right.

Raymond Fowler: How did the objects disappear from view?

Anmarie: They just went straight up and continued their formation. They leveled out, and then went off. Whenever they slowed down, like when they went around that little hill, the largest side of the triangle was on the bottom. As soon as they went to turn, that side dropped about forty-five degrees, almost like the wing on a plane. They went around that way, and then they went straight up. They were in that position when I saw them, you know—in a hovering position with the bottom half with the longest end down. . . . You know those new TR-7's? The weird kind of car that's got almost like a triangle shape? That's the way they are, with the shortest side in the back, the longest one along the bottom and the other one going up. And when they stopped, that end kind of fell down, almost like a slowing motion.

Raymond Fowler: OK, how long do you think you observed the objects from the time you first saw them and last saw them, including seeing them in the distance?

Anmarie: At least a half hour.

Raymond Fowler: Was there much traffic on the road?

Anmarie: At one point there was, and at the New York exit [Route 86], everything thinned out a lot. For a couple of miles, it was like I was the only car on the road.

Raymond Fowler: OK, and the incident in front of the car lasted about how long?

Anmarie: Two or three minutes.

Raymond Fowler: Was your thinking impaired during all of this?

Anmarie: Yeah.

Raymond Fowler: There were no involuntary actions on your part?

Anmarie: No. I squeezed, clutched the wheel so hard—you know, I have long fingernails—I put scars in my palm!

Interestingly enough, the eastbound lane cannot be seen from the sighting area. A view either way is blocked by a hill. Coincidentally, the objects left at precisely the same time as Anmarie noticed distant automobile headlights hit the trees to her right. Apparently the approaching car caused the three craft to leave.

My initial investigation of her sighting lasted over two weeks. During this time, a complete character-reference check was performed to ascertain her reliability as a witness. Anmarie Emery was an excellent example of Gallup's "average sincere American citizen" who has had a UFO experience. She was single, age twenty, employed as an assistant executive housekeeper by a well-known motel chain. She graduated from a Roman Catholic high school and attended Cape Cod Community College, where she earned an associate degree in hotel management. I talked to eight persons about Anmarie, starting with her mother, who herself holds a master's degree in biochemistry. Mrs. Emery told me that she had no doubt that Anmarie had experienced something unusual. She did not believe that she had made up such a story. When I asked what had occurred that evening when Anmarie arrived at her home, she told me that her daughter had not voluntarily related the incident. "She was a little late coming in. I walked into the kitchen, and her face was beet red! She just looked stupefied, amazed, you know? I said, 'What's the matter?' and she said, 'You're not going to believe me!' "

On the following day, both Mr. and Mrs. Emery noticed the minor flaking of skin around Anmarie's eyes and nose. It lasted only a few days. When I personally interviewed her a week later, her skin had healed. (Interestingly enough, a somewhat similar encounter I had investigated in Maine a few weeks before had also caused a mild sunburn effect upon the witness.)

Anmarie's brother confirmed that she had had a scary experience. He called the state police. She did not want to, as she was afraid that they would not believe her.

One friend of the family told me that Anmarie had always impressed her as a "down-to-earth kid—really levelheaded. I'm sure what she saw probably scared her, but I don't think she would exaggerate it. I don't think she would pull a hoax." Another person described her as a hard-working, honest girl, definitely not the type to perpetrate a hoax. He commented "Anmarie is straight as straight can be. That's why I'm intrigued with the whole episode."

My interviews with officials at the high school and college that Anmarie attended bore out all that I had already heard. I talked to teachers who had known her very well. (I often come across other sightings during the course of an investigation. One nun who had a master's degree in aerospace engineering told me that in July 1978, she and other sisters had seen a huge cigar-shaped object pass over the grounds, followed by a disc-shaped object with a purple glowing rim.) I talked with Anmarie's priest and her current supervisor, all of whom gave her high marks for reliability and honesty, and described her as a hard-working young woman.

A number of other UFOs were sighted in Massachusetts on January 5, 1979. Some reports originated in towns very close to Sturbridge, in addition to a number of anonymous UFO calls received by the state police. At six o'clock on that evening, two witnesses at Leicester stopped their car to watch two strangely lit, silent objects hover, perform sharp turns, and move away. An hour later at Worcester, a physics teacher and former Navy jet pilot and his son watched in amazement as a lighted object approached, then reversed direction without benefit of a turn before hovering and then moving away behind trees.

Other interesting sightings were made on January 4 and 9 by witnesses who were not trained observers. However, one must ask if such credentials are required for close-encounters such as that Anmarie experienced, where there is very little leeway for misinterpretation. However, a goodly number of UFO sightings involve *trained* observers.

CHAPTER NOTES

1. Raymond E. Fowler, ed., *The MUFON Field Investigator's Manual* (Seguin, Texas: MUFON, 103 Oldtowne Road, Seguin, Texas 78155, 1975).

2. Allan Hendry, *The UFO Handbook* (New York: Doubleday & Co., Inc., 1979).

3. *National Enquirer*, "Tips for UFO Watchers," June 28, 1978, p. 48.

4. *Gallup Poll*, San Diego *Evening Tribune*, November 30, 1973, and George H. Gallup, Jr., and Tom Reinken, "Who Believes in UFOs?" *Fate Magazine*, August 1974, p. 55.

5. *loc. cit.*

EXPERIENCED WITNESSES

The afternoon of August 27, 1978, private pilot Arthur Silva and a companion took off from Beverly Airport in his Cessna 150. The aircraft carried a transponder that enabled the FAA air-traffic control tower at nearby Logan International Airport to keep the plane under close surveillance. National Weather Service records read that visibility was 15 miles, with thin scattered clouds at 25,000 feet. The wind was from the east-southeast at 10 knots. It was a grand day for flying. Silva intended to touch down briefly at a small airport at Provincetown, on the tip of Cape Cod, and then return to Beverly.

Shortly after takeoff, the Logan tower warned Silva that traffic near him at his 8 o'clock position did not respond to radio calls. Silva glanced around but couldn't see anything. Since Logan's radar did not record altitude, Silva assumed that the traffic was higher and posed no danger. He kept his aircraft on a dead south-southeast heading out over the Atlantic.

At approximately quarter after one, ten miles north-northwest of Provincetown, Silva and his companion noticed a bright reflection directly ahead. He estimated it was about four miles away and at his altitude of 2,500 feet. Both assumed it to be another airplane reflecting sunlight. As it drew closer it became darker in color, and a vague outline could be seen. It didn't have any wings!

Both then felt that it must be a helicopter, until it suddenly picked up speed and rushed toward them faster than a helicopter could fly. As Arthur later put it during my taped interview:

Arthur: I said to Buster, "What in the heck is that? It looks something like a helicopter." Coming towards us, it would have a roundish appearance to it. And then I said, "Hell, it can't be a helicopter. It's going too damned fast!" It zoomed by, heading north, extremely fast. It had no running lights; no lights of any nature. We had a real good view of it. After it went by us, I called traffic control, told them that something went by me like a bat out of hell, and I asked Boston if they had it on radar and whether they spotted it going by me. And they said yes, that they did have traffic. It passed me at three o'clock going north. They didn't say what, they just said "traffic."

Raymond Fowler: What was the object's configuration?

Arthur: My view of it was a round object. It could have been the side of a disc. It could have been something round.

Raymond Fowler: What color was it?

Arthur: Metallic, I'd say, just like burnished aluminum.

Raymond Fowler: Did it have any protrusions?

Arthur: Nope, none whatsoever. No wings. No propeller. No exhaust.

Raymond Fowler: How far away do you estimate it to have been?

Arthur: I guessed that the distance would be about 1,000 feet.

Raymond Fowler: When you first saw it, what was its apparent size as compared to the diameter of the full moon?

Arthur: I would say that it was a full moon, possible a little bit smaller. Not much smaller. Possibly three quarters or better. When it was closest to us, I'd say it looked like the size of a . . . about one and a half times the full moon.

Raymond Fowler: How did the object disappear from view?

Arthur: Well, my plane is one of the few planes that does have a rear-view window. I snapped around as fast as I could, but I couldn't see it. Of course you have ribbing there on your windows and the angle is such that I think the left-hand rib would have been in the way.

Silva's companion, an elderly man, described essentially the same thing, except he thought he saw a blue tinge to it. Silva felt that perhaps the object was reflecting the bright blue sky. The passenger told me that from his quick glimpse of it, "It would almost seem to be like a disc on end, on edge. . . . It didn't have wings. I turned around and I couldn't see it anymore because my vision was blocked from the plane itself."

A character-reference check on Arthur and his companion indicated that both were reliable. Arthur, the owner of a small restaurant, has been a private pilot for eight years and has a flight instructor's rating. A commercial pilot who has known Arthur for a number of years told me that Arthur was a good pilot, not the type who would perpetrate a hoax. He stressed that Arthur would not have misinterpreted a known object.

The FAA told me that there were no military or unconventional aircraft flying in the area. A check with the National Weather Service indicated that only two weather balloons had been launched that day, one at seven A.M. and the other at seven P.M.

On the previous day, Brett and Ellen, a young college couple, were driving along Cape Cod's Route 6 between Hyannis and Barnstable. About ten P.M., a very large, noiseless object slowly crossed the road directly in front of their car. The craft was so low that they thought it would crash into surrounding woods. For a moment it disappeared behind trees, then it ascended and made a second pass in front of the car before making its final disappearance behind trees. The object had a metallic sheen, curved edges, and vertical, rectangular lighted ports along the side facing the witnesses. They noticed moving shadows behind these illuminated apertures or windows. Something like a blue, glowing railing or ring ran around its circumference.

Later that night—actually during the early morning hours of August 27—a woman socialite from a very illustrious family from Wellfleet, also on Cape Cod, had awakened at 4:22 A.M. to use the bathroom and noticed a light source through her bedroom window. She glanced and saw an object with curved sides flying silently from the bay side toward the ocean, its speed slower than that of a conventional aircraft. It emitted a vaguely glowing vapor and carried a number of lights that reminded her of a neon theater marquee.

Later in the day, several hours after Arthur's UFO experience, another sighting was made by a trained observer from Cape Ann, just 40 miles up the coast. The witness was Robert L. Sampson, age 48, who has a master's degree in biology and physics and teaches physics at the local high school. He works for the Civil Defense as a radiologist, and received training in aircraft identification during his tour of duty as a radar-sonar operator with the U.S. Navy:

I had been working in my backyard and was taking a rest, sitting in a chaise on my patio. The mackerel sky and cloud formation were interesting. I spotted an orange circle towards the North, which was too low for aircraft in our vicinity to be at. When I first saw the object, it looked like an orange ball that was falling. Then, as it came into view, it looked like a target sleeve we used during navy gunnery practice, but there wasn't any aircraft towing it! The object moved from north to south. It did not veer from its trajectory and disappeared beyond the tree line. It was in sight for a period of ten seconds and traversed an arc of about 120 degrees . . . I was amazed at the utter silence of the object. It was smaller than an F-100 jet fighter at the same altitude. . . . I could see no apparent controls like rudder, or wings, or ailerons.

Bob estimated that at its closest point, the strange cylindrical object was about 2,000 feet away. It appeared to be on a gently descending flight path that would have caused it to enter the ocean.

By now it should be clear that most witnesses to UFO sightings are perfectly rational people. Several years ago I conducted a detailed analysis of 160 local cases personally investigated.[1] I employed only sightings evaluated in the unknown category that had taken place between 1963 and 1972. My study considered UFO types, configurations, effects, locale, weather, time, and witnesses. A comparison of my local sample with national samples revealed remarkable similarities, strongly indicating that people everywhere were reporting essentially the same things.

My statistics revealed that 291 of a total of 461 witnesses, or 63 percent, were in the young and middle-aged category.

CHILD (7–12)	TEEN (13–19)	YOUNG (20–30)	MIDDLE (31–50)	SENIOR (60–)
9%	25%	24%	39%	3%
42	115	111	180	13

Most of those in the adult category had at least a high school education; 16 percent had received further schooling. This percentage included 21 persons with bachelor's degrees and 4 with advanced degrees.

The 291 young and middle-adult witnesses represented a large variety of occupations, some of which are outlined as follows:

Scientist	Engineer	Technician	Teacher	Police	Other
2%	2%	3%	2%	8%	83%
5	5	8	7	24	242

The *Other* category included the following occupations:

Doctor	Airline stewardess	Minister
Cabinetmaker	Mechanic	Horticulturist
Priest	Dental assistant	Accountant
Nurse	Secretary	Postmaster
Writer	News reporter	Clerk
Truck driver	Administrator	Bus driver
Fire chief	Insurance salesman	Farmer
Realtor	Sweeper	Machinist
News editor	Baker	Airport manager
Taxi driver	Telephone operator	Draftsman
Architect	College student	Housewife

Many of the male adults had also attended a variety of military training schools. Eight were still qualified private or commercial aircraft pilots. But in this local sample, the people who reported UFOs represented a broad cross section of the public at large—which is exactly what one would expect of reports involved in the sighting of real physical objects. The situation has not changed since 1972; the same types of objects are being reported by people from all walks of life.

In the above survey, very few senior adults or children reported UFOs, but there are good reasons for this. Most senior citizens tend to be conservative and less likely to report extraordinary things. Older folks are especially sensitive about maintaining an image of sound mental health, and are also more restricted in their outdoor activities. As for children, however, parents tend to disregard their UFO reports as fantasy—and some, no doubt, are just that. But sincere children make excellent witnesses. Their minds are relatively uncluttered with adult misconceptions, and they describe what they see in simple, childlike terms. One little girl experienced what is now called a close encounter of the third kind. In this case, the parents were understanding; fortunately, so was the investigator.

This event took place on April 23, 1966—just one day after the Beverly affair—in the small rural town of Bingham, Maine.

On May 6, 1966, the *Morning Sentinel* of Waterville, Maine, carried news about the sighting.

BINGHAM GIRL SAYS SHE OBSERVED UFO

Bingham—She's just six years old but states she saw a UFO on the afternoon of April 23 and nobody has been able to "shake" her story. Of course, Kimberly Baker doesn't call it a UFO or flying saucer. To her it looked like a "big ball" or a "bubble." . . .

The news story stated that the area where Kimberly had reported the landed object "appeared as if some object might have landed on it for grass and close-to-ground greenery was flattened." The sighting was investigated by MUFON field investigator Richard Bonenfant, and most of what follows is taken directly from his fine report. Richard himself was born in Lewiston, Maine, in 1944. He spent three years in military service before taking his bachelor's degree at the University of Maine. He earned his master's degree in anthropology from the State University of New York. Since then he has been engaged in the study of birth defects at Albany Medical College, and more recently with the New York State Department of Health. He has published several articles in this field. I mention his credentials to stress that the investigator, a professional who conducted a careful inquiry, was impressed with the witness and her story. According to Bonenfant,

Kimberly Baker and her two cousins, Wendy and Bruce, were attempting to pick pussy willows in a large field south of her cousins' house. They soon discovered that the willow stems were too elastic and tough

to be broken off by hand, so Wendy and Bruce went to their house to get a pair of scissors. While waiting for her cousins to return, Kimberly noted a large, shiny object descend toward her from the direction of Kennebec Mill. Startled and frightened, she froze as the object silently landed several yards from where she stood. Kim quietly faced the object for over a minute before it departed over the roof of a neighbor's house.

When Kim returned home, she went directly to her mother, tugged on her skirt, and said repeatedly, "Mommy, Mommy, I saw something!" Mrs. Baker did not give her daughter's excited comment much attention. Later, she remembered that Kim, as she was nicknamed, had kept unusually close to her that day, as if wanting the security of her presence.

Two days later, on Monday, April 25, Mrs. Baker recalled her daughter's comment. When she queried Kim, "What did you see?" Kim answered, "A big bubble."

"How big was it?"

"Like daddy's car but higher."

"What color was the bubble?" Mrs. Baker asked.

"Shiny." Kim pointed at the family toaster and said, "Like that!" Further questioning revealed that the object had a "sort of door, and a window." The window was later determined to be rectangular in shape and approximately eight inches high. Three distinct lights were observed. On either end of the craft were steady red lights which seemed to emanate from the body of the vehicle. A flashing green light was stationed just above the center of the object. This light appeared to come from a source slightly elevated from the main body. After answering her mother's questions about the craft, Kim proceeded to make some crude drawings of the "bubble."

Mrs. Baker was unnerved by her daughter's account of this strange encounter. Almost for assurance, she notified a family acquaintance, Mr. Allie King, of the sighting. A representative of the Gannett Publishing Company, Mr. King made weekly visits to Bingham in order to make collections for the *Morning Sentinel*. On Wednesday, April 27, he visited the Baker family and reviewed Kim's account firsthand. That afternoon, he tried repeatedly to shake Kim's story by deliberately confusing details. Kim invariably corrected him so that no inconsistencies could be detected. At this time, however, another aspect of Kim's experience came to light.

During the flurry of questions that occurred that afternoon, Mrs. Baker chanced to ask her daughter if she had been afraid. "At first I was," Kim immediately replied, "but not after the man smiled at me." Stunned by this new revelation, Mrs. Baker pressed for details.

Mrs. Baker: What did the man look like, Kim?

Kim: Like Daddy or René [a friend of her father].

Mrs. Baker: What did he do?

Kim: He winked at me, and smiled.

Mrs. Baker: Anything else?

Kim: He said something to me.

Mrs. Baker: What did he say?

Kim: I don't know, I only saw his lips move.

Mrs. Baker: What was he wearing?

Kim: He had a bubble on his head, but he took it off before he spoke to me.

Mrs. Baker: Could you see what else he was wearing?

Kim: When he stood up, I could see that he had lots of black buttons on his chest.

Mrs. Baker: How do you know he stood up?

Kim: Because his head moved up, above the window.

Mrs. Baker: What was the color of his clothes?

Kim: Shiny white.

The introduction of a "man" into Kim's narration only increased her mother's anxiety. Seeking an explanation, Mrs. Baker and Mr. King asked to be taken to the landing site.

Kim, with her blonde hair, blue eyes, and restless energy, led her family and Mr. King to the spot where the object had landed. When they arrived where Kim had seen the object land, physical traces were still evident.

A circular area of compressed greenery about fifteen feet in diameter stood out from the rest of the field. Where irregular patches of pussy willows usually grew to a height of one or two feet, the stems within the circular area were broken off a few inches from the ground. A thorough examination of the surrounding area revealed no tracks that would account for the circle. Mrs. Baker noted that the broken branches within the circle were dark in color, rather than the usual whitish-yellow.

By this time, even Mr. King had begun to entertain some sympathy for Kim's experience. He in turn contacted Mr. Richard Plummer, a newspaper reporter for the Skowhegan branch of the *Morning Sentinel.* The following Wednesday, May 4, Mr. Plummer, Mr. King, and Mrs. Baker once again reviewed the account of Kim's sighting. No flaws in the account could be detected. But when her mother asked if anyone else had seen the "bubble," Kim answered yes . . . a dog saw the bubble and barked at it. A neighbor later verified that a mongrel husky had been barking the Saturday afternoon of Kim's encounter, but that no attention had been paid to this commotion.

Richard's report goes on to check out the witness's reliability, the possibility that she had seen a helicopter, and finally evaluates Kim's sighting as having been in the unknown category. In a discussion relating to the reliability of children, he cryptically remarked, "Perhaps we should remember that in Hans Christian Andersen's fairy tale, *The Emperor's New Clothes,* it was a child's observation that eventually corrected society's view of reality."

My son, David, was eight years old in July of 1976. That summer, the Goodyear blimp had swung in very low over an adjoining golf course at the end of our street. The kids chased excitedly below as it headed for nearby Beverly Airport. The blimp left quite an impression on David's mind.

In August our family wended its way through the White Mountains of New Hampshire. We crossed the Connecticut River just short of the Canadian border and arrived at our favorite vacation spot on Wallace Lake in Canaan, Vermont. Our cottage is set high on an elongated hillock overlooking the lake. Because of a steep embankment, drivers have to be extremely careful backing out of the tiny driveway. David and I were in the car on the way to a favorite fishing hole. David was looking out the side window for me, and I was backing slowly, when he shouted, "Look, Dad. It's the Goodyear blimp!"

"I can't look now. It can't be the Goodyear blimp. It doesn't come way up here."

"Where did it go?" David exclaimed in a puzzled tone.

By this time I had made my turn safely and stopped the car to see what he was talking about. As he gave me a description of a typical UFO, I felt as if I were jinxed! Why, oh why did it have to appear then? I took David in the house and had him draw it. He carefully sketched an oval object with a central dome. In his own words, it was the "Goodyear blimp with a hump on its back." I then asked him to show me on paper how the object moved. He traced an upward steplike flight path and told me that it moved like "it was going upstairs." Then he drew wiggly lines around it and said, "It stopped and wiggled all over," and then "It was gone!"

My heart sank. The typical domed disc, the typical zigzag movement—the typical wobbling on the axis before changing direction or darting! I feel that there was no way David could have concocted such a story. He did not even call it a flying saucer—to him it was merely the Goodyear blimp!

Children *do* report UFOs: Their carefree play keeps them out-of-doors for long periods of time, and they are probably more apt to see UFOs during the daylight hours than the majority of adults. But few reports are investigated as in the case of Kim's sighting.

Up until now, we have overlooked those persons who are considered to be the most reliable and highly trained observers in the world—military pilots and astronauts. The account that follows is a direct transcript of a recorded interview with former astronaut Gordon Cooper, who recounts his experience when he served as a jet fighter pilot at an unnamed U. S. Air Force base in Germany.

While tracking a weather balloon, a weatherman sighted some strange objects flying at a fairly high altitude. Before long, the entire fighter group was out peering through binoculars at these groups of objects coming over, all heading generally from easterly to westerly... and all in very strange patterns resembling fighter formations. But unlike fighters, they would almost stop in a forward velocity and change 90 degrees sometimes in their flight path... Within the next two or three days we'd had practically all the fighters on base we could muster up climbing as high as they would climb with guys with binoculars in them still trying to spot these strange devices flying overhead.... They were round in shape and very metallic looking.[2]

In one case, a UFO took a military helicopter in temporary tow! This now-famous incident on October 18, 1973, near Mansfield, Ohio, involved an Army Reserve UH-1H helicopter under the command of Captain (now Lieutenant Colonel) Lawrence Coyne and his crew of three. Coyne is commander of the 316th Medical Detachment (Helicopter Ambulance) and is flight facilities supervisor at the Cleveland Hopkins Airport. Lieutenant Arrigo Jezzi, the copilot, had about five hundred hours flying time and is a chemical engineer. The medic aboard that night was detective John Healey, a member of the Cleveland police department's police intelligence unit. The crew chief, Sergeant Bob Yanasek, is an IBM repairman. The following is a transcript of an interview with Colonel Coyne.

We were flying along at about 2,500 feet when the crew chief on the helicopter observed a red light, on the east horizon. He then informed me that the light was closing on the helicopter, coming at us on a collision course.... I looked to the right and observed that the object became bigger and the light became brighter, and I began to descend toward the ground to get the helicopter out of the collision course....It looked like we were going to collide with it, and we braced for impact.

I observed this craft stop directly in front of us, hovering, right over the helicopter. At this time, a light came out of the aft end of this vehicle, swung 90 degrees and came into the cabin of the helicopter. It was a bright green light... This craft, from the angle we saw it, was cigar-shaped, had no wings, no vertical or horizontal stabilizer and was approximately 60 feet long, 15 to 20 feet in height.

When I had last looked at our altimeter, we were at 1,700 feet... and I looked at my altimeter and my helicopter was at 3,500 feet, climbing a thousand feet a minute with no changes in control. We went from 1,700 feet to 3,500 feet in a matter of seconds and never knew it! The helicopter topped out at 3,800 feet and there a bump, like turbulence, at which time we had control of the aircraft. I had control. We took it back down to 2,500 feet.[3]

At ground level, several witnesses watched the strange encounter in utter amazement. One stated that the UFO looked like a blimp and was much larger than the helicopter.

Listen to Astronaut James McDivitt describe what he saw while orbiting the earth in Gemini 4 on June 4, 1965.

At the time that I saw it, I said there was something out in front of me, outside the spacecraft, that I couldn't identify. I never have been able to identify it and I don't think anybody ever will.

We were in drifting flight and my partner Ed White was asleep. The spacecraft had all flight control systems turned off except the radio. I noticed something out in front that was a white cylindrical shape with a white pole sticking out of one corner of it . . . I thought I might run into it so I turned on the flight control system . . . in the meantime, I grabbed two cameras which were floating in the spacecraft and I grabbed one, took a picture, and let go of it and I grabbed the other one and took a picture. . . . I never did find out what it was and nobody else did either.[4]

McDivitt, an Air Force general, has made it absolutely clear that NASA never did show him any pictures of the object he photographed.

The United States Air Force-sponsored University of Colorado UFO Study concluded:

The training and perspicacity of the astronauts put their reports of sightings in the highest category of credibility. They are always meticulous in describing the "facts," avoiding any tendentious interpretations. . . . Especially puzzling is . . . the daytime sighting of an object showing details such as arms [antennas?] protruding from a body having a noticeable angular extension. If the NORAD listing of objects near the GT-4 [Gemini 4] spacecraft at the time [of McDivitt's sighting] is complete, as it presumably is, we shall have to find a rational explanation or, alternatively, keep it on our list of unidentifieds.[5]

Dr. Hynek has pointed out that the typical UFO witness is often a respected member of the community whose report is unlikely to have been motivated by a desire for publicity or gain. He may well be a personal acquaintance of the local editor, may have children in school, likes to watch the same TV programs as you and I. A person who discharges his daily responsibilities honorably, and has no record of dishonesty or mental imbalance, would have nothing to gain but ridicule in making his experience known. In short, people who know them find it harder to conceive that such individuals "went off their collective trolley" than to concede that they had some very unusual experience.[6] Unfortunately, statistics indicate that "only 12 percent of those persons who have seen flying objects they cannot identify actually report the sighting."[7] This is only a slight improvement over Air Force statistics gathered in the 1950s, but this percentage should increase yearly as the subject of UFOs gains more public respectability. You should never be ashamed of reporting a UFO sighting—you are certainly in good company!

A minority of persons deliberately perjure themselves when they take the stand, however, and my next chapter addresses several personal encounters with this wasteful and frustrating type of witness.

CHAPTER NOTES

1. Raymond E. Fowler, *UFOs: Interplanetary Visitors* (New Jersey: Prentice-Hall, Inc., 1979), pp. 201, 202.

2. *UFOs: The Credibility Factor,* L-P Record, Columbia House, Rising Sun Music, Inc., 1975.

3. *loc. cit.*

4. *loc. cit.*

5. E. U. Condon, director, *Scientific Study of Unidentified Flying Objects* (New York: E. P. Dutton & Co., Inc., 1969), p. 208.

6. J. Allen Hynek, "UFOs," *Christian Science Monitor,* April 22, 1970.

7. Condon, *op. cit.,* p. 77.

WILD-GOOSE CHASES

A few years ago, a twelve-year-old boy sent the Center for UFO Studies a set of photographs showing a disc-shaped object hovering over some woods. They boy and his companions wrote that they had spotted the object while playing. One allegedly ran into the house, got his Polaroid camera, and took several pictures of the object before it departed at great speed.

Our local investigating team dispatched an investigator. Much to our surprise, the boys' parents were unaware of their UFO experience—but upon learning about it, they had no reason to doubt their sons' story. Thus, an initial analysis was undertaken at the local level.

Polaroid photographs of UFOs are not highly desirable, since there are no negatives to subject to the techniques normally used in photoanalysis. So we enlarged the UFO image to see if the object became recognizable. Indeed, the magnified "UFO" displayed the exact shape and contours of a familiar hand-thrown Frisbee. Confronted with this evidence, the boys admitted that they had faked the photographs to see if they could fool CUFOS.

Hoaxes comprise a very small percentage of reports, but the vast majority of them originate as schoolboy pranks. Recently I received another Polaroid photograph, from another twelve-year-old boy, who related that he had not been feeling well and so had stayed home from school. Glancing out his bedroom window, he saw an oval object darting over the neighborhood. He quickly grabbed his Polaroid and snapped a picture of it as it hovered over nearby trees.

Compared with the window frame and distant trees, the UFO image was grossly large. Had the object really been hovering over nearby trees, its size would have been immense. I wrote to the boy, returning the photograph and telling him I thought the object's plastic visor indicated that it was nothing but a motorcycle helmet. Soon I received a phone call from the boy's father, who told me sternly that the family wanted no publicity. He insisted his son had indeed photographed a UFO, and "that was all there was to it!" In such nonpublicized cases, it's best to just agree to disagree, and go on to the next item. After such a prank has been publicized by the media, however, the reading public should be accurately informed— if the children's parents are cooperative.

As far as the public was concerned, one case of this kind started with a fascinating news story in the Morristown, New Jersey, *County Daily Record* of January 24, 1967:

YOUTH PHOTOGRAPHS UFO
Mystery in Florham
Florham Park—Photographs of an unidentified flying object taken by an alert youngster Saturday morning disappeared into the maw of government secrecy yesterday after they were reported to the Office of Strategic Information. . . .

According to the boy, about 7 Saturday morning he was going up to his room, when he saw the UFO hovering a few feet off the ground at the end of the family driveway. He described the UFO as about 50 feet in length and looking something like a submarine. He said the machine made a slight humming noise as it moved.

The exterior, the boy said, was covered with lumps of black carbon-like material mottled over a greenish blue substance which was the hull covering. He said the UFO appeared to have a window at the front end which was pointed toward the house as if someone in the UFO was inspecting the window from which he was taking the pictures.

Police who inspected the photographs said one defined an object which tallied with the boy's description as submarine-shaped with another oval perched on its top. Reports of four other UFO sightings have been received by the police department within the last three months.

This intriguing account contains many of the elements of typical UFO cases: government secrecy, a domed oval object, and other reports in the same area. Later, however, the boy told his parents that he had photographed a flying-saucer model dangling in front of his bedroom window! The embarrassed parents stressed to me that their son had intended it to be a joke on his friends at school. He hadn't anticipated that the whole episode would be taken seriously by adults, or that the concocted story would get completely out of hand.

It's to his credit (and his parents') that a public confession was made at the school he attended. The reporter of the article was also notified, and he rendered the public a good service by writing a follow-up story the very next day, titled "Florham UFO a Hoax." The boy's mother told me that their son had constructed a very realistic clay model. She philosophically told the *County Daily Record*, "I guess all that can be said is that people want to believe in flying saucers. We didn't doubt it at first, and neither did our neighbors, who streamed through the house all day Sunday to look at the photos."

Some parents are not so understanding. A similar event involving youngsters with a Polaroid camera occurred in New England. They too convinced their parents that they had really photographed a UFO, and the local newspapers printed several large stories on the incident. Soon the photographs and the boys' sighting account were picked up by the wire services, and with the full consent of the parents, NICAP launched an investigation.

Analysis revealed that the photographs were close-ups of the glowing filament within a light bulb! Confronted with this evidence, one youngster confessed that the pictures were fakes. Strangely enough, he insisted that they *had* really seen a UFO. But his confession had been taped, and the parents were told the news several hours later. They consulted a lawyer, who advised them not to release the truth to the press. As a result, the photographs and accompanying story were accepted as authentic around the world. To avoid possible legal entanglements, investigators were forced to neither confirm nor deny the incident.

At dusk on March 17, 1967, a cylindrical object spouting a fiery exhaust danced and skipped over the streets of South Lawrence, Massachusetts, continuing into adjoining Andover where it passed over Route 495—a major highway—before blazing over the Raytheon manufacturing plant. The weird sight interrupted the busy rush hour below.

My news-clip service picked up local media coverage, and soon I was questioning persons who witnessed the strange object. One housewife described it as a flying plank with its lower end burning. Some young men told me that it looked like a toothpaste tube on end, performing violent maneuvers. A truck driver excitedly related to me how he had pulled over to watch a flaming "fish-shaped object" as big as an airliner bounce across the sky. In reality, this UFO—which amazed so many people—turned out to be literally full of hot air!

During this time, TV shows and magazines were describing in detail how college kids were constructing and launching hot-air balloons. All it took was a common plastic garment bag, a coat hanger, a bit of tinfoil, string, and lighter fluid. In the case just cited, two young boys decided to build one of these improvised UFOs. First they bent a coat hanger into a rectangle and covered the metal with the drinking straws, then taped the open end of the bag to the straw-covered frame. Next they shaped the tinfoil into a cup and taped it to the frame. When lighter fluid was poured into the cup and ignited, the hot air filled the bag with a snap. The pillow-shaped balloon quickly rose to the end of its string tether. But the fire burned through the string, and the balloon moved rapidly away, at the mercy of the prevailing wind.

The launching in this case was accidental, though most such balloons are sent aloft deliberately to cause false UFO reports. The most commonly-employed heat source is a cluster of birthday candles supported by a light balsa-wood frame attached to the coat hanger. The majority of launches take place at night, usually during school vacations. The most common description is that of a slow-moving, orange glowing ball. The plastic bag sometimes catches fire, giving the impression of a crashing, flaming object.

I remember a certain newspaper reporter who sighted this type of UFO and wrote a front-page description of a bright orange-red object moving erratically, which ejected a number of smaller glowing objects before disappearing. I phoned and told him that he had seen a prankster's hot-air balloon, with the nearly expended candles falling from the frame. He found my explanation funny and hard to believe. I challenged him to search the area under which he had sighted the UFO. He did, and found the garment bag high in a tree! To his credit, his byline appeared beside another newspaper story, featuring a telescopic photo of the garment bag wrapped around a tree branch. Some burned-out candles were plainly seen attached to the wire frame.

When these devices are seen in the daytime, descriptions include flying tubes, fish, cylinders, and pillows. In another case, some boys sent a number of them aloft near the end of a private airport's runway. Lacking a reference point for comparison, pilots who saw the objects described them as being as large as an airliner! Needless to say, untethered hot-air balloons can set destructive fires and present a threat to aircraft. One night the FAA phoned to tell me that ground and air observers were reporting two extremely bright red objects dancing in formation along the coastline north of Boston. In cooperation with the local police, we discovered that in-dividuals had affixed lighted railroad flares to two large kites. At least they had the sense to fly them over the ocean.

After one of my UFO lectures, some young men came up to tell me they had constructed a crude object of sheet metal, attaching to it battery-powered flashing lights. One warm summer evening, they transported it across a field to a relatively untraveled road not too far from their homes. When no cars were in sight, they quickly "landed" their UFO in the middle of the road, activated the flashing lights, and dashed behind a stand of nearby bushes.

They did not have to wait very long. Distant headlights marked their first victim—a lone woman driver who brought her car to an abrupt halt about fifty feet away from the object. One very long minute passed.

Then the car suddenly backed up, turned around, and sped off at great speed. Much to the boys' delight, this scenario repeated itself—until oncoming flashing lights indicated that someone had called the police!

A cruiser rolled up to within about fifty feet of the flashing contraption. Again, about a minute passed. It was deathly quiet except for the methodical chirping of crickets. Then the cruiser doors slowly opened on either side. Two policemen emerged with drawn weapons.

The now-frightened boys watched breathlessly as the two uniformed armed men advanced cautiously toward their blinking work of art. Suddenly they stopped and lowered their service revolvers. One then walked briskly up to the saucer and kicked it over to the side of the road. When the officers peered out over the surrounding fields, the boys were quietly edging their way back toward home.

I couldn't help laughing with these young men. Nonetheless, obstructing the road could have caused a serious car accident. And even if UFO pranks aren't dangerous, they often cause the wasteful expenditure of investigators' time and money.

Adults should know better; a few don't. Their motivations can be very complex: They may need personal recognition, gaining some attention in a lonely environment. They can also want to increase their status among UFO believers; or make a fast buck via magazine articles, books, and lectures. Or course a smaller number of UFO reports are generated by mentally unbalanced, self-deluded people who aren't really responsible for their actions. One young man I know has been in and out of a mental institution because of his almost daily reported encounters with UFOs and their occupants. One woman used to phone to tell me that the UFO people had built a huge city under Brockton, Massachusetts, and chosen her to be their leader!

Then there are some who really *do* have a genuine UFO experience, who become frustrated because no one seems to have satisfactory answers for what they have seen. Night after night they go out, looking skyward, hoping to have a repeat experience. Sometimes anything that moves becomes a UFO because they so badly want it to be one.

In July of 1964, our family set off for a week with my parents at Surry, Maine. When friends of my parents came over to visit, they related a fascinating story: About six years before, a man I'll call Alex had told them that strange objects containing little men had overflown his property on many occasions. He showed them photographs of the objects and told them that the FBI had investigated these strange occurrences. When I telephoned Alex, he seemed more than willing to talk with me, so Margaret and I set out for his home during the early evening of July 28.

As he lived several towns away, it was a rather long drive along a narrow, winding back road. Suddenly my clutch pedal made a scraping sound, then gave way completely. Fortunately we managed to coast into the town of Bucksport, where a garageman informed me that I needed a new clutch. I phoned Alex, who insisted on driving to Bucksport to pick us up.

About a half hour later, Alex and his wife, Myrna, picked us up. A tall, burly fellow with a weathered face and rough voice, he stood in striking contrast to Myrna, a small, rather frail-looking and very soft-spoken woman.

During the drive, Alex rattled off descriptions of UFO sighting after UFO sighting. Finally the fast-moving car exited onto a bumpy dirt road that stretched endlessly across field and marshland until it terminated at a large, wind-battered house. As we stepped out of the car, a huge German shepherd bounded up to us with a threatening growl. Alex assured the dog that we were friends. I wasn't too sure.

Inside, the lonely house was graced with plain but sturdy old furniture. Shutters creaked in response to a sudden sea breeze over the marsh. Darkness soon arrived, and we sat listening to some very strange tales.

Alex told us that in March and September of 1958, many residents of this small coastal town had sighted strange aerial lights that hovered, darted, and swooped down at people. On one night, one of these bright lights landed briefly in his field before taking off again. Then the flying lights began regular periodic flights over and around his property. Worried, he reported the incidents to the state police, who sent an officer to investigate. Alex related to us that the police officer also saw the lights and notified Dow Air Force Base at Bangor.

The Air Force responded by sending two air policemen to spend a night in a staff car at the edge of the huge field. At 2 A.M. they were alarmed to see a low-flying ball of fire pass directly over the field. The following day, an Air Force lieutenant and sergeant arrived with questionnaires for Alex, Myrna, and the state policeman to fill out.

Laughingly, Alex told me that the lieutenant had asked them if they wanted the air police to patrol the area for their protection. Alex replied that the lights had never harmed anybody; besides, townspeople often came out to his field at night to watch for the lights. At this information, the Air Force officer instructed him to tell these people that the Air Force knew what the lights were.

I was looking Alex straight in the eye. He seemed quite sincere. Once in a while he glanced toward Myrna, who would nod in agreement.

It was now pitch black outside. The solitary lamp in the room barely illuminated our surroundings. As the evening wore on, Alex excitedly told me how the commanding officer at Dow AFB had provided him with a special telephone number so that Alex could report any UFO sightings directly to him. On the few occasions that Alex called this number, he said, two jets would soon arrive over his property. However, the lights would always disappear before their arrival, as if they knew they were coming. Alex told us that he began sleeping days so that he could spend his nights watching for the lighted objects. On several occasions he said he had approached within one hundred feet of lights near the ground, whereupon they would just blink out.

Then, grinning, he reached for a folder and dumped a large

number of photographs onto the table in front of us. Most of them portrayed blurred lights and vague images. Excitedly he pointed out what he called faces on some of them. In order to get some of these pictures, he said, he had pointed his flash camera where the lights had been.

One especially intriguing photo depicted an elongated cigar-shaped object with vertical bands encircling its center portion. I found this quite exciting, as I had read of reports describing similar objects. But some of the other photographs showed only an elaborate string of light bulbs with makeshift reflectors set up around his field. His plan had been to turn them on when an object landed, but after this the objects stopped coming.

I began wondering if I were listening to a deluded man. Alex pulled out some papers from another envelope and showed me correspondence with *Life* magazine and the Air Force about his photographs. Upon request, he gave me an extra carbon copy of the Air Force correspondence. Addressed to him, it was from the commanding officer of Dow Air Force Base; on the surface, it seemed to provide some actual support to his strange stories:

12 February 59

Dear Mr._____:

I am writing in reply to your query concerning your photographs. Shortly after your initial sighting, I sent a qualified officer to investigate the situation. His information, together with the photographs that you sent me, were given to Air Intelligence for their review and analysis.

Past records have shown that sightings such as you have made are usually attributed to natural phenomena. Even so, the Air Intelligence takes great pains to study all available information and photographs in order to ascertain the innocence of such incidents. As of this date, I have not received your photographs from the Intelligence people. Upon receipt, however, they will be forwarded to your residence.

Sincerely
Boyd B. White
Colonel, USAF
Commander

The Air Force had never returned Alex's photographs and negatives. Very hesitant to let me borrow his prints, he finally relented and gave me some of them. It was getting late, so I phoned my father and asked him to meet us at Bucksport.

As we drove back, Alex told me in quiet tones how he had seen a craft buzz his field in broad daylight. He actually saw little men waving to him from its windows! Then—as if saving the best for last—he told me that one had actually landed and left traces behind. He described the grass and leaves turning brown where the lights had settled down onto the field. After the object had taken off, he found on the ground a substance resembling scorched corrugated paper. When I asked him for samples of this residue, he told me that he had given it all to the Air Force, on their request. When it occurred to me that he had never given me any of the other witnesses' names, Alex said that he would talk to them first and send me their names later by mail.

Back at my parents' home, I examined Alex's photographs in good light. One glowing ball over the field looked suspiciously like the rising sun. One mechanical contrivance looked like an obvious made-on-planet-earth item! The others were so blurred that one could see in them whatever one wanted. The large cigar-shaped object still looked interesting, though it was also suspect because of the dubious nature of the others.

Soon after returning to Massachusetts, I wrote Alex that his photographs looked like exposures of common man-made objects or natural phenomena, stressing that I needed other witnesses' names, addresses, and telephone numbers. His prompt reply further aroused my suspicions:

August 25, 1964

Dear Ray,

Your letter received & would have answered sooner, but have been away.

In regard to this coming Sat. the 29th I will not be able to see you, as I expect to be away for the week end & maybe longer—so think for the time being we'd better just forget the whole thing, & if any "events" occur, I will get in touch with you—furthermore, the ones who saw the most have refused to admit anything anyway & would be unavailable in any case—of course, after five years, it's rather vague.

Guess this will have to be all—thanks for writing what information you received from others.

Sincerely,
Alex

Disappointed, but even more determined to get to the root of this matter, I arranged for my brothers to pay Alex a surprise visit. Much to poor Alex's dismay, they wandered about the house commenting rather freely upon a number of "very interesting things" he had that obviously coincided with his UFO photographs. The mysterious picture of the banded, cigar-shaped UFO turned out to be a photograph of an old-fashioned elongated desk lamp! It really wasn't necessary to accuse Alex of perpetrating a hoax—he had been caught, and he very well knew it.

Anyone can file a UFO report and get official response with related letters. I half wondered about the reporter from *Life*, who had traveled so far for so little, but I dismissed the case from my mind—until much later, when I came across some curious information.

In 1958 and into 1959, I was told, Alex had indeed informed friends about strange objects coming in off the ocean and reconnoitering his property. He became the butt of local jokes, and as far as could be ascertained, no one else witnessed these sightings. However, Alex suddenly began buying expensive photographic equipment, wire, lights, and other related material. He was not well off financially, and those who knew him were surprised at his rashness.

Alex's doctor knew him very well and was personally convinced that initially, Alex and his wife had observed real UFOs. But because nobody believed him, the doctor theorized, Alex took the matter into his own hands. He set up lights at the landing site and lay in wait for the objects to return so he could photograph them. Unfortunately, his work and expenditures were in vain. To save face, Alex then, according to the doctor, turned to producing fake photographs. Those who analyzed them were probably just being charitable by not commenting on their obvious unauthenticity, but the photos created the attention and respect that he craved. Myrna's apparent supporting testimony could very well have been forced; I also found out that she was afraid of him. My arrival upon the scene resurrected the whole matter once again, and my intense interest provided yet another outlet for his past frustrations.

10
IDENTIFIABLE
FLYING OBJECTS

Shortly after midnight on August 10, 1966, Nellie had just retired in a summer camp at Moultonboro, New Hampshire. Suddenly the bedroom became illuminated. Bewildered, she saw a red-orange globe of light emerge *through* the adjoining wall of the cabin. The globe was about three feet in diameter and had within it what looked like a dark mark. When the luminous ball began to move about the room, she told me, during my investigation, she was so frightened she could not utter a sound. Nellie watched petrified as the globe skirted along the walls and ceiling—then crawled deliberately toward a small closet, squeezed through the crack around the door, and disappeared!

A similar event was investigated just a few days later by NICAP astronomical consultant Walter Webb. Around 10 in the evening, June 16, 1968, a woman was walking across the hallway to her dining room at her home at Revere, Massachusetts. Abruptly, a strange orange glow illuminated the hall floor. Glancing around, she traced the light source to the dining room windows. At this very moment her nephew, watching TV in the darkened living room, was startled by the same glow shining through the front windows.

Quickly stepping over to the window, the woman saw a ball of fire "like a big bowling ball" slowly descending out of the southwest toward her neighbor's backyard. Thinking it would crash and explode, she screamed. The cat flew about the house and the dog began whining. The descending fiery globe halted momentarily in midair, about twenty feet from the ground. Its round shape was clearly outlined in front of a maple tree. It was a deep orange color with a paler center, lighting up the whole yard. Then it again began moving back up into the southwestern sky.

The nephew joined his aunt and they both watched the object retreat, spewing a tiny white exhaust. Suddenly it began wobbling. There was a brilliant flash, and it totally disintegrated in a shower of white sparks. The whole episode so unnerved the woman that she had to take a sleeping pill in order to settle down that night.

Both the Moultonboro and Revere cases were evaluated as possible events of ball lightning, or BL. BL is rare and, like the UFO, not completely understood. Atmospheric physicist James E. McDonald has written that only recently has "BL been admitted as a real phenomenon rather than some kind of illusion."[1] As McDonald further pointed out:

In this sense, the history of ball lightning studies is amusingly parallel to UFOs. . . . Students of atmospheric electricity have not yet succeeded in developing an adequate theoretical understanding of the baffling phenomena reported under this heading. . . . The range of ball lightning characteristics is so wide that no single mathematical model has fit very satisfactorily the reported effects.[2]

Authorities believe that the phenomenon is a stable arrangement of ionized gases and electric currents. Not at all like the transitory, brilliant, jagged lightning flashes, the ball represents an unknown mechanism for storing energy.

Witnesses consistently describe BL as a ball of light—usually about the size of an orange or small grapefruit. However, some reported BLs have ranged from a few centimeters up to many meters in diameter. Durations of reported observation vary from a fraction of a second up to tens of minutes.

A NASA survey of BL noted two different categories. In one, the ball appears after a normal lightning stroke to the ground. It remains and dissipates slowly and silently—or erupts with an explosive report. I was fortunate enough to observe such an event when I was twelve years old. Paul and I were fishing at a little pond when the sky began to darken, and we heard the ominous distant rumble of thunder. We realized we'd best run home before the thunderstorm hit.

As we picked up our can of worms and headed for the road, it was hot and very close. No sooner had we reached the road than there came a brilliant flash of lightning and a simultaneous clap of thunder. A bright object blinked on in the air. Running, we glanced at it sideways: It was ball shaped, and slowly floated down into a gravel pit. There was a dazzling flash, and a deafening roar that echoed over the countryside. I don't think my legs had ever moved faster. When I arrived breathlessly at home, my parents told me that I had seen ball lightning.

In the other category, the glowing ball is first seen in midair and it remains aloft, vanishing without noticeable disturbance.

Historical reports of apparent BL indicate a variety of movement: hovering; moving slowly through air (with or against the wind) at speeds estimated anywhere between 5 and 60 miles per hour, but mostly below 15 miles per hour; and rolling along the ground, floors, walls, and tops of roofs or fences.

Some observers have an impression that the ball rotates or spins. Others report an associated hissing sound, and sometimes an odor like ozone or burning sulfur. Rarely is more than one ball seen at a time. A few have caused radio interference and physical damage to persons and property. In a research paper on BL, Walter Webb writes that:

A Soviet plane flying between 12,000 and 15,000 feet in a storm cloud encountered a ball that exploded, causing an engine to stall momentarily. . . . Another Soviet plane flying at 10,000 feet in stormy weather also encountered an exploding ball. It wiped out radio communication and caused the radar operator to receive a shock when he tried to disconnect the antenna. The ball melted a propeller-tip. In Britain, a ball hit an iron gate during a thunderstorm and shocked a boy whose hand was on the gate. He couldn't lower his arm for a few hours. . . .It almost *always* occurs during a thunderstorm and usually materializes after a lightning stroke.

According to all I have read, my own BL experience is a textbook example, though the Moultonboro and Revere cases are not, since there were no electrical storms in progress. According to the National Weather Service, the weather for the Moultonboro area was clear with unlimited visibility. At Revere, it began raining heavily about ten minutes after the event, but with no normal electrical-storm activity. Some atmospheric physicists would claim that the clear weather at Moultonboro would rule out BL entirely, but the closet into which the ball disappeared contained an electrical junction box, and it would appear that this scurrying ball of electrical energy was seeking a ground upon which to discharge itself.

Another theoretical but highly dubious phenomenon might account for clear-weather incidents. UFO debunker Philip J. Klass has proposed that UFO sightings are caused by plasma, an artificially induced atmospheric phenomenon. He speculates that under the proper conditions, a corona discharge on power lines might detach itself as a "plasmoid" and float about like BL. Scientists who worked on the University of Colorado study confided with me that they had examined his hypothesis and concluded that "Klass was dismissed!" James McDonald also concluded that this hypothesis had no scientific foundation.[3] It is quite true that the corona discharge sometimes formed on power lines might appear as strange flashing lights, but a close observer could readily identify this as an electrical phenomenon. A NASA report on BL concluded that only a small percentage of these plasmalike balls were reported to follow power lines.[4] This NASA conclusion is quite pertinent, since to an observer, the theoretical plasmoid and BL would appear identical.

Like BL, Saint Elmo's fire—another real and apparently flaming atmospheric phenomenon—is usually observed during electrical storms. Its glow, caused by the brush discharge of electricity in the air, appears at an object's prominent terminal points, such as an aircraft's wing tips, a ship's mast, or a tower. This phenomenon could conceivably cause a UFO report if observed from a distance. Even some types of tornadoes could give rise to UFO reports. A few have variously been described as featuring a vertical luminous column, a blue halo, rotating lights, or a glowing object ejecting balls of orange fire![5] But usually a tornado would be recognizable because of its very nature and storm-associated winds.

Until recently scientists had scoffed at strange luminosities reported prior to and during earthquakes. Some have theorized that it is a piezoelectrical effect caused by varying pressures upon the earth's crust. The scientific world finally took notice when a team of scientists studying a series of repetitive earthquakes at Idu, Japan, witnessed the phenomenon firsthand.

... at the time of the Idu earthquake ... scientists were able to observe those luminous phenomena so often described by the witnesses of the very great shocks. Until then, in spite of the abundance of eyewitness accounts, there was some doubt as to the reality of those long flashes of lightning, balls of fire, spreading beams, pencils of light, and curtains of varying color and intensity ... ordinary explanations for phenomena of this kind—storm lightning, aurora borealis, electric arcs between high-tension cables, and above all the witness's own emotion ... could be refuted one after the other at Idu, and the luminous manifestations attributed to the earthquake. It still remains to explain their mechanism.[6]

Swamp gas is normally seen on damp, still nights in the summer or early fall, shortly after sunset. Other names for these curious lights include marsh fire or swamp fire, will-o'-the-wisp, ignis fatuus, jack-o'-lantern, spunkie, feu follet, corpse candle, witch light, and friar's lantern. Swamps, marshes, bogs, and cemeteries are their prime breeding grounds. There have been reports from both temperate and tropical latitudes, and accounts have come from as far north as Scotland.

Like BL, swamp gas—which apparently ignites spontaneously—is not fully understood. Never collected or analyzed, it is generally believed to be generated by decaying organic matter. The gas phosphine (PH_3) and methane (CH_4) are considered likely candidates. Phosphine is spontaneously inflammable in the presence of hydrogen phosphide (P_2H_4), which may in turn ignite the methane.

In reality, the phenomenon resembles a tiny luminous globe or candle flame varying in size from about ½ inch to 5 inches in length and not more than about two inches in width. Usually it is about the size of a fifty-cent piece; its color is generally blue, but some witnesses have reported green, red, and yellow. A clear white color has never been reported.

Most often, swamp gas shines with a steady light, but on occasion it has been known to flicker or pulsate. Its light is usually faint, but some reports indicate a luminosity similar to that caused by a flashlight. It may occur singly or in groups. Witnesses report that it can remain nearly motionless, waver to and fro in a breeze, or move about horizontally or vertically. It may appear to advance, recede, separate, and recombine, or constantly appear and disappear. Its height normally varies from ground or water level to two or three feet. One report estimated it as being ten feet off the ground.

Individual globules have reportedly lasted anywhere from three seconds to a few minutes. A display involving many globules may last for hours. The slightest breeze may extinguish these globules, but reignition often occurs when the breeze calms down. Usually no noise is associated with these mysterious-looking lights, though some have reported a tiny popping sound concurrent with the appearance or disappearance of the phenomenon. In most cases investigated, no heat was felt. However, in one nonauthenticated case, a person claims to have ignited hemp fiber with one of the lights. Some have reported an associated odor like sulfur, phosphorus, or ammonia. Perhaps significantly, I do not have one case in my personal files where swamp gas has been reported as a UFO!

A mirage is an optical illusion of a distorted or displaced real object. It is produced by vertical layers of air which vary in temperature. The resulting temperature inversion causes light rays to bend. Thus an object normally out of view, beyond the observer's horizon, may appear to float above the horizon. Because light waves from the top and bottom of the object might travel in totally different paths, an object with a considerable vertical structure may be especially distorted. Examples of non-astronomical objects affected by temperature inversion include distant towers; anticollision lights; automobile, truck, and train lights; and ship lights at sea. When ghostly floating lights or objects are seen near the horizon at night or day, a possible temperature inversion is given serious consideration, especially when the reports involve UFOs over flatland areas or over the ocean. Fortunately for the investigator, the local U.S Weather Service will provide temperature-inversion data upon request.

Sun dogs and moon dogs are reflections from a layer of ice crystals suspended in the atmosphere. This natural mirror causes one or more mock suns or moons to appear beside the real one. This phenomenon is most often observed from high-flying aircraft; in temperate zones it is usually seen only during the cold winter months. I saw a sun dog several years ago, but even when I pointed it out, the others about me seemed indifferent to the curious sight!

A few citizens—and on one occasion, even the police—have phoned me to ask about the strange lights in the northern sky. My reply is simple—they are the Northern Lights! The proper nomenclature, of course, would be the aurora borealis. Seen only at night in the northern sky, this interesting sight is both an atmospheric and an astronomical phenomenon— the earth's magnetic field interacting with energy from the sun. It may resemble a glowing patch of diffused light, a luminous curtain, light, or wavy shimmering bands of light. White, yellow-green, and occasionally red, blue, gray, and violet colors may be seen. The phenomenon is visible in the northern hemisphere within a zone of about 23 degrees of latitude from the North Pole. It is less commonly observed below 45 degrees of latitude. The aurora borealis is rarely reported as a UFO.

I customarily receive many calls about UFOs in the dead of night. The voice of one young lady was clearly agitated. She told me that she had gotten up to go to the bathroom and decided to step out onto the apartment veranda to get a breath of fresh air. She was startled to see a V-shaped formation of glowing objects moving overhead with a fluttering motion. I tiredly asked, "Did you hear any noise associated with the objects?" "Why, yes," she replied quite matter-of-factly, "I heard a honking sound like geese!" "What makes you think they *weren't* geese?" I asked. "Oh!" she replied, "I didn't think geese would fly over a city!"

This young lady was dead serious. I explained to her that night-migrating birds, especially ducks and geese, may reflect moonlight or city lights. When flying overhead, these birds appear as diffuse moving light sources. The oft-reported fluttering motion is due to the movement of their wings.

In another incident, a driver reported a fluttering object that suddenly rose up from beside the road and disappeared from view. The sighting area was near water, and it is easy to imagine a passing motorist scaring up sleeping ducks. The frightened bird would rise up suddenly, briefly reflect the oncoming auto's headlights, and would appear as a large fluttering light source making a pass at the car.

I myself have been momentarily startled by streetlights reflecting off the body of a flying squirrel. Even the erratically moving, self-lumines-cent firefly has caused me brief consternation. One time in my backyard, I was demonstrating to a visitor how to view through a telescope. Suddenly he shouted, "An object just passed in front of the moon. There's another one!" I took a look through the scope myself. Sure enough, an object darted across the lunar disk. The telescope had magnified the size and movement of swallows! Since its eyepiece was focused for the distant moon, the familiar shape of this common bird was distorted. Even without the telescope, one could easily be confused by night-feeding birds or bats.

Some birds, like the seagull, have highly reflective white feathers. In the day, they reflect sunlight and appear as silent-moving, bright, unresolved points of light. I have personally taken more than one curious glance at gulls whirling high above on thermal currents.

October 22, 1973; 1400 hours; temperature 56 degrees; wind, southeast at 9 knots; ceiling, zero with 13-mile visibility. In the town of Sudbury, Massachusetts, Jane was housecleaning when her four-year-old son burst into the house to proclaim that huge spiderwebs were falling from the sky. She stepped outside to see masses of weblike material draped over the bushes, telephone lines, and on the lawn.

June had a background in biochemistry. Dashing back into the house, she grabbed some construction paper, rolled it into a tube, and returned outside, wrapping strands of the webbing around it. While collecting samples, she glanced upward to see where the wispy threads were coming from:

I noticed sort of a globe, a ball-shaped object in the sky. I tried to figure out what that was. I thought, it doesn't look like a plane, and I noticed other things just directly over me, floating down. . . . They were floating around in the air like a light web, and some of them landed in the yard. Some of them I picked up. I put a couple of the more tangled-up, thicker ones onto the construction paper.[7]

The gleaming sphere remained in view for about a minute before disappearing into the distance. The wispy threads continued falling. After about thirty minutes they became sparse, and June returned into the house, shaken and nervous. Even after placing the material in the refrigerator, June noticed that the strange webs partially dissipated, leaving strong white threads that remained stable.

Such material, sometimes associated with the passage of UFOs, has been called angel hair. A spectacular incident took place on October 17, 1952, at Oloron, France. At 12:50 P.M. crowds of observers gazed at a huge white cylindrical object in the sky. Tilted at a 45-degree angle and flying silently, the weird object was accompanied by about 30 domed disks traveling in pairs. Electriclike flashes arced between each pair. The top of the cylinder spewed out white vapor while large amounts of wispy filaments of material fell slowly to the ground, vanishing into nothingness as they touched the earth. The apparition, nevertheless, was tracked by the radar station at Mont-de-Marsan. Then, ten days later, 16 discs clustered around a similar vertical cigar-shaped object, which hovered for 10 minutes over Gaillac, France. Again and concurrently, a whitish substance showered down, covering trees and houses before dissipating into nothingness.

French UFO investigator Aimé Michel records still another similar event in his book *Flying Saucers and the Straight-Line Mystery.* The witness, M. Carcenac, described the sighting on October 13, 1954, above Graulhet, France:

At 4:30 P.M. I noticed at a high altitude toward the northwest moving southward . . . a white object. . . . I got my opera glasses. I could then see very distinctly a sort of huge, flexible, soft disk, white, swaying as it moved along at tremendous speed. I had been following the bizarre craft for several seconds when it exploded in full flight. At the same time, a circular object, very much smaller and silvery, seemed to spurt out of the mass and continued straight toward the south, where it soon disappeared, while the burst fragments of the soft disk scattered out through the sky . . . to fall gently like shreds of cloth or paper.[8]

Michel describes the fallen debris covering the ground and sometimes catching on trees or telegraph wires. When witnesses handled the wispy threads, which clung together like cobwebs, they evaporated. Analysis was attempted by a local chemist, but subjected to heat, the material disappeared.

In the summer of 1957 a trained biologist of the U.S. Fish and Wildlife Service witnessed a similar fall about three miles off the Florida mainland. His report to NICAP stated:

For a period of two hours we observed . . . very fine cobwebs up to two or more feet in length, drifting down from the sky. . . . I assumed that some phenomenon of temperature or timing had resulted in the mass hatching and exodus of a certain type of spider . . . on the mainland. . . . Although we captured a number of these strands on our fingertips, no spiders were to be seen, despite the likelihood that a percentage of them would have spiders attached.[9]

This gentleman, like others, was thwarted in his attempt to analyze the wispy material.

I carefully placed several of them inside a mason jar. . . . Under high power, I had hoped to see the tiny adhesive droplets that adorn most but not all spiderwebs, and were these present, there would be little doubt of their true nature. However, when I uncapped the jar later in my office, *no trace of the web material could be found.* [italics mine][10]

Puzzled, the Department of the Interior biologist ended his report to NICAP with the following statement:

This phenomenon is to me still unexplained, and I have seen nothing comparable to it before or since.

I will mention . . . that I have always been interested in the biology of spiders and their webs. . . . I would say that it is possible that the strands . . . were something other than spider web, and that I have no explanation for the apparent disappearance of the collected material in the mason jar.[11]

Similar aerial material has fallen without corresponding UFO activity in the affected area. On November 9, 1958, Humboldt, Trinidad, Rio Dell, and other northern California towns were inundated with showers of weblike material with strands up to forty feet long! A biologist at Humboldt State College ruled out the possibility of it being a mold growth or animal product.

On October 18, 1973, just after dawn, at Watson and Zachary, Louisiana, a fast-maneuvering object emitted swirling white material described as a "long, silky substance" with some strands as long as six feet. One worried mother removed the fallen substance from her little boy, but it evaporated on contact with her skin! The October 19 *State-Times* of Baton Rouge expressed authorities' bewilderment over the continuing showers of wispy material:

UFO stood for "unknown falling objects" around Northwest Louisana Thursday, and official sources were baffled. The filmy, string-like substance dropped from a clear blue sky. They were like the threads of spiderweb, sometimes five to six feet in length.

Now, let us go back to the case at Sudbury, Massachusetts. Needless to say, I was quite excited over the prospect of obtaining some of this material for analysis. An immediate investigation was launched, and on the day after the sighting, samples of the substance were collected throughout the neighborhood. Since the character of the witness and neighbors was beyond repute, a hoax was ruled out. Balloon-launch records revealed no weather or research balloons had been responsible for the "globe, ball-shaped object" that June had seen; the nearby Army laboratories at Natick said that they had not conducted any experiments that could have caused the phenomenon. A check with various fiberglass and asbestos industries also proved negative. Industrial wastes caught in an updraft and blown along by prevailing winds were ruled out.

A sample of the material was first brought to the University of Massachusetts field station, examined under a microscope, and determined *not* to be spiderweb. However, a local zoologist who read about the incident in the newspapers informed the media that it *was* spiderweb! Small samples of the wispy material were sent to several local laboratories. There was not enough of the threadlike substance for a wet chemical analysis, but samples were nonetheless subjected to mass spectrometer analysis, thermal gravimetric analysis, X-ray fluorescence scan analysis, and X-ray diffraction analysis.

One laboratory report indicated that the threads were comprised of 95 percent organic and 5 percent inorganic matter. Potassium, silicon, calcium, and phosphorus were listed as major inorganic constituents. Aluminum, oxygen, and chlorine were detected in smaller amounts. The organic material remained unidentified. A few labs took photographs of the material through electron microscopes. One examiner, a chief of general medical research, stated that:

The smallest strands . . . are 25 microns in the 5000 times magnification and are smaller than any asbestos fibrils. . . . It seems to be composed of fibers . . . surrounded by a transparent matrix . . . and has changed in size with time. . . . No spiders were found.

Not one of the laboratories could identify the source of the material in question.

Just 18 days later eight witnesses—including a science teacher—observed another low-flying silvery disc pass over the same neighborhood. One witness noticed white clouds surrounding the disc, but no material was observed falling to the ground. On October 8, 1969, via a short-lived phenomena news card, the Smithsonian Institution had reported that the St. Louis, Missouri, area was blanketed with spiderweb. The card mentioned that the St. Louis Health Department attributed the fall to a mass migration of ballooning spiders. In my study of this phenomenon, I came across an interesting statement by Dr. Jacques Vallee:

It has been suggested that cases of *angel hair* . . . are due to the migration of huge clouds of very young spiders; this hypothesis has had little support, especially among biologists.[12]

Curious, I decided to consult with two leading authorities on spiders: one at the American Museum of Natural History in New York City and the other at the Smithsonian in Washington, D.C. I was told that certain species of young spiders, after breaking out of their egg case en masse, climb a tall object and secrete a strands of silky web from their bodies. This silk is then caught up into the air by the wind, which carries the young spiders for miles. "Ballooning" spiders have been found up to 200 miles over the ocean. I found that the optimum migratory seasons in North America are in the spring and fall months. Much to my dismay, however, the two scientists disagreed on certain questions: Would the spiders be obvious to a person retrieving the web? The Smithsonian thought so; the AMNH disagreed. Would the web be hard to preserve? Both said no. Could strands join together into a floating mass which could appear to an observer as a floating object? No, said the AMNH; possible, said the Smithsonian. Would it be possible for an entire neighborhood to be blanketed with such spiderwebs? No, said the AMNH; yes, said the Smithsonian.

I next turned to NICAP records for more clues, and found that a statistical study within the document *The UFO Evidence* recorded falls of such material back into the 1700s! Adding my own data to this study, I discovered that 27 of 47 cases involved simultaneous sightings of flying objects, the most common of which were cigar shapes and silvery balls.

Significantly, about 80 percent of the sightings were reported in the fall; 50 percent—including the Sudbury case—were reported within the month of October! Thus the majority of angel-hair cases coincide exactly with the optimum migration period of ballooning spiders. This is especially true of the orb-weaving spider.

I believe that the Sudbury case is a prime example. The ball-shaped shiny object was indeed moving with the wind, as would be expected of a sun-reflecting globe of spiderweb. Although local attempts at analysis of the Sudbury material were inconclusive, follow-up laboratory analysis of the remaining fibers, arranged by Dr. Hynek, added further weight to the spider hypothesis.

The scientist who performed this analysis told me that although he could not positively identify the Sudbury material as spiderweb, it nonetheless contained some of the same proteins. In retrospect, I realized that the inorganic materials found by local laboratories were probably contaminants picked up from lawn fertilizer, telephone wires, bushes, hands, the paper used for collection, and so forth. My evaluation of the Sudbury case was "probable spiderweb."

Cases like that which took place at Oloron, France, do remain baffling. The material that rained down from those objects seems to have been of a different nature than that recovered at Sudbury. The Oloron material evaporated upon contact with human hands; the Sudbury material dissipated only partially. Could this be because of June's speedy collection and refrigeration of the wispy threads? Dr. Vallee suggests that real angel hair might be composed of ionized particles in an unstable state. French researcher Aimé Michel elaborates further:

We might imagine that under some conditions the means of propulsion by the saucers can produce a *polymerization* of atoms of the surrounding atmosphere, forming a sort of high-molecular-weight plastic that solidifies in filaments . . . a peculiar and unstable sort of atmospheric *ice,* which can crystallize out of the cold upper air only under the unusual conditions existing in the vicinity of a flying saucer. . . . When the substance falls to the ground, normal warmth would soon depolymerize it and release the atoms in their original gaseous state, so that in the end there would remain nothing but the ordinary gases of the atmosphere. . . . Instead of trying . . . to make a chemical analysis of these fibers, we should . . . preserve them at low temperature . . . and . . . investigate the crystal structure by X-ray diffraction.[13]

Easier said than done, Monsieur! The years since 1954 have come and gone without an official, well-documented analysis.

A young woman was driving a dark, lonely road between Hamilton and Ipswich, Massachusetts. The sky was clear with excellent visibility. Suddenly a huge, bright white, glowing object appeared to her right. It looked as if it were settling into the adjoining field before it blinked out. She streaked home at top speed to report the incident to the police, who patrolled the area soon after, but found nothing. The desk officer passed the case on to me. I visited the site, but found no markings that indicated an object had settled. I took compass readings and returned home to study a topographical map of the area. Plotted on the map, the witness's line of sight did not reveal any clues, so I added the next matching sectional map. All of a sudden, I realized I should have deduced the probable answer to this case based on the witness's description alone. I continued plotting her line of sight—across the additional map to the main runway of Beverly Airport!

I knew the landing approach well. The descending aircraft with its powerful landing lights had approached the witness's vantage point head-on. Then to line itself up with the runway, it took a sharp left turn. The girl's excitement and utmost assurance that the object had landed nearby (and it had!) colored my initial impressions.

Conventional aircraft reflecting sunlight inevitably give rise to some UFO reports. However, most UFO reports involving aircraft take place at night. An inexperienced observer does not always recognize a conventional airplane's strobe and landing lights which on a clear night can be seen for miles. Many times the brilliance of these oncoming lights outshines the more recognizable identification and anticollision lights. Often the landing lights on a distant oncoming aircraft appear to be one or more hovering bright objects. Some airline companies illuminate the upright tail section of their aircraft to display their monogram, presenting a strange sight unless viewed at close range. And a night-flying helicopter's reddish interior lights, reflected through the transparent bubblelike cabin, appear totally unconventional when viewed from a distance. Should the aircraft turn suddenly or shut off its lights, the "object" appears to recede, dim, or blink out. Temperature inversion, clouds, and fog all add to the apparent strangeness of aircraft lights. But usually an aircraft at close range can be identified by its noise and flight characteristics.

The standard lighting configuration for both fixed-wing and rotary-wing aircraft are similar. First, the forward-position lights—a steady red and green light—spaced laterally as far apart as practicable, are installed forward on the aircraft. On an airplane they are located on the wings; on a helicopter, they are on the struts. From the pilot's viewpoint, the red light is always on the left (port) side and the green to the right (starboard).

The rear-position light, also steady, is white and mounted as far to the rear as practicable. All aircraft are also required to bear at least one red rotating anticollision light mounted on the craft's top or bottom. Sometimes one or more supplementary blinking, high-intensity strobe lights are mounted on the leading edge of the wing. When conventional aircraft are misidentified at night, strobe and landing lights are most often the culprits.

According to a statistical report prepared by CUFOS, misidentification of aircraft accounts for the largest segment of IFOs. During the first six months of 1978, the Center found that 210 reports out of a total of 452 identifiable sightings (in other words, 46%) were attributable to aircraft. For the same period in 1977, 174 of 397 IFOs (or a total of 44 percent) were aircraft. However, out of the combined total of 384 identified aircraft, 48 percent concerned a certain type of conventional aircraft carrying extremely unconventional lighting.

Since 1963 people from many walks of life dogmatically insist that they have sighted a UFO, claiming that it performed fantastic hovering maneuvers, fluttering, reversing in flight, even right-angle turns. They generally describe it as being cigar- or disc-shaped, and invariably it bore a row of bright rectangular windows or lights revolving around its perimeter like a theater marquee. When I inform these would-be witnesses that it *was* a marquee, I sometimes get incredulous looks and nasty remarks.

The above-described IFO is none other than a night-advertising helicopter or plane—usually a small one-engine Cessna carrying an electronically controlled lighted billboard of several hundred flashing lights. The aircraft's standard lighting is often lost in the glare of the sign, which usually cannot be read, much less identified, unless it is overhead.

Joe Budina is one of the pioneers in the aerial night-advertising business. The specially designed rig he used in the early 60's was a forerunner to the more sophisticated mass-produced type used today throughout the United States. Once he decided to use his aircraft to advertise Unequaled Formula Oil. You guessed it! It was the product's initials that caused the stir: When told that she had sighted the advertising plane, one woman retorted: "I *know* it was a UFO. It lit up with the *word* UFO!"

The Goodyear blimp displays a similar lighted sign. Its configuration, lighting, and relatively silent motors cause both daytime and nighttime UFO sightings. Such reports are easy to identify, since the Goodyear Company at Akron, Ohio, keeps meticulous flight records that are available for the asking.

It was about 4:45 A.M., September 6, 1977. Jerry reached out to silence the alarm clock. He got up, put on slippers and gown, and stepped out onto the second-story porch for a breath of fresh air. Then he blinked and looked again. A tight formation of silent white and red glowing objects was moving slowly across the sky! Some were flashing white, while the others glowed a steady red. They darted back and forth in formation as they glided silently along.

Directly behind them—and approaching rapidly—were several jet fighters. Jerry's pulse quickened. He recognized the engine sound and their navigational lights. As the Air Force interceptors caught up to their quarries, they disappeared into nothingness! Not a sign of the fighters could be seen as the flotilla of strange glowing objects continued off into the distance. Jerry went to the phone and called the state police—who in turn referred him to me. Jerry said it looked as if the UFO formation had disintegrated the pursuing aircraft. He was very excited and sincere, and I felt certain that he had witnessed something very unusual.

I called the FAA Air Traffic Control center at Nashua, New Hampshire, and asked the watch supervisor if the radar operator for that sector had tracked any unusual targets. He informed me that there was a military exercise in that area, and referred me to the FAA military liaison officer, who explained that a refueling mission had taken place involving air tankers from Pease Air Force Base.

This kind of report was a first with me, so I placed a call to Pease AFB and reached an officer belonging to the 715th Air Refueling Squadron. "Would you kindly describe the lighting effects that would be associated with such a mission?"

The officer told me that the light on a standard KC-135 tanker aircraft's refueling boom would probably not be visible from the ground. Nor would the light on the receptacle of the aircraft being refueled. However, the lights that caused the UFO report were probably two rows of three lights affixed to the bottom of each tanker's fuselage.

He stated that the middle two lights lit up with a steady green only when both the tanker and the refueling aircraft were properly aligned. Apparently when Jerry was gazing upwards, they were a steady red—because the approaching fighters were not yet properly aligned for re-fueling. The outside lights were white, flashing vertically or horizontally to provide visual directional instructions to the oncoming pilots. This caused the glowing "UFOs" to appear to dart back and forth in formation!

During actual refueling, the interceptors' conventional lights were dimmed and strobes were shut off, causing the interceptors' apparent disappearance.

Military experimental aircraft are yet another stimulus for false UFO reports, but such craft do not usually stray from official testing grounds. It's the amateur aircraft builder who's more likely to have his handiwork misidentified.

On the way back from summer vacation one year, I spotted what looked like a silvery oval object circling high above the highway. We stopped—along with other cars—to look at it. As it descended, I easily recognized it as a hang glider! I would never have thought that someone would be hang gliding in this mountainous area, but the pilot had jumped off Mt. Washington, the highest mountain in New England! Others who didn't stop to watch may still think they saw a UFO.

One evening I received a phone call from a perturbed resident of Amherst, New Hampshire, who had sighted a "batlike flying object" flying low over power lines at dusk. Somehow attached to this strange object was a definite humanoid figure. The witness reported a dull roaring sound as the object flew by, following the swath cut through the woods by the power lines.

The following morning I called the local police to obtain names of additional witnesses, whereupon the police told me they'd captured the UFO occupant—an enterprising young earthling who had been testing a homemade, *powered* hang glider. One would have thought that he would choose a safer flight path.

A common thing seen under unusual circumstances is almost like seeing a local friend while traveling in a foreign country. You might pass by without speaking because you *know* that it couldn't be her. It was almost midnight on September 28, 1979, when several persons returned to their apartment courtyard at Jamaica Plains, Massachusetts. They heard a strange crackling sound coming from above and saw a ghostly white, triangular image dancing to and fro overhead. By the time the report reached me, the UFO had crashed—and our investigator found the remains! But who would have expected someone to be flying a kite at that time of night?

Commercially produced weather and research balloons are more predictable than their makeshift cousins. The National Weather Service faithfully launches its run-of-the-mill weather balloons at seven A.M. and seven P.M., local time, all over the United States. Weather balloons are usually orange or white, but appear disclike or globular when reflecting sunlight or moonlight. This type of balloon carries an instrument package and is designed to rise to an altitude of about 30,000 feet. Then when it descends to 28,000 feet (or fails to reach the desired height), the balloon automatically bursts, and a parachute returns the instruments safely to earth.

All the phone calls I received concerned a bright object hovering high in the west just after sunset. One of the callers was from the adjoining town of Danvers, Massachusetts. I really didn't expect to see anything, but when I stepped off the front porch to look for myself, I saw a bright, silent glowing ball that reminded me of Venus. It was still very light out, and no stars could yet be seen in the sky. I dashed inside, brought out a six-inch astronomical telescope, and turned it on the hovering yellowish globe. What an amazing difference a 40-power eyepiece makes! The object was a weather balloon, the instrument package clearly visible. No sooner had I focused the eyepiece than the balloon exploded, and the instrument package dropped from view. All that remained were a myriad of golden pieces reflecting the setting sun as they quickly dissipated.

Many groups launch a variety of research balloons, and it's nearly impossible to keep track of them all. Moreover, they can attain very high altitudes and traverse thousands of miles, far from the original launching site. Such devices may reach a diameter of up to 200 feet, and are especially noticeable around sunrise or sunset. They too reflect sunlight and moonlight and may appear as cones, discs, or ovals. Since the upper wind direction and speed may differ markedly from the wind at lower levels, a research balloon may move contrary to winds plotted at ground level. I have yet to investigate a research-balloon case, and have never seen one myself. However, man launches other devices that produce UFO reports from uninformed witnesses. One warm summer's evening, a young couple was crossing a dark field when a glowing object approached them at low level. They both instinctively ducked, only to see it back off again. Frightened, they ran home and phoned the police. The object, gradually dimming, was still visible in the southeastern sky.

Unknown to them, police, radio, and TV stations were receiving similar reports on the same object—*all along the eastern seaboard of the United States.* There had been no need to duck, for they had witnessed a glowing cloud of gas over 500 miles away!

Periodically, NASA launches rockets from Wallops Island, Virginia, to test reentry devices and to perform certain experiments. The glow from reentry can be seen as far north as Canada along the eastern coast, and up to 600 miles inland. Even more spectacular are launches that release glowing clouds of sodium and barium for atmospheric tests. Usually the cloud appears as a bright pinpoint source of white, green, red, or yellow light, then rapidly expands—which can indeed give the impression that a fast-moving object is approaching head-on. Next, it quickly shrinks in size, giving the impression that the object is receding. This scenario varies if upper winds cause the "object" to change shape.

Rocket firings of this type also originate from Eglin Air Force Base, Florida, and the Churchill Test Range in Manitoba, Canada. (In 1978, such launches were made from Soviet ships off the coast of Virginia in cooperation with NASA.) Other rockets are launched from special test ranges like Vandenberg Air Force Base, California. Intercontinental ballistic missiles such as Minuteman travel thousands of miles out over the Pacific in long-range tests, and the sunlight reflecting off their bodies and contrails is often reported as UFOs.

At last count, this planet is being orbited by some 700 satellites, some of which are clearly visible to the naked eye. They appear as starlike objects moving steadily along a straight path (usually west to east, because it's easier and more efficient to launch them in the same direction as the earth's rotation). Satellites sometimes may appear to zigzag in flight—an illusion caused by autokinesis and/or atmospheric conditions.

Transit time of the artificial satellite varies from a few minutes to about twenty minutes, depending upon its distance from earth. Variations in brightness may be caused by changes in the reflecting surface of a tumbling satellite. This man-made moonlet will blink off at the end of its visible flight as it passes into the earth's shadow.

Sooner or later, a satellite's orbit gradually decays. It will be attracted back into the earth's atmosphere and burn up like a meteor. The appearance of a reentering satellite is similar to that of a meteoric fireball except that it appears to move slower and remains visible longer. Its trajectory is also flatter, and almost always in an easterly direction. NASA and NORAD track satellites, and both will provide the investigator with transit and reentry data.

A widely-witnessed incident at Cape Ann, Massachusetts, on August 2, 1967, caused a local uproar. I investigated the case concurrently with scientists of the Air Force-sponsored University of Colorado UFO Project. The following is excerpted from their final report:

Case 29
Northeastern
Summer 1967

Background:
At least 17 witnesses in ten independent groups reported seeing six to 16 bright objects or as many lights associated with a single object, in the northeastern sky at about 9:30 P.M. EDT. Most of the reports indicated that the lights were visible for 10–15 sec., although a few claimed durations up to five minutes.

... A group of six teenagers said they saw a noiseless *flying saucer* with 6 yellow lights 200 ft. in the air over the concession stand on the beach. They reported the object to be about 20–35 feet across with a "round thing on the top and bottom." ... Similar observations... made at the same time ... were from four different beaches, an airport, and a fishing boat off-shore. The reports varied in detail, but ... all agreed that the lights appeared in the northeast. Elevation angles that were indicated varied from 5–30° above the horizon. The lights were described as blinking on and off; some descriptions indicated that they appeared in sequence from left to right and blinked off in reverse sequence, right to left. Most observers saw 5 or 6 yellow lights in a roughly horizontal line, each light being comparable in brightness with the planet Venus. One private pilot observing from the ground saw a horizontal string of 6 to 8 pairs of lights, one yellow and one red light in each pair. The array moved toward the horizon and seemed to get larger for 5–7 seconds, stopping 4–5 seconds, then beginning to retrace the approach path before blinking out about 4 seconds later. ... at least one witness, in addition to the teenagers at the original beach, reported seeing a large disk-like object encompassing the lights. Other of the witnesses "had the feeling the lights were attached to an object. ..."

Reports of these UFO sightings, when they had been telephoned to the nearest Air Force Base by observers, had been disregarded there. No unusual unidentified radar images had been recorded at the nearest FAA Center. The observations as described did not resemble airplane activity or meteorological or astronomical phenomena. No blimps or aircraft with lighted advertising signs were in the vicinity of the sighting at the time.[14]

When Drs. Craig and Levine returned to the University of Colorado, they had checked with the FAA, Air Force, and the United States Navy, but no one had any known aircraft in the Cape Ann area.

About a month later similar sightings occurred along the coasts of Connecticut, Rhode Island, and Cape Cod. Most witnesses described strings of bright lights that appeared and disappeared in perfect sequence. The Air Force informed the press that the strange lights were caused by a B-52 bomber dropping high-intensity flares along the coastline.

I immediately placed a call to Headquarters 8th Air Force (SAC), Westover AFB, Chicopee Falls, Massachusetts. Information officer Captain William J. Ballee was most cooperative. He had just finished reading John G. Fuller's book *Incident at Exeter,* and recognized my name. I asked him if he would contact all SAC bases and ask for detailed records of Air Force flare drops between July 1 and September 13, 1967. (I decided to keep the Cape Ann sighting date confidential, since I didn't want the Air Force to come back with a prefabricated answer.)

Several weeks later I received a large envelope containing dozens of teletype messages from SAC bases all over the United States. Each contained records of flare drops. Scanning them quickly, I found that a flare drop had occurred on August 2—the time and coordinates coincided exactly with the phenomenon sighted at Cape Ann!

Why hadn't the scientists from University of Colorado found out about these flares? They were traveling under military orders and presumably were given complete cooperation in their investigations. Perhaps the flares were dropped intentionally as a test of public (and investigator) reaction![15] In any event, the University of Colorado study concurred with my evaluation in their final report.

The Chairman of the NICAP Massachusetts Subcommittee, Mr. Raymond E. Fowler, continued the investigation and subsequently learned that an aircrew from the 99th Bomb Wing, Westover AFB, had dropped 16 white flares while on a practice mission about 30 miles NE of Cape Ann. The flare drop coincided in time and direction with the observed UFO. As Mr. Fowler suggested, the "object" enclosing the string of lights must have been constructed by imagination.[16]

Later, a test of these flares' visibility was planned with the cooperation of the Air Force and the NICAP subcommittee. At a predetermined time, one of my field investigators watched from a beach on Cape Ann as an Air Force B-52 dropped the same type of flares off the coast of Maine. He saw and photographed them, and his photographs were sent to the people at the University of Colorado.

The flares used had a rating of 2,000,000 candlepower and a burning time of about 3 minutes. Each is equipped with a parachute. With its chute open, it falls at a rate of 450 feet per minute and can be seen from a distance of over 50 miles, depending upon the aircraft's height and atmospheric conditions. At close distances, between 1 and 2 miles, the light emitted from the burning magnesium appears as brilliant white. As distance increases, however, the flare looks yellowish. At even greater distances it may appear reddish. As each flare ignites and expends itself, one at a time, the impression given is that of a forward-moving circular craft with rotating lights around its perimeter. These flare drops are conducted over the ocean, the Great Lakes, and military test ranges.

Even common fireworks such as rockets and Roman candles may cause UFO reports when launched at inappropriate times and places. Everyone expects to see them on the Fourth of July, but not in a rural area in the dead of winter! Other possible IFOs are attributable to lights from distant autos, snowmobiles, trains, or buildings on elevated terrain. Even anticollision lights on distant towers might seem unusual to strangers in the area. On April 29, 1976, JoAnn was driving north on Route 1 at Topsfield, Massachusetts. Visibility was 15 miles that night, according to the U.S. Weather Service. I am familiar with this stretch of road. It is very dark as there are no streetlights. At about 11:05 P.M. she was climbing a steep grade and observed what she first thought was a single headlight approaching on the southbound lane. She was traveling at about 50 miles per hour, and the light seemed to be doing the same. As it came nearer, it took on the size and shape of a basketball. Then at an estimated distance of 10 feet, at an altitude of about 3 feet, the round white light abruptly turned sky-blue, smoothly diminished to a brilliant blue pinpoint of light, and disappeared into nothingness!

No vehicle was seen; no other traffic was on the road at that moment. The total sighting duration had been about 10 seconds. When she reached the crown of the hill and started to descend, JoAnn then observed two separate white lights approaching, which she easily identified as motor-cycle headlights.

My theoretical explanation for this sighting was that the first light had also been the headlight of a single motorcycle coasting downhill. This would account for no noise being heard. Just before the vehicle passed her car, I deduced, its headlamp blew out. The light's extraordinary brilliance and apparent size would have been caused by the filament suddenly burning up. This would also account for the bluish color and the rapid recession to a pinpoint of light as the filament burned out completely. But JoAnn insists that she saw nothing pass, nor did she see a vehicle in her rear-view mirror.

I believed that because of the very dark conditions and the after-image in her eye caused by the brilliant light, she just did not see the motorcycle. She did easily recognize the two motorcycles that passed her about a minute later, but these vehicles were coming uphill, not coasting, and were probably making lots of noise as their engines strained on the upgrade. Most likely, all three motorcycles were traveling together; the first one had probably just pulled ahead of the others.

March 10, 1977, at approximately two P.M. a young man was taking advantage of warm, springlike weather, and sat outside on the flat roof of an apartment building, reading a book. He put the book down, gazed up dreamily at the deep blue sky, and was shocked to see a silver cigar-shaped object drift slowly overhead, followed by smaller disc-shaped objects. Quite agitated, he finally reached me by phone via the local police.

His description was similar to many others I had read about. This sighting had been made in broad daylight; would others be reporting it? Our conversation went something like this:

"What were you doing when you saw the objects?"

"Reading a book."

"On what subject?"

"UFOs."

"Oh. How come you were reading it up on the roof?"

"I was smoking pot."

Relatively few cases seem to be caused by a natural hallucination. Some are probably caused by an artificially instigated hallucination, as in the following instance.

Phil had left the party none too soon—he'd had too much to drink, and he knew it. He decided to pull off the road and sleep it off. Suddenly, in the early morning hours, Phil woke up with a start. He had heard a noise, and for one panicky instant did not know where he was. Recovering his senses, he gazed out the car window and was shocked to see a brilliant spray of sparks at the corner of the field in which he'd parked. Startled, he watched the streetlights bordering the field flicker a few times before going out. The whole area was plunged into blackness.

Still half asleep and sluggish, Phil tried to fathom what was going on. Then, horrified, he saw a flashing red glowing object float across the other side of the field. He remembered hearing about UFOs and associated power blackouts. They weren't going to get him! He quickly started the car and drove off.

When I investigated this intriguing report, I found that another car (probably driven by another party goer) had smashed into a utility pole. The crash woke up Phil, who saw the crossed high-tension wires arcing before settling to the ground. The flashing red light was a repair truck moving along the road on the opposite side of the field. There was nothing wrong with Phil's description of these events—it was his interpretation that was literally way out in left field!

CHAPTER NOTES

1. J. E. McDonald, *UFOS: An International Problem,* p. 19.

2. *Ibid.*

3. *Ibid.*

4. W. D. Rayle, "Ball Lightning Characteristics," *NASA Technical Note D-3188* (Washington: NASA, January 1966), p. 13.

5. Roger N. Shepard, "Tornadoes: Puzzling Phenomena and Photographs," *Science,* January 6, 1967, p. 27.

6. Haroun Tazieff, *When the Earth Trembles* (New York: Harcourt, Brace & World, Inc., 1966), p. 114.

7. Personal files.

8. Aimé Michel, *Flying Saucers and the Straight-Line Mystery* (New York: Criterion Books, 1958), p. 170.

9. R. A. Hall, ed., *The UFO Evidence* (Washington: NICAP, 1964), pp. 99, 100.

10. *Ibid.,* p. 100.

11. *Ibid.*

12. J. Vallee, *Anatomy of a Phenomenon* (Chicago: Henry Regnery Company, 1965), p. 62.

13. Michel, op. cit., p. 171.

14. E. U. Condon, director, *Scientific Study of Unidentified Flying Objects* (New York: E. P. Dutton & Co., Inc., 1969), pp. 339, 340.

15. Raymond E. Fowler, *UFOs: Interplanetary Visitors* (New Jersey: Prentice-Hall, Inc., 1979), pp. 159–61.

16. Condon, *op. cit.,* pp. 61, 62.

Not every strange light or shape in the sky is a genuine UFO. Following are a number of "Identifiable Flying Objects"—as well as some genuine unknowns.

The Planet Venus seen against a dusky sky. Bright stars and planets—especially when viewed near the horizon—give rise to a number of UFO reports *(Allan Hendry)*

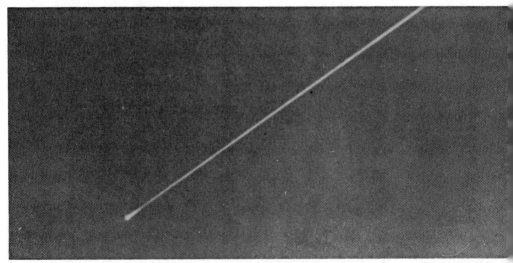

A Meteor moves very quickly, usually down the sky, and is gone in a second or less. Larger fireballs or bolides may take longer to cross the sky, however *(Allan Hendry)*

Coronal Discharges from power lines can mimic the shape and behavior of reported UFOs—which, coincidentally, are often sighted in the vicinity of high-tension wires [simulated] *(Coral Lorenzen, Aerial Phenomena Research Organization)*

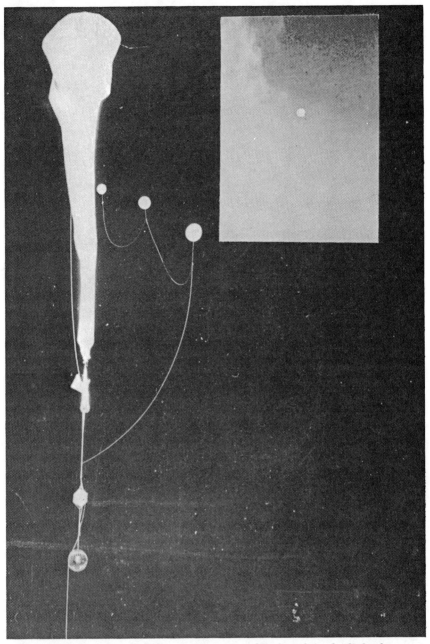

A Research Weather Balloon is a large gas-filled sock in daylight, but at dusk or dawn can been seen as a slowly-drifting sphere of light
(Allan Hendry)

Nighttime Advertising Planes are quite recognizable in the daylight . . .
(Sky Ads, Burlington, Massachusetts)

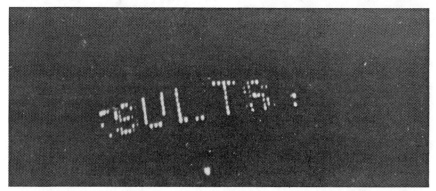

. . . and at night, as long as their glowing messages are read from directly
underneath . . . *(Allan Hendry)*

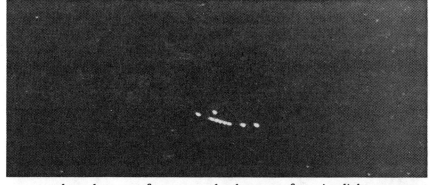

. . . but when seen from an angle, the rows of moving lights suggest a
rotating disc-like craft *(Allan Hendry)*

Homemade Hot-Air Balloons can be assembled from balsa wood struts, a few birthday-cake candles, and a plastic laundry bag (above: *G. J. Gelineau,* Lawrence Eagle-Tribune); but it can look like a flaring, blazing source of light—especially when either the balsa wood or plastic catches fire! (below: *Allan Hendry*)

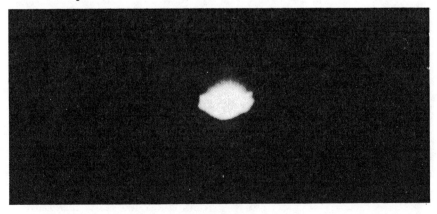

A Model of a UFO was hung by a string from overhead telephone wires in Walpole, Massachusetts, sometime in 1966. Seen against the empty sky, it's hard for a photo analyst to determine the little object's true size *(Harold Hope)*

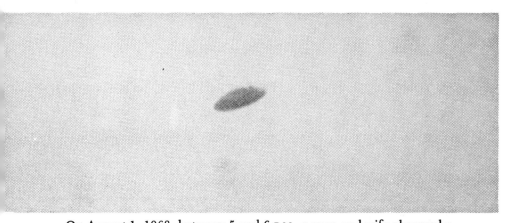

On August 1, 1968, between 5 and 6 P.M., a man and wife observed a domed disc passing over their homesite west of Charlotte, North Carolina. Their use of a Polaroid camera—which produces no negative—makes analysis difficult *(NICAP)*

These two photographs were taken on May 11, 1950, in McMinnville, Oregon. An USAF-sponsored study concluded, "the [photographer] is an honest individual and the negatives show no signs of having been tampered with. . . .The accuracy of . . . photometric measures of [the] original negatives . . . argue against fabrication" *(UPI)*

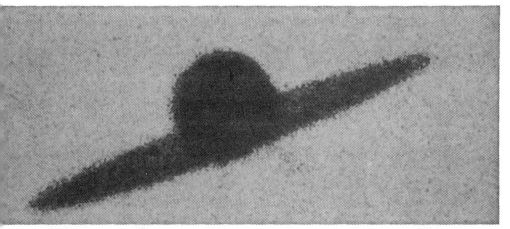

On March 18, 1975, a man was photographing birds near an abandoned quarry in Hamilton, Ontario. He saw this object zig-zagging above him and snapped three photos. An enlargement shows a domed disc with struts or antennae (The Spectator, *Hamilton, Ontario, Canada*)

A most provocative photo of an apparent unknown. On November 22, 1966, a Ph.D. biochemistry consultant watched this UFO rise from a cluster of trees in Willamette Pass, Oregon. The photo itself shows a triple image. NICAP analysts doubt that any object could stop three times in 1/100th of a second, but. . . .*(NICAP)*

11
CELESTIAL
EXPLANATIONS

Late one evening a student called from a phone booth in front of Endicott Junior College at Beverly, Massachusetts. The young woman was so perturbed that I had to interrupt several times to get the gist of what she was trying to tell me. She shouted that a UFO was hovering near the college, and lots of people were out on the street watching it. Even the police were there. One officer viewing it with binoculars said he could see four smaller UFOs orbiting the larger one, which kept moving up and down and side to side.

After asking several questions, I proceeded to tell her what I thought it was. She would not accept my explanation and said the police wanted me to come down. So I put my coat on and drove to Endicott College. It was about midnight. I had to get up early for work and should have been in bed. I'm afraid that I wasn't in the best of moods when I pulled over to the curb beside the flashing cruiser.

About fifty persons were gazing upward. A police officer standing beside the squad car with binoculars shouted, "What is it, Mr. Fowler?" I glanced up and asked what they were looking at. They all pointed at Jupiter! Before I could answer, someone shouted, "It's moving again!" Concurrently, I watched some ocean mist pass in front of the shining planet.

I turned to the crowd and politely explained that the four objects the officer could see with binoculars were four of Jupiter's larger moons. A murmur of utter disbelief rippled through the crowd, and no one except the police officer believed me. I bade them all a hearty good night and returned home.

How, one might ask, could this crowd of apparently intelligent young men and women be fooled by Jupiter? Apart from the mild mob hysteria that often develops in such situations, some singularly bright planets and stars are extremely prominent in the nighttime sky. Moreover, under certain atmospheric conditions celestial objects exhibit apparent movement and rapidly changing colors. In the case just cited, Jupiter's movement was attributable to three basic reasons:

1. *Autokinesis*—When a stationary person stares at a planet or star without a visual stable reference point for comparison, the star or planet appears to move and dart about. In reality, this is caused by the minute movements of the observer's head and eyes.

2. *Refraction and dispersion*—As the light of a planet or star shines through the air enveloping our planet, rays of varying wavelengths bend at different angles. This can cause the celestial object to twinkle, change color, or even seem to move up and down and back and forth. Atmospheric turbulence and changes in density and temperature aggravate this effect, which is most prominent when a planet or star is rising or setting near the horizon and the observer is looking through a thicker blanket of air. (In the Endicott College case, Jupiter was rising over the ocean.) Usually by the time a star or planet reaches a position close to the zenith (overhead), it takes on a normal appearance.

3. *Clouds*—The superimposed movement of windblown clouds can make a planet or star appear to move in the opposite direction. At Endicott College, the windswept mist off the ocean caused precisely this effect. The star or planet's gradual appearance through varying thicknesses of cloud cover may cause the shining object to appear to move toward an observer.

One cold wintry morning before sunrise, a truck driver was making early morning rounds. The sky had cleared rapidly after a late winter snowfall. The oncoming dawn had bleached out the starry night. As the driver rounded a bend in the road, he saw a yellowish, hazy ball of light, seemingly just above treetop level. Curious, he stopped at the side of the road, stepped out into the crisp morning air, and cautiously walked across the road to get a closer look. Not a whisper of sound came from the diffuse glow.

Suddenly there was a whooshing sound, as branches directly under the object released their snow. A sparkling cloud of white crystals scattered in all directions. When it had settled, the object was gone!

His immediate impression was that its rapid departure had caused the tree branches to sway. But the time, direction, elevation, and weather conditions indicated that the glowing object was none other than Venus, shining through remaining clouds on the horizon. The cloud cover must have thickened and obscured Venus; a coincidental spurt of wind dislodged snow from adjoining tree branches.

Stars seen in the nighttime sky differ from season to season, because the earth revolves around the sun every 365¼ days. Thus we look out upon the universe in different directions and see changing scenery along the way. Our distance from stars (other than our sun) is so vast that their relative position in the sky appears to remain fixed. We see the same constellations (or star patterns) at the same positions and times, year after year. The earth also rotates west to east on its axis every 24 hours, causing the stars to appear to rise in the east and set in the west about 4 minutes earlier each night. Bright stars (especially Sirius, Capella, and Arcturus in the Northern Hemisphere) are often reported as UFOs.

Planets, unlike stars, journey around our sun, outlined against a band of constellations called the zodiac. The rotation of the earth also causes planets to appear to rise and set, easterly to westerly. Our own earth is only one of nine known planets orbiting the sun. Whereas stars are distant, hot, self-luminous bodies of nuclear-fired gases; planets are close, cool bodies that reflect the sun's light, shining with a steadier glow. Only the four brightest planets—Venus, Mars, Jupiter, and Saturn—are often reported as UFOs. Of these, Venus is the chief culprit. Venus becomes visible annually, and is seen in the east as a morning "star" or in the west as an evening planet. It has been fired on by antiaircraft batteries and chased by jet interceptors. Mars ranks a close second every twenty-six months, when its orbit brings it near the earth. Under proper conditions, it blazes like a beacon in the nighttime sky. At times Venus is bright enough to be seen in the daytime if you know where to look for it. Saturn is least likely to be reported as a UFO, but Jupiter runs a close third to Venus and Mars.

A young dating couple was returning home late at night. As they approached a major highway at Danvers, a brilliant object was hovering over the intersection. Frightened, they turned onto the highway and sped away at great speed to escape this strange apparition—but the object was now to their right and matching their speed!

They pulled into an all-night service station and ran inside for help. When the station attendant came outside with them, he saw in the sky a stationary light that seemed much too bright to be a star. He ran back into his office and phoned the state police, who in turn referred the witnesses to me.

They excitedly related the car chase and told me how the car would not start when they first tried to leave the gas station. Not only that, but their gas tank was abnormally low! They attributed both of these factors to the UFO. I told them I'd check and get back to them. The next day I phoned the young lady to tell her that she had seen the planet Venus. On the next clear night she took another drive and saw the same bright object in approximately the same place—but she never told her boyfriend!

Years later I was giving a lecture at a meeting of UFO buffs. Afterward a young man got up and told the audience how he and his girl friend had been chased by a UFO. His story sounded familiar, and after asking a few questions about the time, date, and place, I ascertained that this was the same young man who was with the girl that eventful night. When I told him that it had really only been Venus, he replied that I didn't know what I was talking about. One lady jumped up and gave me a lecture on how I was probably working for the Air Force and was getting paid to explain UFOs away.

Another brilliant, scintillating, multicolored light chased a young couple's car all the way to a restaurant. They ran from the parking lot into the building, but when they left later on, the object was higher in the sky and looked like merely a very bright star. In this case, direction, time, azimuth, and elevation indicated that it was Sirius.

What causes the illusion of being chased by a star or planet? Apparent movement is caused by the real movement of an automobile's changing direction along a winding road. Bright planets and stars appear larger when rising or setting, when they often appear to give off rapidly changing colors, and their strange appearance is compounded when viewed through eyeglasses, windowpanes, curved windshields, and nonastronomical binoculars and telescopes.

For the first six months of 1978, CUFOS identified 452 UFO sightings reported via their hotline. A total of 127, or 28 percent, were attributed to stars and planets. For the same six-month period in 1977, a total of 116 out of 397, or 29 percent, were identified as stars and planets.

To the trained investigator, any point-light source having a long sighting duration is an immediate astronomical suspect. Fortunately, the predictability of annual star and planet positions in the sky allows for easy identification.

Returning home in the early morning hours from train station, a very well-educated woman was shocked to see a huge, bright red, flattened oval object hovering silently over the trees behind her home. She told me that it was as large as the moon—which I told her it was! She found this very hard to believe until I demonstrated with almanac and compass that the direction, elevation, and phase of the gibbous moon were a perfect match to where she had seen her UFO.

This is just one of several moon-on-the-horizon sightings that I have investigated personally. As in the case of stars and planets, viewing the moon near the horizon through clouds or fog, or from a moving vehicle, can give the illusion of movement. Many a person's car has been "chased" by the moon. But investigators are able to give pertinent identifications because most witnesses are able to give accurate descriptions.

Comets are worth only a brief mention, since those that can be seen with the naked eye are quite rare. Masses of frozen gas and solid matter moving through space, most comets travel in enormous elliptical orbits around the sun. As one approaches the sun, its gases vaporize, forming a glowing, ghostly white halo around the frozen nucleus. The glowing tail usually trails the nucleus until it rounds the sun, whereupon the pressure of the sun's photons and particles (or solar wind) causes the tail to stream out in front of the nucleus. A comet's tail always points away from the sun. Comets within our solar system have predictable orbits. Others come from vast distances outside the limits of our known solar system.

About a half-dozen comets are discovered each year. Most can be seen only with telescopic aid; only several conspicuous comets appear in the course of a century. Significantly, I have received just one "unidentified flying comet" report during my tenure as a UFO investigator. Comets— even the vastly overrated Kahoutek—usually receive much publicity, and the public at large is usually aware of them.

During the early morning hours of September 11, 1975, dozens of people, including eleven police officers, witnessed a glowing streak across the Boston skyline. The amazed observers saw it break into three separate pieces. Each piece seemed to move off in a different direction before blinking out. Area newspapers carried the event as a well-witnessed, spectacular UFO sighting. All the local witnesses had the impression that the object flew directly over Boston at a low altitude.

However, our investigation revealed that people in adjoining states saw a similar object at the same time—and heading in the same direction, indicating that the object was hundreds of miles above the earth. Meteors, commonly called shooting stars, are gravitationally attracted pieces of matter from outer space which burn up by friction in our earth's atmosphere. They vary from particles the size of a grain of sand to pieces weighing tons. Billions of meteors enter our atmosphere each day, but relatively few survive their searing flight, and fewer still are recovered as meteorites. Most ordinary meteors are visible for only a fraction of a second, described merely as streaks of light or as short-lived, fast-moving starlike objects with or without a fiery trail.

On rare occasions, several meteors may travel briefly across the sky together. Once in a great while, a person may observe a meteor head-on. During a major meteor shower, I once saw a bright motionless pinpoint of light near the constellation Lyra suddenly brighten and dim to nothing. The parent meteor may fracture into individual parts, as did the one in the Boston case just discussed, or explode in a shower of fiery pieces. A few meteors may be observed on any clear night, but showers occur at predictable times throughout any given year. A single observer may sight fifty or more per hour. These occurrences are caused by our planet's annual passes through areas of space debris and remnants of comets. These meteor showers appear to emanate from "radiant points" within or near that portion of the sky framed by a certain constellation. A list of major showers can be found in most almanacs or astronomy textbooks.

During the rush hour on the evening of April 25, 1966, tens of thousands watched a huge ball of fire move slowly and deliberately along the horizon, leaving a glowing contrail in its wake. Police, newspapers, and governmental agency switchboards lit up solid red. My phone rang continually as witnesses described the crash of a flaming object "just over the hill," "a few miles away," and so forth. The object was visible long enough for one quick-thinking astronomy professor to phone his observatory while the event was in progress! He had immediately recognized the "UFO" for what it was—an extraordinarily bright meteor called a fireball or bolide. These uncommon visitors cause the bulk of meteor-type UFO reports, though, of course, most are not so spectacular.

Fireballs may exhibit brilliant shades or combinations of white, green, blue, yellow, and red. Although the fireball is sometimes seen over an area of a thousand square miles or more, each individual observer may believe it's passing close by or has landed a few blocks away. Bolides can appear as a brilliant fiery ball, an edge-up disc, or an elongated teardrop. Observers have described them as being the "size of a full moon," or as "a plane crashing." Although most fireballs last only several seconds, there have been cases in which they have traveled from one horizon to the other. Some, as in the Boston case, leave large luminous trails which have been known to last several minutes before fading. Sometimes a sonic boom is heard during the fireball's passage. Those overtaking the earth during the evening hours travel slowly and are fewer in number. Ones entering the earth's atmosphere head-on during the early morning hours travel much faster and are more plentiful. A few are bright enough to be noticed in broad daylight.

Statistically, meteors finish behind stars and planets when it comes to misinterpretation. During the first six months of 1978, CUFOS found that 54 reports (or 12 percent) of a total of 452 identified sightings were attributable to meteors. For the same period in 1977, a total of 45 reports (or 11 percent) of a total of 397 identified sightings were meteors.

Sometimes, extenuating circumstances may mask the reality of an otherwise run-of-the-mill meteor. The parents of one of our local investigators, physicist David Webb, sent him news clips describing a sighting. The November 5, 1971, copy of the *Alliance* (Ohio) *Review* sported a rather spectacular headline: UFO SUSPECTED AS "CULPRIT" IN SHED BLAZE HERE.

According to the newspaper account, numerous individuals—including two police officers—had sighted a bright blue glowing object with a fiery trail descend over the city of Alliance. One customer at an automobile sales lot excitedly told a salesman that she saw the glowing object crash near a small vacant building on an adjoining hill. The busy salesman paid her tale little attention until about ten minutes later, when he thought he saw a small brushfire on the hill. Discovering that the shed was ablaze, he phoned the fire department.

When the fire truck arrived, the building was engulfed in flames. A bystander told the fire chief that he had seen a fiery object come in from the east and crash through the shed roof! The chief stated that the area where the fire started contained "a white fire like you couldn't imagine. It was really bright, almost to the point where it hurt your eyes to look at it." Once the fire was out, firemen found remnants of a "magnesium-like" substance. "We are not sure what this material is," the chief said, "but it was confined in one area and was the only substance of that nature found in the garage." He added that a piece of this material had been found lying on an iron bar. It had heated the bar white hot!

The incident must have seemed highly significant, because NASA and the Air Force soon became intimately involved. Assigning David Webb to the case, I called the company which reportedly was analyzing the material, and was told that the substance contained aluminum, magnesium, and silicon. (I also found that an Air Force captain had phoned asking for the same information!) The company representative informed me that the material and their report had been sent to the Alliance fire inspector.

The fire inspector was very cordial when I finally reached him by phone at home on Friday evening, November 12. He stated that a NASA official had already examined the material and had concluded it was not part of a reentering satellite. I then asked him if NICAP could have a sample of the material. He graciously agreed to send me a piece on Monday morning from his office, where it was stored for safekeeping. He added that on Monday, USAF Captain Lawrence McKinney from the Foreign Technology Division at Wright-Patterson Air Force Base was visiting his office. I groaned—Project Bluebook came under this division. I pleaded with the inspector not to give all of the material to the Air Force. He chuckled and promised that he would send me a piece first thing Monday morning, before the good captain ever arrived.

Deciding not to take any chances, I phoned the inspector early Monday morning to remind him to send me samples of the residue before the Air Force arrived. But I was too late. Captain McKinney had paid him a surprise visit at his home—on Saturday. The inspector had to accompany the officer to his office downtown, where the material was kept. The good captain told him that the material was not unusual and did not come from a satellite, but nevertheless proceeded to confiscate all of the metal. Before I hung up in utter dismay, the inspector told me casually that no one admitted seeing an object hit the building. He added that the juvenile officer blamed five boys for setting the shed fire.

At the time, I thought this was all very strange indeed, and hoped that David's forthcoming on-site investigation would get to the root of this intriguing matter. I also couldn't help wondering if the Air Force paid the fire inspector that unscheduled visit because of my phone call on Friday night? Strange coincidences like this have happened quite often.

The Air Force base operator gave me Captain McKinney's extension and rang it for me. "Foreign materials," said a young lady's voice on the end of the line. Eventually Captain McKinney came to the phone. He stated tersely that the material was not unusual and had nothing to do with satellite reentry. He would not send me a sample; that was that.

I sent for copies of the Alliance Fire Prevention Bureau report; the fire department report, and the research company's analysis report. They added little that I didn't already know. They did, however, contain some names and addresses of UFO witnesses, which I relayed to David Webb. He found that most witnesses had sighted the fiery aerial object low in the southern sky at about 8:15 P.M., some 15 to 20 minutes before the fire was noticed. Since most witnesses observed the object south of the shed, it was quite apparent that the object they were watching did not hit the building.

Newspaper stories from other Ohio communities strengthened Dave's suspicions. The Cleveland *Plain Dealer* and the Elyria *Chronicle Telegram* carried stories of dozens of similar sightings all over northeastern Ohio. David interviewed a high school planetarium director who, with his wife, had seen the object during the same time frame and direction from 42 miles northwest of Alliance. In his final report, David Webb concluded that:

No direct evidence for arson could be found at the fire scene. . . . Five boys were interrogated ; . . but did not confess to arson. . . . The actual cause of the fire does not appear to be related to any material found in the shed. . . . Therefore, ignition due to a meteorite, fireworks rocket, airplane or space hardware fall appears unlikely.

It is likely that the molten material found in the shed is associated with a magnesium/aluminum alloy dolly . . . in the shed . . . The angle iron, wheels and axle . . . [were] found. . . . Several local manufacturers . . . [stated] that these are constructed of a steel frame and wheels with a supporting lattice of a magnesium/aluminum alloy used for light weight. These were the major constituents of the . . . samples.

After numerous interviews by the Alliance Fire Department NASA, the Air Force . . . and myself, there remains only the *one* confirmed report of an unknown man seeing something *impact* the shed prior to the fire. I believe it likely that this man was sincere in his report, but misinterpreted the altitude and distance of an exceptionally bright Fireball.

Lest anyone think this a remarkable coincidence, an acquaintance at the Smithsonian Institution told me their team had investigated a fireball falling in line of sight with a barn fire in New England. Again, the object was actually hundreds of miles away: In this case, the barn fire was attributed to the spontaneous combustion of stored hay.

But what *are* the characteristics of objects evaluated in the "unidentified" category?

12
CONSISTENT CHARACTERISTICS OF REAL UFOs

The final report of an Air Force study of 286 cases evaluated in the unknown category, classified Secret, concluded that:

The objects sighted have been grouped into four classifications according to [physical] configurations: 1) Flying Disks 2) Torpedo or Cigar-shaped 3) Spherical 4) Balls of light. ... The most numerous reports indicate the daytime observation of metallic disk-like objects, roughly in diameter, ten times their thickness.[1]

An earlier classified memo sent to the commanding general of the Army Air Force read that most of the objects were "circular or elliptical in shape, flat on the bottom and domed on top."[2] In 1955 another Air Force study concluded that of 2,199 UFOs reported between 1947 and 1952, 47 percent of the objects were oval, 5 percent were cylindrical, and 24 percent were light sources and other shapes. In the remaining 24 percent of the cases investigated, no shape was denoted.

NICAP statistics are strikingly similar. Of a total of 333 cases documented between 1942 and 1963, 58 percent were discs, ellipses, etc.; 8 percent were cylindrical; and 34 percent fell into the category of light sources or other shapes.[3] Many of the discs were reported to have the typical central dome or superstructure on top.

In 1974 I performed a detailed analysis of sightings during the period from 1963 to 1972 in my personal files to see if local statistics were similar to national statistics. The results were nearly identical with the NICAP and Air Force conclusions. Out of the 160 unknowns examined, 59 percent were elliptical or oval, 8 percent were cylindrical, and 33 percent were balls of light and other shapes. The similarity within such comparisons illustrates that the phenomenon has remained basically the same for years.

Similar analyses of thousands of UFO reports have revealed typical maneuver patterns: hovering, or very slow motion, followed by rapid acceleration; circling and pacing human-made vehicles and structures; satellite objects associated with larger parent objects; a wobbling on the axis, especially when stopping suddenly; a pendulum or falling-leaf motion when descending; a forward up-and-down movement similar to a sine wave; and right-angle turns without benefit of a curve radius. UFOs also show a peculiar affinity for certain environmental situations: swampy areas; power lines and power stations; freshwater bodies; locales around military installations, especially where nuclear material is being stored or used; and other areas of apparent technical interest.

UFOs also exhibit certain strange effects: electromagnetic (on compass, radio, ignition systems, etc.); radiation (burns, induced radio activity, etc.); ground disturbance (dust stirred up, leaves moved, standing wave peaks on the surface of water, etc.); sound (none, hissing, humming, roaring, thunderclaps, etc.); lights (colored lights around perimeter, plasma-like glow over the surface of the object, etc.); vibration (weak, strong, slow, fast); smell (ozone, burned matches, sulfur); flame, smoke, or cloud; strange beams of light that extend and retract like solid tubes; and the inhibition of voluntary motion by observers.

The alert reader will already have recognized many of these characteristics in some of the UFO sightings already described in this book; obviously many other reported details are not so consistent. For immediate comparison, however, let's summarize a number of sightings our local MUFON team evaluated in the unknown category. Over and over again, witnesses reported basic characteristics and other consistent traits.

On June 6, 1974, Vivian (47), her son Richard (11), daughter Barbara (10), and niece Helen (30), were driving home from a PTA meeting at Amesbury, Massachusetts. They were going north on Route 150 (the Exeter road) to their homes in South Hampton, New Hampshire. Richard and Barbara called attention to a bright red beaconlike light in the sky a few miles ahead. While proceeding northward, they noticed that the light was getting larger. It was soon lost behind trees. However, as they approached a large open area where Midway Excavators, Inc., was located, they could see it shining through the branches.

As they passed the open area Helen, curious, slowed the Volkswagen station wagon, fully expecting to see a beacon light on a tower or tall crane. To their amazement, a large red illuminated dome was hovering over the edge of the clearing. Beneath the dome was a bright rectangular opening with something like "blades spinning around inside." The whirling blades seemed to protrude outside as well. Within this lighted rectangle was centered a dark square, like a darkened window. From the bright opening spewed white, blue, and yellow sparks in simultaneous double bursts, 180 degrees apart. They became frightened, and Helen sped off. Her passengers glanced behind and, to their horror, saw that the noiseless and completely unconventional object was following their car! As they slowed, approaching a junction, the craft descended rapidly right at them. As their car turned right onto Locust Street, Helen instinctively braked as the red-domed, sparking vehicle passed directly in front of them. Proceeding ahead of them above the road and into a field, it stopped around 400 feet away and hovered with a "bobbing, fluttering motion" about 30 feet above a 90-foot elm tree.

Helen brought her car to a full stop. As soon as she cautiously stepped out (the others felt safer observing from inside), a band of soft-glowing colored lights appeared around the object's perimeter—greenish-yellow, then deep red, pinkish-red, dark green, and finally a deep blue—like a "string of beads." The colored lights flickered on and off, one by one.

The reflection from these multicolored lights revealed a lower, larger, inverted bowl-shaped section, to which a central dome was attached. After the colored lights blinked off and on a bit, then all of the lights would go on at once with just one solid color: first red, then blue, then green. Helen stood transfixed at this unearthly sight until the object began moving around the field with a "jerky motion" and began to descend toward the ground. Helen thought it was going to land! As Barbara dived onto the backseat floor, Helen jumped back in the car and drove quickly to Vivian's house to call the police.

When they rushed into the house, Vivian's son Todd (17) and his girl friend Kathy listened incredulously to the excited witnesses. Todd persuaded his mother to put the phone down; he felt the police wouldn't believe such a story unless the object was there for them to see. He suggested that he and Kathy drive down to the field: If the object was still there, then they would call the police.

Todd and Kathy drove immediately to the sighting area. As he suspected, the object had left. He continued to Amesbury where he dropped Kathy off at her home. Todd then headed back home along Route 150.

As he approached the Locust Street junction, he could see a light in the sky shining through the trees. He lost sight of it momentarily because of tall trees bordering the road. But when he turned right onto Locust Street, he saw the colored, illuminated bottom of a "bowl-shaped" object hovering over the same elm tree in the field. Todd stepped on the gas and drove home at great speed to alert his family.

In the excitement, no one bothered to call the police! They all rushed out and tumbled into his car. Todd headed for the field. The object was *still* there. No one wanted to stop at the edge of the field; they were too scared. Todd continued by the hovering object and parked on a hill on an adjoining road that looked down upon the field.

The object remained hovering below them, over the tree. Vivian noticed lights on at a house on the hill and ran over to alert its occupants to the strange sight. Helen told me that she too stepped outside the car, but no sound could be heard from the craft. Then the lighted, domed disk began to alternately hover, bob, and zig zag back and forth above the field.

In the meantime, Vivian had dashed into the strangers' house without even knocking! While she was inside, the others heard the sound of a low-flying jet aircraft. Glancing eastward, they watched a single-engine jet traveling north to south, heading directly for the hovering object. The object immediately reacted to the oncoming intruder, retreating back over a swamp bordering the field. Then it descended quickly with a jerky step-by-step motion, like a falling leaf, settling on or near the ground. All of its lights blinked out, except for a red glow that lingered momentarily before it too faded away. The aircraft overshot the field and made a few wide circles around it before flying away.

At this point Vivian came rushing out of the nearby house with the husband and wife who lived there. They saw only the aircraft moving away into the distance. The group watched for some time but when nothing further could be seen, they headed home. Vivian reported the sighting to Pease Air Force Base, and later to the police, who in turn informed the *Amesbury News*, which in turn informed me.[4] I investigated the case jointly with John P. Oswald, a MUFON investigator for that area. Later Stephen Webbe, staff writer for the *Christian Science Monitor,* conducted an inquiry and wrote a feature story based on this fascinating sighting.[5] The Pease AFB command post told Vivian that she was being recorded during the telephone interview, but when I phoned to secure a copy of this recording, they denied any interest in the sighting. Vivian's telephone call was acknowledged, but they wouldn't admit to taping it. I was told that none of their aircraft were involved.

A thorough character-reference check indicated that the witnesses were stable, honest individuals. A house-to-house survey located no other witnesses. Most were not at home at the time or had been busy indoors. The FAA told me that no unusual radar tracks had been noted in that area. (However, the UFO was well below the altitude covered by FAA radar in that sector.) We concluded that no man-made or natural object could account for the weird craft. Investigator Oswald and Vivian's son attempted a ground search of the swamp for physical evidence, but when Todd sank up to his hips in water and mud, at the outset, both agreed that the going was too treacherous.

Interestingly, Route 150 had already been host to a classic UFO sighting: On September 3, 1965, Norman Muscarello had hitchhiked this same stretch of road. Historically, UFOs have an affinity for northeastern

Massachusetts and southeastern New Hampshire. I have many good cases on file from this area, including twin Massachusetts incidents that occurred on February 12, 1976. One sighting at Salisbury was investigated by John Oswald; I investigated the other at nearby Newbury.

It was about 6 P.M. when a young Amesbury housewife noticed a slow-moving bright white light over the bordering town of Salisbury. It looked unusual enough for her to report it. About a half hour later, someone else also noticed a strange bright white light. Kevin, age 12, was doing homework in his family's trailer home at Salisbury.

The trailer park was relatively new, and they had moved in only about a week before. No one was in the trailers on either side. His mother sat across the table from him, her back to a window. At first Kevin paid little attention to the bright white light in the sky behind them. When it didn't move out of his view, however, he asked his mother what it was. Jeanne glanced behind her and dismissed it as just an airplane.

Kevin continued working; the bright light remained stationary. Kevin mentioned it again, so Jeanne got up and went to a larger window for a better look. She stared for one long moment, then called Kevin. Together they saw a large disc-shaped object hovering over the trees bordering the adjoining field, about 600 feet away. Around its perimeter was an intensely bright white band of light; just above was a ring of individual red and green lights. Jeanne's daughter, Suzanne, joined the vigil at the window. As they watched, the circular object abruptly tipped on edge and descended toward the field, dropped behind trees, and turned out its lights. Then, in less than a minute, it rose back up above the trees with its lights on.

Terrified, Jeanne and her children ran out of the trailer park to Steven's house, about three minutes away. The clock on a nearby church read 7:05 P.M. Steven and his wife were not home; their son and three friends were watching TV when Kevin burst in. Jeanne and Suzanne arrived soon after and alerted Steven's parents, who resided next door. The group watched the object, still visible about 2,500 feet away. One boy went in and got a camera, but his attempts to photograph it proved unsuccessful.

All of the witnesses described the UFO as a disc with individual rings of red, green, blue, and yellow lights. At times a white light would appear, uncomfortable to watch because of its brightness. The object performed amazing maneuvers. It would go up and down vertically, move incredibly slowly, or not move at all. All of its lights would blink out at times, then they would blink on as the object appeared elsewhere in the sky, having moved rapidly back and forth. At times the entire craft seemed to rotate. Finally it shut off its lights and moved away.

Steven arrived home to find the excited witnesses talking about their strange UFO experience. He quickly drove into Newburyport to tell a friend who worked for the local newspaper. Later, the field over which the object hovered was examined, but nothing was found. Jeanne and her children then warily returned to their trailer. At about 8:45 P.M., the reporter, Kevin, and a teenage friend briefly viewed the same or a similar object about a mile away.

Other UFO reports made this night may very well have involved the same object. At 8:02 P.M. another reporter at the *Newburyport Daily News* received a call from his son, who reported that an extremely bright, low-flying light had come in from the ocean, heading for the mouth of the Merrimack River. Then an unnamed coastguardsman phoned the paper to report that he had watched the same object move inland from the ocean at an estimated altitude of 1,000 feet. The object overflew the Salisbury Beach State Reservation and headed toward the mouth of the Merrimack River.

Only one other witness became known to us: He got a close look at it after it arrived on the other side of the river. Carlton, a schoolteacher with a bachelor's degree in history, served in Naval Intelligence and had training in aircraft identification. At the time of the sighting, about 8:45 P.M., he was driving along dark and desolate Old Point Road, returning home to his winterized cottage on Plum Island. A loud hissing sound "like a ship blowing its stacks" jolted Carlton. Simultaneously, the luminous bottom of a circular craft descended into view about 500 feet above his car! He first thought it must be a helicopter, but there was no engine sound and it did not display running lights. Out of curiosity, Carlton slowed the car to a near stop.

The object, matching his forward speed, glowed with a strange combination of amber and blue with a metalliclike sheen. It continued above the road with him, ascending, descending, and swinging back and forth like a pendulum. Then it suddenly spurted out ahead of the car, climbed to about 1,000 feet, and stopped in midair. From the hovering craft, a silvery light beam "as bright as a navy cruiser's searchlight" blinked off and on in four different directions—up, left, bottom, and right, one after the other. The light or lights exhibited this strange sequence only once. This shining ray was unusual in that it was shaped like an inverted bottle with a long neck, and seemed to be enveloped in a fibrous cloudy substance "like white wool." (Was this the mysterious angel hair?)

When the last light beam blinked out, the whole object suddenly was enveloped in a reddish-pink "coronalike" glow. Viewed edge on, it was a sharply defined disc-shaped craft. Abruptly, the glowing object drove toward the mouth of the Merrimack River Bay area at tremendous speed and disappeared.

Again, a full-scale investigation included checks of character reference, man-made and natural phenomena, and civilian and military helicopters. These sightings at Salisbury and Newbury were evaluated in the unknown category.

Carlton allowed no publicity about his UFO experience, but the Salisbury sightings received wide local coverage because of the personal involvement of newspaper reporters.[6] In his evaluation of the Salisbury sighting, John Oswald alluded to the many other UFO reports originating in this area:

This region of the coast has expansive tidal marshes, one arm of which reaches to within 1000 feet of [the witness's] home. . . . To the NE along the coast, 17 miles from Salisbury, there is a nuclear submarine base and a Strategic Air Command Base near Portsmouth, New Hampshire. The *Incident at Exeter* occurred just 8.5 miles to the NW of . . . [the witness's] home. Indeed, the area within a 20-mile radius of Salisbury, has for the past 15 years been, in all probability, one of the most active areas in the United States. . . . In addition to the *extreme* activity in 1965, 66, and 67 . . . significant UFO activity also was present in the early 60's, the Spring of 1971, the Fall of 1973, the Spring of 1974 and then again in the Fall of 1975.

Oswald alludes briefly to other close-encounter cases that he has investigated in this haunted locale, including a provocative case that took place at Stratham, New Hampshire—interestingly enough, only a few weeks after the Salisbury and Newbury incidents. The following information has been obtained from John Oswald's detailed report. (The witness's name has been changed, at her request.)

On the evening of February 24, 1976, I had a phone call from the FAA concerning a UFO report from Auburn, New Hampshire. A husband and wife had watched an extraordinary-looking pinkish-white light stop and hover before angling upward at a 30-degree angle and out of sight, at fantastic speed. After talking to the witnesses, I faithfully logged the report. What they had seen seemed unusual, but not worth an on-site investigation. Then at about 8 P.M. another strangely maneuvering light was sighted from York Beach, Maine; witnesses had reported this to the U.S. Coast Guard and to Pease Air Force Base. Both sightings were a prelude to something much more bizarre.

About 9:28 P.M., Darlene had just left the Richi-McFarland Children's Center at Exeter and had entered the town limits of Stratham, New Hampshire. Driving alone, she turned left onto the westbound ramp of the Route 101 bypass and, proceeding along the ramp, glanced to her left to check for merging traffic. A strange motionless craft hung in midair, only 12 feet above the pavement, opposite the eastbound lane and only 30 feet from her car! She braked to a stop. For one fleeting moment she thought it must be a helicopter. But the object was disc-shaped and as large as a small four-room house. Its surface was smooth but not shiny. Its body color could not be discerned due to a yellowish light directed downward from small hooded fixtures around the perimeter of the craft. However, a very prominent silver-colored, metallic-looking rim encircled its midsection.

The bottom of the vehicle appeared nearly flat. On the edge nearest her was a marking that looked like a black cross, about an inch or so wide, painted on a lighter surface. Since she could not see the entire bottom, she couldn't discern how far this mark extended. From the outer portion of the craft's circular bottom, four darker-colored legs or struts extended vertically. Each was estimated to be about 4 feet long and 2 by 4 inches in cross section. They were equally spaced at 90-degree intervals and extended directly into the object without braces. To the end of each protrusion was affixed a horizontal foot, about 15 inches long.

Centered on top of the craft, an illuminated dome had distinct dark-bounded sections that glowed with the same yellowish color. The dome appeared translucent, but nothing could be seen within it. The craft's surface was covered with many small bumps that reminded Darlene of the "beaded surface on some glass shower doors." At the left side of the dome was attached a steady, red circular light, roughly twenty inches in diameter, with a shade and intensity similar to a red traffic light.

As if mesmerized, Darlene sat still, observing the object. The UFO was absolutely stationary. The unaffected car engine idled quietly, and her AM radio continued playing softly. She heard no sound and felt no effects. This strange standoff lasted about two minutes, during which time she was able to scrutinize the hovering craft very carefully. Suddenly the unsettling feeling that she was being watched welled up within her. Darlene careened out onto Route 101, and sped home to wake her sleeping husband. John had never seen her in such a state before, and he first thought she had been involved in an accident. After calming down, she described the frightening encounter. They decided, for the time being, not to report such a bizarre incident. But Darlene found it difficult to sleep that night; she kept waking up in panic. Two days later, on the morning of February 26, she walked hesitantly into a local police station and reported the incredible episode. The officer in charge referred her to John Oswald, who performed a detailed investigation and concluded that Darlene had observed a totally unconventional object at close range.

Some close encounters involve multiple and independent groups of witnesses. One such incident occurred on April 4, 1976, a little over a month after the Stratham case, and again in the northeast corner of Massachusetts. (Interestingly enough, most reports placed the object in near proximity to certain Air Force installations.)

As the temperature dipped near the freezing mark, cloudy skies quickly gave way to a crystal-clear night. The crescent moon hung low in the west, illuminating the vast salt marshes bordering the seacoast towns of Essex and Ipswich. On Sagamore Hill, two huge Air Force radio telescopes stared passively at the star-studded sky, their 84- and 150-foot faces capped with red anticollision lights. Route 133—known locally as the Essex road—cuts through this outlying marsh, woods, and open pasture-land. About 9:30 P.M., two schoolteachers, Jean and Patricia, were returning to Ipswich from church activities at Fairhaven Chapel in Essex. Jean was driving. Pat, visiting her parents in Ipswich, sat to her right. In the backseat, Donald, Pat's fourteen-year-old brother, gazed dreamily into the night sky.

Their report to the Ipswich police was relayed to me shortly afterward. I rushed to the police station to conduct an initial interview and visit the sighting area. As we approached the site, the look of terror in the witnesses' eyes made it quite apparent that they had undergone a terrifying experience.

Donald had been the first to notice an intensely bright white light suddenly appear in the south-southwestern sky. Asked what it was, Jean and Pat dismissed it as just a bright star or perhaps a light on one of the nearby radio telescopes. However, the light grew larger, and they soon realized that it was moving toward them.

Jean parked on the shoulder of the dark, deserted road. As the fast-approaching object flew low over the treetops, closing rapidly on the parked car, a double horizontal row of lights now could be seen. "I saw more and more lights," Jean told me, "and I was fascinated at what it could be, and as it got closer, it looked like maybe 20 to 50 double rows of white lights."

Then the silent object slowed abruptly and hovered about 300 feet away. The twin rows of bright shimmering lights, tilted to the observers' left, cast a glow that temporarily hid the shape of the hovering object. Jean quickly rolled down her side window and gazed in awe. At that instant, all the white lights blinked out and they saw what was bearing the lights: Poised motionless above the trees was a silvery saucer-shaped vehicle, reflecting a blue luminous haze that enveloped a central dome capped by a blue halo! From the disc's leading edge—which, like the previously observed white lights, was tilted to the witnesses' left—shone steady blue, green, and red lights. Not a sound could be heard.

Patricia and Donald told me that Jean was staring at the object as if literally spellbound. She was totally oblivious to their hysterical cries to drive away, and the strange look in her eyes, "like she was hypnotized," added to Patricia's fright. Frantically she pounded Jean's back to "snap her out of it." Jean related to me later that the object's appearance flooded her with a strange but wonderful feeling of utter awe. She had been totally unaware of the commotion of the others in the car until she began to feel a "pain in my back"—the blows of Patricia's fists. Was Jean's reaction natural, or still another example of apparent mind control? Repeated questioning didn't produce a satisfactory answer. To Jean, the reaction was natural; but it seemed abnormal to the others, who felt she had temporarily lost contact with reality. When she suddenly snapped out of it, she too was immediately caught up in the others' collective fear, and rapidly drove away without even looking back!

The total episode had lasted for only about 3 to 4 minutes. The frightened witnesses headed directly for the home of Patricia's parents in Ipswich, arriving at about 9:40 P.M. Patricia's mother urged them to phone their pastor; he urged them to file a complaint with the police. They left for the police station.

Shortly after their departure the mother's two cats, usually docile, went utterly wild, running all over the house, jumping up on furniture, crawling under beds as if being chased by an unseen enemy. Finally they had to be caught and put outside. There was no apparent stimulus for their fright. But in light of similar animal reactions to the nearby presence of UFOs, one could speculate that the alien craft, unlighted and unseen, was following the witnesses' car.

I estimated that the trio traveled to the police station between 9:50 and 9:55 P.M. At about 9:50 a similar lighted object was seen hovering at tree top level less than a mile from the police station. At 9:55, while Jean and Patricia were inside the police station filing a report, a similar object was sighted hovering above a tall tree only 750 feet away! Then at about 9:50 a husband was driving his wife home from a friend's house on Town Farm Road in Ipswich. She was asleep in the passenger's seat, when he noticed an unusual string of white lights up ahead. He first thought they might be some new kind of streetlights. But as he drove closer, they became larger. About 1000 feet away, 6 large, oval white lights hovered about 50 feet above a deserted playground. The glowing ovals had the appearance of white light shining through large windows wrapped around a curved surface. He stopped the car and tried to wake his wife to see this extraordinary sight, but she felt sick and demanded to be taken home. Reluctantly, he left the area.

During a house-to-house check for additional witnesses, I found that at 9:55 P.M. Ronald and his girl friend Cheryl had been driving approximately the same route Jean and Patricia had taken to the police station. First the couple sighted bright white lights shining through the trees. When they rounded a corner and headed toward the South Parish Green, they were astonished to see a circular pattern of intense white lights, about 50 feet in diameter, hovering about 1,000 feet over this open expanse. About 200 yards from the tree over which the object seemed to hover, Ronald slowed his truck. Just as the truck came to a stop, the object seemed to move away so fast that all they could see was an afterimage!

Interestingly enough, my house-to-house canvass revealed that one household, directly across the street from the green, had experienced severe TV interference just before 10:00 P.M. A young mother whose son's bedroom window faces the green told me that at about 9:55 P.M. a light so bright that it penetrated the thick curtains suddenly illuminated the room, then subsided. But both the TV interference and the light were experienced at the time the object was observed hovering across the street.

In the meantime, Jean, Patricia, and Donald were inside the nearby Ipswich police station, completely oblivious to the events occurring in the immediate vicinity until Ronald and Cheryl walked into the station to report what *they* had witnessed.

The area of the initial sighting contains three United States Air Force antenna sites, forming a triangle with legs about 6 miles long and a base of about 2 miles. Sagamore Hill, on the Hamilton-Ipswich border, is the home of the Air Force geophysics laboratory's radio telescope observatory. The lighted, domed disk had passed over this antenna site and its huge radio telescopes just before approaching the lone parked car on the Essex Road. About 6 miles to the north is the Air Force Geophysics Laboratory's experimental radar station, located atop Ipswich's Great Neck Hill. Then about 2 miles north-northwest of this site is this same agency's Radio Astronomy Unit 1 Antenna site. Although this particular site had recently been deactivated, two of its large antennae protrude prominently into the sky from a hilltop jutting out of the surrounding marshland. Perhaps significantly, this night's next UFO sightings took place in the center portion of the strip between these two installations.

Town Farm Road, on the outskirts of Ipswich, penetrates deeply into a vast salt marsh. Along this lonely road, which terminates at USAF Radio Astronomy Unit 1, houses soon become sparse and widely separated. Wayne and his wife Nancy are one of the few families that live in this desolate location. The USAF radar station lies about 2 miles east of their house; the radio astronomy unit is about a half mile north-northwest of it. On this same evening, at about 9:57 P.M., Nancy was standing at the glass combination storm door, looking east-southeast over the marshland. She had the radio on and was waiting for a 10:00 P.M. newscast to come on.

Without any warning, an intense bright white mass of many lights appeared as if "out of nowhere" about 1,500 feet over the marsh. The lights, forming a cluster about the width of a house, moved slowly and silently down the marsh about 2,500 feet away. Nancy yelled for Wayne. He arrived just in time to see the lights disappearing behind the trees in a west-southwesterly direction—heading toward the rustic home of Lyle and Ruth, another young couple, whose house lies at the end of a built-up driveway jutting 800 feet into the marshes to an area known locally as the island.

According to a clock on the wall, it was just about 10:00 P.M. Ruth was seated on a couch, watching a movie on television. All of a sudden, a bright flash of light shone through the huge picture window. Glancing up to her left, she saw a horizontal string of four reddish-orange lights shining down from the sky through bordering trees; the TV was not affected. Dismissing the sight as oncoming aircraft lights, she resumed watching the movie. But a few moments later, she was startled to see the formation of lights still there, in exactly the same position!

Ruth turned down the TV and walked to the picture window. No sound could be heard, and the lights were unnaturally motionless. More curious, she went outside to obtain an unobstructed view. When she rounded the corner of the house, four large, distinct illuminated ovals stared down at her, glowing like hot coals. The area was deathly quiet. The craft staring down at her was absolutely motionless and only 50 feet above the marsh—too close for comfort. She quickly walked, then half ran back to the house where, from behind the picture window, she again observed the object shining through the trees. Then each glowing red oval simultaneously switched to a bright white color. Concurrently, her phone began ringing, and she ran to answer it. When she rushed back to the window moments later, the object was gone! Running upstairs, she went from window to window, but whatever it had been had completely disappeared. The clock now read 10:11 P.M.; the craft had hovered for over 10 minutes without making the slightest sound or movement!

When the Ipswich police notified me of the initial sightings, I departed immediately for the station and conducted initial interviews, had the witnesses fill out and sign UFO report forms, and then accompanied them to the sighting area to take azimuth and elevation readings. Later, a full-blown investigation lasted a full month. During this time, ads were run in local papers for other witnesses. Routine checks were made with other police stations, the FAA, and a nearby Coast Guard installation. Extensive house-to-house canvassing was initiated. In regard to the activity of unconventional aircraft, helicopters, flare drops, satellites, reentering space debris and atmospheric tests involving glowing barium gas, checks were made with local airports, radio and TV stations, commercial companies, the National Guard, the Coast Guard, the Navy, Army, and USAF North American Air Defense Command, the USAF Strategic Air Command, the USAF Geophysics Laboratory, state agencies, the Smithsonian Institution, and NASA. Interviews with friends, neighbors, employers, and a pastor indicated that the witnesses were honest and reliable. Detailed reports written up for each incident included area photographs, tape transcripts, annotated topographical maps, and a most thorough documentation of both the sightings and my investigation. My conclusion was that six independent reports of aerial phenomena the observers considered highly strange were reported in the same general area, on the same date, and within the same 30 to 45–minute time slot. The sightings were evaluated as being in the unknown category.

Why do such objects appear over a given sighting area? On the surface, this case seems to have involved reconnaissance of three USAF antenna stations. Interestingly, the Sagamore Hill radio telescopes had monitored signals from outer space (dubbed LGMs, Little Green Men) a number of years ago. At that time some theorized that these signals might be from some extraterrestrial civilization, but they turned out to be from a natural celestial object called a pulsar. However, people on Town Hill Road told me that in the past, contingents of Air Force personnel and equipment would roll down Town Hill Road to the lonely radio astronomy station, coming and going at certain times. In light of the huge concentration of sightings in northeast Massachusetts and southeast New Hampshire, I sometimes wonder whether such installations could be covers for secret detection or communication experiments.

Ipswich, for example, has been a frequent host to other spectacular UFO sightings. One took place on the same night as the incident at Exeter, at 1 A.M. It too took place along Route 133 near the radio telescope installation on Sagamore Hill.

As his car approached the crest of the hill overlooking Candlewood

Golf Course, Dennis felt the hairs rise on the back of his neck. As he reached the top of the hill and started down the other side, a feeling like static electricity coursed through his body. Simultaneously he was startled by a strange glow just off the road to his left. Moments later he was almost broadside to it. Over the green floated an object like an "inverted saucer with a flat dome"! Surrounded with a weird grayish glow with a reddish tint, it seemed about 40 feet in diameter. Dennis kept on going. He wanted no part of it.

One year later, on September 17, 1966, at about 4:45 A.M. Susan woke, coughing, and got out of bed to get a drink of water. Her and her husband's home overlooks Crane's Beach where the Ipswich River enters a bay. Passing by a window, she noticed a strange glow coming from the beach, and called for her husband to come quickly. Both watched a huge yellowish-glowing, cigar-shaped object hovering vertically over the deserted beach. From time to time it would slowly tilt to about 60 degrees from the vertical, then back to an upright position.

Suddenly two small glowing, ringed oval objects approached the larger object from over the bay, moving with an up-and-down skipping motion, and entered the cylinder's upper end! Fascinated, Susan and her husband watched similar objects enter and leave the larger object before it suddenly faded into nothingness. Earlier that same morning the police at Brookline received two separate calls within just a few minutes of each other, concerning a bluish-green oval object hovering over Larz Anderson Park.

A current investigation is underway concerning another glowing cylindrical object sighted from Martha's Vineyard on the night of March 27, 1979. The witness reported seeing a 30-foot-long greenish-glowing, cigar-shaped object emerging horizontally out of the ocean only 100 feet from the shore of deserted State Beach! It seemed to be the cause of loud static on his AM car radio. He left the car to shine a spotlight on the object, but inexplicably he became totally immobilized. The object continued out of the water, and streaked upward and out of sight. Only then could he move again.

Some close encounters take place in broad daylight, such as the following case from Medway, Massachusetts, investigated by MUFON investigator Joseph Nyman. On June 25, 1978, several Main Street residents were gathered in a neighbor's backyard to watch their children play ball. At nearby Logan Airport the weather bureau recorded broken clouds at twenty thousand feet. At 8 P.M. the temperature was a balmy 76° F., the sun still well above the horizon.

One of the kids batted a ball and a father stopped conversing to follow its flight. Through a gap in the tall pines bordering the property, he noticed what appeared to be a balloon. It moved closer very rapidly, and in a matter of seconds it was only about 300 feet from the amazed group. As if in response, the noiseless object slowed to a complete stop. About thirty feet in diameter, it looked like a silvery-gray disc with a central dome. For about five seconds it hovered, bobbing and wobbling "like a floating ball on disturbed water," then sped away very rapidly into the distance. Even though newspaper coverage was given the incident, no other witnesses could be found to this transitory occurrence.[7] After his investigation, Mr. Nyman evaluated the sighting as being in the unknown category.

In some cases, creatures are sighted in or near the object. An Air Force textbook used at the United States Air Force Academy in 1968 states that:

The most commonly described alien is about three and one-half feet tall, has a round head (helmet?), arms reaching to or below the knees, and is wearing a silvery space suit or coveralls. Other aliens appear to be essentially the same as Earthmen, while still others have particularly wide (wrap-around) eyes and mouths with very thin lips. And there is a rare group reported as about four feet tall, weight of around 35 pounds, and covered with thick hair or fur (clothing?). Members of this last group are described as being extremely strong.[8]

Witnesses have consistently reported that communication with these beings was accomplished by telepathy. Often the creatures are reported to have floated as if moving on an invisible elevated trolley. (For examples of this type of case, see my book, *The Andreasson Affair*.)

In the early days ground observers and pilots reported the uncomplicated flyby of distant unconventional objects. Then came reports of close encounters with structured vehicles, which left no room for misinterpretation or misidentification. Then reports of UFO landings became prevalent. Physical traces supplemented the anecdotal testimony of unimpeachable witnesses. In the end the evidence of their authenticity was overwhelming, and I found myself being raised into yet another level of thinking. Then witnesses began to report UFO occupants. Up until this time, many researchers had accepted the theory that extraterrestrial UFOs were remote controlled. Nonetheless, evidence mounted for the reality of alien creatures actually piloting the craft. In 1967 Dr. William T. Powers, former Air Force UFO investigator and consultant, revealed some thought-provoking statistics about such reports to the readers of *Science*:

In 1954 over 200 reports concerned landings of objects, many with occupants. Of these, about 51 percent were observed by more than one person. In fact, in all these sightings at least 624 persons were involved, and only 98 of these people were alone. In 18 multiple-witness cases, some witnesses were not aware that anyone else had seen the same thing at the same time and place. In 13 cases, there were more than 10 witnesses. How do we deal with reports like these? One fact is clear: we cannot shrug them off.[9]

The problem was that many civilian researchers (especially those in NICAP) *had* shrugged them off! Then during the early 1970s a new breed of contactees gained serious attention by conservative UFO researchers. Unlike the previously stereotyped individuals, these persons appeared quite sane and normal. Their backgrounds differed greatly, but general and subtle similarities existed between their reported experiences. The first such case dated back to September 19, 1961, when postal worker Barney Hill and his social-worker wife, Betty, were reportedly abducted by the crew of a UFO near Woodstock, New Hampshire. The case received wide attention, mainly because of John Fuller's excellent documentary, *Interrupted Journey.* The Hill case, initially investigated by Walter Webb, stood out from the typical contactee-type case from the very beginning.

Shortly after their UFO experience, the Hills had sent NICAP a written description of the UFO and of humanoid figures seen behind its lighted windows. NICAP dispatched a local field investigator, Walter Webb, who submitted his six-page report on October 26, 1961. During their sighting, Walter discovered, the Hills experienced a two-hour memory blackout. Betty complained of weird, recurring dreams concerning their abduction by creatures from the UFO. Barney, on the other hand, suffered symptoms of high stress about the incident. In the summer of 1962 both sought and received therapy from Dr. Duncan Stevens of Exeter, New Hampshire. Later, on his advice, the Hills initiated a series of visits with Dr. Benjamin Simon on December 14, 1962. Under hypnosis, the Hills relived a mind-boggling UFO experience.

I was fortunate to have met the Hills just prior to their visits with Dr. Simon. On November 4, 1963, a small group of interested people gathered to hear them discuss their conscious memories of the UFO sighting. Betty told us of her recurring, detailed, and quite vivid dreams. Both expressed fear that they had been taken aboard the alien craft for a physical examination.

I attended this meeting with an engineer friend of mine—a laser specialist. I can clearly remember asking him, "How can two people stand up there, look you in the eye, and lie like that?" Most conservative UFO researchers tended to shy away from such reports. Since then, however, many other similar cases have been documented by competent investigators. (In fact, the sheer abundance of such reports helped instigate the spectacular and successful movie *Close Encounters of the Third Kind.*)

On December 3, 1967, Police Officer Herbert Schirmer of Ashland, Nebraska, had a close encounter with a hovering UFO. There was a period of time for which he could not account afterwards. Under hypnosis, however, Schirmer relived an abduction experience similar to the Hills'. Taken to the University of Colorado for further tests, Schirmer has stated that his case received very serious attention and was compared with others by scientists on the project. Nonetheless, the Condon Report publicly put little credence in his report.

With the new interest created in cases like this, MUFON consultant Dave Webb, a solar physicist, along with his coworker Ted Bloecher, began the enormous work of collecting reports where entities were sighted in the presence of UFOs. Some involved time lapses and alleged abductions. During the 1973 wave of sightings, Webb recorded 70 cases involving entities and UFOs in his excellent paper, *1973–Year of the Humanoids,* which may be purchased from CUFOS. Of these cases, 55 took place in the continental United States, 36 in October, and 7 on a single day—October 17—with two others occurring on the night of October 16. Webb comments, "This represents the largest number of humanoid reports from one country since the famous French wave of 1954," meticulously documented by UFO researcher Aimé Michel, whose findings were summarized in a book translated into English in 1958. However, the reports were so strange that his work was largely ignored until others took time to investigate similar incidents.

Two shipworkers, Charles Hickson and Calvin Parker, were abducted from the end of a dock on the night of October 11, 1973. On October 16, 1973, a woman and several children were allegedly abducted from their home at Lehi, Utah. Air Force Master Sergeant Charles Moody reported that occupants of a UFO took him forcibly from his automobile during the early morning hours of August 13, 1975. Sandra Larson, her daughter, and a friend were abducted from their car in the wee hours of the morning near Fargo, North Dakota; a similar case involved David Stevens and his friend on August 27, 1975, at Norway, Maine. On November 5, 1975, six woodcutters fled when they saw their coworker Travis Walton struck down by a beam from a hovering UFO. When they returned to the scene, the object and Travis were gone. Travis showed up 5 days later, claiming that aliens had taken him off on the UFO. On the night of January 6, 1976, Louise Smith, Mona Stafford, and Elaine Thomas were abducted from their car at Danville, Kentucky. All of these reports had striking similarities that made one wonder. How many of the scores of seemingly purposeless car-chasing cases of the past also involved abductions erased or blocked from the abductees' minds?

I personally investigated in great depth one of these cases, which involved a family at South Ashburnham, Massachusetts. On the night of January 25, 1967, aliens took the mother from the house; the rest of her family was put into a state of suspended animation and guarded by another entity until she was returned. Most of this experience was recovered through the use of hypnotic regression. My book *The Andreasson Affair* was based on the final 3-volume report, numbering 528 pages of carefully investigated documentation. The events encompassed within this particular CE-III strain one's credulity almost to the snapping point. But, there may be even stranger UFO events ahead of us.

CHAPTER NOTES

1. G. E. Valley, "Some Considerations Affecting the Interpretation of Reports of Unidentified Flying Objects," *Project Sign Technical Report No. F-TR-2274-IA, Appendix "C"* (Wright-Patterson AFB, Dayton, Ohio: AAF Air Material Command, February 1949), p. 19.

2. E. U. Condon, director, *Scientific Study of Unidentified Flying Objects* (New York: E. P. Dutton & Co., Inc., 1969), p. 894.

3. R. A. Hall, ed., *The UFO Evidence* (Washington, D.C., NICAP, 1964), p. 143.

4. "Strange Flying Object seen in South Hampton," *Amesbury News,* June 12, 1974, p. 1.

5. Stephen Webbe, "Mystery Object stirs New Hampshire folks," *Christian Science Monitor,* July 30, 1974, p. 48.

6. *Newburyport Daily News,* February 14, 17, and 18, 1976.

7. "UFO spotted in Medway?" *Milford Daily News,* June 26, 1978.

8. Donald G. Carpenter, Major, USAF, ed., "Unidentified Flying Objects," *Introductory Space Science,* (Department of Physics, USAF Academy, 1968), Volume II, pp. 461, 462.

9. William T. Powers, Letter, *Science,* CLVI, April 7, 1967.

13

HAUNTED
WITNESSES

Shortly after one o'clock in the morning on December 16, 1978, our bedside phone jolted me out of a sound sleep. I desperately tried to clear my mind for intelligible conversation. It was a man who sounded very upset, beginning with an all-too-familiar apology for the account he was about to relate, assuring me that he was sane, and practically begging me to hear him out.

John's UFO experience had taken place during the cold, moonlit night of December 14. He had kept the episode to himself until late Friday night, when he felt that the events were just too much for him to handle alone. First, in desperation, he phoned his estranged wife, who urged him to call the police, who in turn advised him to phone Charleston Air Force Base in Maine, where a Sergeant Feehan listened to his story before informing him that the Air Force didn't investigate UFOs anymore. The telephone operator didn't know of a number where one could report a UFO, so he placed a call to a local newspaper, which advised him to call the FAA at Bangor. Putting him on hold, the FAA contacted the New England FAA Air Traffic Control Center at Nashua, New Hampshire, who gave him my telephone number.

By that time, it was 1:15 A.M. No wonder John was at his wits' end. I promised to interview him in person at my earliest convenience and I phoned the FAA at Nashua and Bangor, as well as Charleston Air Force Base. Each source confirmed that John had called them; they felt he was serious about his experience. I rose early in the morning of December 31,

1978, and drove six hours straight to John's home. Much of the story that follows is excerpted directly from our taped interview:

On December 13, I had had a good day at work, and on the side here at home, I give individual karate lessons. I had one of my students come over, and I guess he left about nine o'clock. I was sitting around paying bills, and I—I don't know, I just felt uncomfortable to myself. My daughter was in bed and it was getting late, around 11:30. I went to bed, laid there, and I just couldn't sleep. I got up two or three times to have a smoke and went back to bed.

Sometime between 1:00 and 1:30 in the morning of Thursday, December 14, 1978, John finally succumbed to an overwhelming compulsion. Looking back, he cannot understand his action. He was then separated from his wife and told me he would never leave his daughter alone in the house late at night.

I just felt that I had to get out for some reason. I didn't know why. I got dressed, got in the car, and drove out of the yard. I've never left my daughter alone like that.

John drove "as if in a daze" out along Route 9E, a desolate stretch of road known as the Airline.

And all of a sudden my car went dead completely, motor went out and I coasted to a stop. I tried to start my car. It wouldn't turn over. My battery wasn't dead because my lights were [still] on.

John tried unsuccessfully to restart the car, both in neutral and park. Then he turned off the radio and again tried to start the engine. There was no response at all. He had left the lights on because although this road was little traveled at that time of night, it was possible for a fast-moving logging truck to hit him head on. But when he turned the key, the lights did not even dim.

All of a sudden I heard this noise. . . . I use the word crackling because I can't explain the sound. It sounded similar to [castanets]. A steady click-click-click, you know? The sound didn't scare me; I said, "What the hell is that?"

John turned his head to the right, where the sound seemed to be coming from. Slightly ahead of his car and off to his right, about 50 feet from the road, a huge elongated, rectangular dark object was hovering 30 feet above the ground. Almost as soon as John saw it a rectangular portion on the object's front end lit up and shone a soft green light through the car's front windshield. Simultaneously John felt a strange sensation like "pins and needles" course through his body, and felt himself sink into a trancelike daze. He remained fully aware, but couldn't move a muscle. Strangely enough, his initial fear upon sighting the huge object had disappeared. He felt calm and unafraid.

Abruptly, the soft green light changed color and began pulsating—first slowly, then faster and faster.

The second color looked like a reddish-pink. . . . The colors blinked faster and then I heard a voice—"Do not be afraid. We will not harm you. We are from the 17th star"—I can't forget that voice. Then the lights started flashing fast again, and every time these lights seemed to flash rapidly, it just seemed like I was in a daze. At first, when I first saw it, I was scared; at the end, I was scared. While this was going on, I didn't really have any feeling.

Then, after the lights slowed down again, John heard the voice say, "We will return," and felt a strong impression that this statement was true. The lighted rectangular opening suddenly blinked off, and John heard the strange clicking sound again. The object backed away.

It seemed to rise, but on an angle. . . . The crackling noise came back again, once it started to go, but it was very fast . . . and as soon as it went, I turned my key and my car instantly started. . . . I felt like I had a toothache. . . . On the way home . . . I felt cold, very cold. . . . The next morning I noticed skin peeling off around the nose and in back of the ears, and on the forehead. I've been getting headaches since I've seen it, pretty regular.

Although there were no other known witnesses to John's UFO encounter, there is strong circumstantial evidence that the Air Force was attempting to intercept the huge object with interceptors from Otis Air Force Base. On December 18, 1978, I phoned Ed Walch, watch supervisor, at the FAA Traffic Control Center. Asked if the log showed other UFO reports or anomalous radar targets, he referred me to Mr. Cushing, FAA military liaison, who told me that during John's sighting there had been a military exercise aloft involving B-57's, F-101's and F-106's. Curious, I asked him where the interceptors were during the sighting time frame. He referred me to Mr. Bob Hurley, FAA coordinator with NORAD at the Air Development Center, Griffiss AFB, Rome, New York, who told me that his records pinpointed the presence of F-106 interceptors just about twenty miles west of the sighting area, in central Maine, at two o'clock local time on December 14, 1978! A remarkable coincidence, indeed, to have Air Force fighter aircraft on a defense exercise almost directly over a UFO encounter in progress!

I phoned the 101st Fighter Squadron at Otis AFB, where a Colonel Provost insisted that there were no UFOs or radar targets connected with the defense exercise. However, it seems certain that something strange was going on in the New England skies that night. A friend of mine who monitors the Pease AFB command post intercepted the following message about a "postbriefing conference" held by a Captain Brewster.

At 0447 local there was a loud booming noise associated with a light in the sky. We received numerous calls from it. Radar Approach Control said there were no aircraft within 100 nautical miles of the base at the time. At this time, we are receiving numerous calls from . . . [the] wire services and they are being referred to the information office.

Later on that same morning I received another UFO report from a gentleman from Peabody who had watched a high-flying, noiseless object that did not look like an aircraft. In any event, John was drawn to the UFO for the apparent purpose of receiving a message that echoes in his mind: *We are from the 17th star. We will return.* Significantly, the 17th and 18th stars from our sun are estimated to be Lacaille 9352 (11.7 light-years away) and Tau Ceti (11.9 light-years away). Because of the allowances for inaccuracies, Tau Ceti could just as well be the 17th star; according to astronomers, it is one of the prime suspects for harboring planets supporting intelligent life as we know it!

Since the incident, John has had recurring dreams concerning the incident, including getting out of his car and climbing a ramp into the object. The dreams always end at that point, leaving him frustrated at not knowing what happened inside. At times, flashbacks of a lighted control panel with wires come to his conscious mind, but quickly slip away. For several weeks after, the same compulsion to leave the house nearly overcame him. Once he actually dressed and went to the car, but fought off the desire and returned to the house. Over and over again the message about the 17th star comes to mind.

It's a hell of a thing to try to live with. It doesn't leave. It's in your head every single day. I really don't know if I want to find out more about it.

The lonely site of the encounter was a flat-topped high hill. The UFO had hovered over a huge gravel pit just off the road, above a stand of small trees. When we approached, John became visibly nervous and his voice quavered when he talked. He began to have the same cold feeling he had experienced that fateful night. I clocked the time and mileage to and from his home. We estimated that there could be over an hour missing from John's conscious memory. His dreams and fleeting flashbacks of alien instruments are typical of other victims of a UFO abduction. In such cases, memory is mercifully erased from the witnesses' minds, and usually can be recovered only through hypnosis.

Is John a psychotic? A publicity seeker? No, I found that he has a good job. His house in a nice neighborhood was well kept, inside and out. Nine character references, including his priest, a prominent businessman, neighbors, and former employers all described John as totally honest and industrious. Even his estranged wife vouched for him. His hobbies are music and teaching karate. In his younger days he enjoyed racing cars, had been involved in many demolition derbies, and emphasized that he wasn't easily frightened. I was impressed with his not trying to embellish his experience. If I deviated in the least from what he had told me, he corrected me. I have suggested hypnotic regression, but up until this time John has refused to become further involved.

Witnesses who have had a close encounter with a UFO often experience paranormal events prior to, during, or after the sighting. Such witnesses are literally haunted by strange impulses, apparitions, and a variety of weird phenomena. Many of these persons have never had prior interest or experiences in the occult. It would appear that their close proximity to the UFO and/or its occupants has somehow heightened their psychic awareness. Such experiences indicate that UFOs' technology embraces a wedding of mind and matter, often including the disturbing ability to control human physiological and mental processes. Dr. J. Allen Hynek aptly comments upon such abilities in his foreword to *The Andreasson Affair*.

Here we have "creatures of light" who find walls no obstacle to free passage into rooms and who find no difficulty in exerting uncanny control over the witnesses' minds. If this represents an advanced technology, then it must incorporate the paranormal just as our own incorporates transistors and computers. Somehow, "they" have mastered the puzzle of mind over matter.[1]

A *close* encounter of the first kind involves an alien object sighted within an estimated 500 feet of the observer. A CE-II differs only in that there are definitive UFO effects upon the environment, observer, or instruments; including burned, baked, or impacted areas of the ground, temporary paralysis of the witness, and interference with fixed, mobile, or airborne electrical apparatus. CE-IIIs involve the *sighting of alien entities* in association with the UFO. CUFOS has computer-coded a total of about 60,000 UFO reports from 113 countries and 250 sources. About 3 percent—or 2,000 of these reports—involve CE-IIIs, of which there are seven types:

TYPE	ENTITY RELATIONSHIP TO UFO
A	Seen inside the UFO
B	Seen entering or leaving the UFO
C	Seen in close proximity to the UFO
D	Seen in an area of general UFO activity
E	Seen, but with no established association with an observed UFO
F	Not seen, but the witness receives an intelligible communication
G	Seen during an on-board UFO experience by the witness

Witnesses to Types C, F, and G are most apt to become hosts to a variety of unearthly phenomena. John's case concerns the rare Type F which represents 40 (or 2 percent) of the CE-III's on file at CUFOS. *The Andreasson Affair* was a Type G, which type represents about 10 percent or 200 of the 2,000 CE-III cases on file at CUFOS. The following witnesses have requested pseudonyms to protect their family from bad publicity and probable ridicule.

Sounding rational and very sophisticated, the woman on the telephone told me that UFOs and strange beings had been seen on their property. I told her that unless she identified herself and gave me the details of times, dates, and places, there was nothing I could do. She said that her family must remain anonymous, but that she would talk over with them the matter of my investigating the incidents.

It wasn't until April 1978 that Joanne LeBel called me again. A new series of strange happenings had convinced the family that something had to be done. A priest's blessing of the house had been fruitless, and they had decided not to call the police anymore lest they get a reputation for being crazy. Completely frustrated, they didn't know where to turn next. I assigned David Webb to this fascinating case. A physicist and one of the leading experts concerning CE-III's, David is cochairman of the MUFON humanoid study group and was one of the principal investigators of the Andreasson affair.

I accompanied David on his initial interview. Joanne and Joseph LeBel have three children: Allan, Nancy, and Douglas. A carpenter by trade, Mr. LeBel originally emigrated from Canada to the United States; he served as a medic for four years in the Royal Canadian Air Force. When David and I arrived at the LeBel home, we were kindly greeted by Mrs. LeBel, Nancy, and Douglas. Joseph and Allan had gone on an errand and were expected back shortly. The family was well dressed, the house clean and attractive. One immediately got the impression that these typical middle-class people were not the type to perpetrate a hoax. The LeBels told us about one incredible event after another involving UFOs and man-like apparitions. They seemed very sincere. There was cross talk between them as they described the events.

Had I not investigated the matter myself, I'd probably pass it off as either a hoax or the product of sick minds. Later, I personally conducted a careful character check that indicated that this family was well respected in the community. A priest, a leading businessman, the local chief of police, and others all attested to the honesty of these hardworking, devout Roman Catholics.

The LeBels own about eight acres of land, much of it wooded but accessible by logging roads. It is set well back from a lonely road in a small New England town. Mrs. LeBel's mother lives next door. Joanne lived in her parents' house for 28 years before she and Joseph built their own house in 1967. As early as 1962 Joanne's mother had sighted a brilliant glowing object over this property, one of the highest points of land in the area. In 1974 the LeBels' son, then only 17, was terrorized by a UFO outside his bedroom window. Mrs. LeBel told us that the series of weird events seemed to have started with Allan's UFO experience. When Allan arrived with his father, I asked him to describe what he had seen.

Allan: The light, basically, was our first sighting. It must have come down in the backyard or close to it. The light was so penetrating! My drapes were down—same heavy drapes that are in there now, and the white shades were down. Yet the light was so intense that it lit the room up like infra-red lighting.
Ray Fowler: What did you do?
Allan: I looked out the window . . . and a big cigar shape was up behind the pool. The pool was an eighteen-footer and it made it look like a drop in the bucket for size.
Ray Fowler: And how long did it stay there?
Allan: Not very long. . . . I had just pulled the shade back, I couldn't stick my head out the window or anything like that to see. To my knowledge, it went straight up.

Later that summer, while on the way to a campsite in Colebrook, New Hampshire, the family saw a gigantic object seemingly take off from a mountainous area at about 11:30 P.M. Very few aircraft are seen at all in this desolate, remote area. They reported the incident to a priest, who told them that many strange things had been seen in the Colebrook area, but that witnesses were reluctant to publicize their experiences.

In 1977 and again in 1978, the LeBel family began sighting a strange prowler who exhibited a number of abilities. The police were called on many occasions, but before they arrived, he would disappear. This mysterious manlike figure turned up again and again during the summer months of 1977.

Nancy LeBel: It was so hot, I went out on the piazza. Just after I sat down in the rocking chair, I saw someone coming along the side of the house where my window was, crouched over. I didn't know who it was, but he had a white shirt on and dark slacks on. Just as I was watching, my mother came out.... I stood up. When I got up out of the chair, he heard the noise. He turned just his body. He didn't move his feet at all!

Mrs. LeBel added that he moved away very slowly, with his hands straight down at his sides. They did not move as an ordinary person's hands would when walking.

I called him and said, "Look, if you want to come in and look through the house, you're welcome. I just would like to know what you want. We're getting pretty fed up with this." But he kept going. He never turned his head or anything. He kept it straight, walking toward the woods. And after he got to the woods, it seemed like his whole body turned in the strangest manner.

Ray Fowler: Did you seen his eyes, nose, and mouth?

Nancy: No. I really couldn't see. The lights were not on.

Joanne: But you could see him because the shirt seemed so white. So many times my mother would walk across from next door and be upset that someone was standing up near the trees. And she said, "he has a white shirt on and dark slacks."

Ray Fowler: Now, when you were closest to him, did you hear any noise when he walked?

Joanne: No. There was no noise, and from what I could see, there was no shadow.

Ray Fowler: Did the grass move when he went through the field?

Joanne: I couldn't see. It was too dark.

Ray Fowler: Did you notice whether he caused some physical effects on anything—grass, dirt, anything?

Joanne: That reminds me of something that has really baffled my husband for so long. No matter where he is, there's no footprints.

David Webb: No one in the family has ever seen footprints?

Joanne: No. My mother had an incident last summer. ... She thought it was my husband. His back was to her, and then she heard a noise and turned around. ... My husband and his brother came out of the cellar. When she turned back again, the man was gone—and there was no noise, footsteps or running or anything!

Joe LeBel: I lost sixty pounds chasing that son-of-a-gun last year and I haven't caught him yet.

Joanne: He took a baseball bat, cut it off, and made a billy club out of it. And he went around with that all summer long.

Joe LeBel: I'd start walking along right behind him, and then when I figure I'm close enough to grab him, as I go to put my hand on him, he's not there! I thought I was going crazy.

The strange activity ceased with the summer months. In November 1977 a number of even stranger incidents began, continuing off and on into the spring of 1978. In November, Douglas had set afire a toy plastic car in the backyard.

The smoke started to bother my eyes so I went into the piazza for a minute. I walked back out. As I was putting the model out, coming across the yard I could hear footsteps, like crushing. I looked up, and there was this person all in white, the head and everything. He went behind my little tepee shed that I used to have and he was gone, just like that.
Joe LeBel: **We never found any footprints.**

Douglas ran in the house and told his father. Mr. LeBel came right out and found the strangely dressed man standing near his car. At last he had managed to sneak up behind the stranger. Joe said "I had a Thunderbird out there, a '64, and he was right at the back of the Thunderbird. I walked around the Thunderbird and I went to put my hands on him, and he's gone!" The strange man slowly dissipated into nothingness before his very eyes!

Ray Fowler: **And he seemed solid to you?**
Joe LeBel: **Right.**
Ray Fowler: **Can you describe the back of his head?**
Joe LeBel: **Look, there's no hair! It's a helmet! It's gray and the suit is white.**

Joe continued to see this strange man several times. He called in the police but they could never find the interloper. Finally the local police sergeant told the family, "We've had it!" A relative who works on the local police force said that at the station, the LeBel property was laughingly referred to as the "combat zone."

For about a month things seemed to calm down, then the hauntings returned with a vengeance, this time involving people outside the immediate family. On January 9, 1978, Joanne's mother was hosting her granddaughter Marilyn; Marilyn's husband, Jerry, then on furlough from the Army; and their two children—Carol, age 6, and Johnny, 4. Except for Douglas, the rest of the LeBel family was home next door with Carol and Johnny when suddenly a bright light shone through the dining room window. Glancing out, Joanne and Nancy LeBel saw a large yellowish-white light angling toward the ground. Nancy ran out the back door in time to see the object disappear behind trees some distance behind the house. As the light dipped out of sight, it seemed to "wink out." She went inside and phoned a friend, but five minutes later, the telephone inexplicably went dead, remaining inoperative for about twenty minutes. During this time Joanne's mother tried to phone them, to no avail.

As she pondered about what was wrong with the phone, little Johnny began screaming from the upstairs bedroom. His father jumped out of his chair and dashed up the stairs. "Daddy," Johnny cried, "a man was trying to touch me." The little boy told him that he had seen a man dressed in white standing at the foot of his bed.

Jerry assumed the boy had been dreaming. As he turned to go back downstairs, he heard a knocking sound in the adjoining empty bedroom. Then he heard the sound again from just outside the window. Alarmed, he strode across the room and pulled back the curtains. There, on the roof of the back porch adjoining the first floor, was a white-suited figure, only about four feet away from the window. Its face appeared hooded by what seemed like a mask. Jerry stared at a pair of eyes staring back at him. Recovering, he dropped the curtain and quickly went downstairs. Not wanting to frighten the children, he quietly told the others what he had seen. The porch door began banging, and he cautiously stepped outside to check. There was nothing there. He closed the door and glancing back, he again got a brief glimpse of the strange figure. Whatever it was disappeared, and no one else saw anything strange that night.

The next day, January 10, displayed high, broken clouds. As usual, the nocturnal visitor left no tangible signs. A few snow flurries fell from time to time, and Joe LeBel spent much of the day working about the property. In the afternoon Joe drove his truck down among the trees to chop wood:

Joe LeBel: I knocked down a tree and cut about four or five hunks out of it, and I stopped to light up a cigarette. And I happened to look over and there's this man standing there in a white suit, with a battleship gray helmet. It looked like mittens that he had on, just one finger and a thumb. It looked like it was part of the suit he had on. The other fingers were together, like if I were wearing a mitt with one finger and a thumb.

The weird being—exactly the same type seen several times during the previous month—was about four and a half feet tall and was standing about seventy-five feet away.

Joe LeBel: I kept cutting wood for about a good hour and a half. He never moved. He stayed right there in that one position.
Ray Fowler: You never challenged him?
Joe LeBel: No. I spoke to him in English, and nothing, he's just standing there. When I spoke in French, he moved, like, so I'm wondering if he speaks French.
Ray Fowler: You weren't afraid of this guy standing there at all?
Joe LeBel: No. Then when I got a load of wood cut, I got into the truck and I started coming out. I looked to the left to where he was, and he wasn't there anymore. But then I spotted this *thing*. I said, "Gee, there's no boulders that size over there," so I pulled the truck up and took a

walk down the road. Then I came in back of that boulder, and it was a ship! I went, oh, fifty feet from the ship. It looked almost egg shaped. It's wider at the front than at the back, and it's got little windows all over the sides of it. Except the windows look like a frog's eye. It's got a hood, like, over the windows. It was right on the ground, on the snow at that time.

Ray Fowler: Were there any legs or struts?

Joe LeBel: I couldn't see anything.

It was getting dark. Joe went back to the truck and quickly drove home. When he told the others about it, they laughed and said that he must have been mistaken. Joe works mornings, but as soon as he got back home the next day, he went down into the woods.

Ray Fowler: Did you see an imprint where the ship set?

Joe LeBel: There was no imprint! There was nothing! Then I came down to the house with the load of wood. Later, when I went back up again, it was still in the same place.

Ray Fowler: You didn't notify any authorities about this strange object?

Joanne LeBel: No. I didn't know who to contact. You see, we had spoken to my brother-in-law, a policeman on the force here. Of course, he doesn't believe in this at all.

Joe LeBel: If it wasn't there, then they would say I'm crazy, right? I mentioned it to her brother-in-law, and he just laughed.

Joanne LeBel: I thought, "Oh, well, maybe he *thinks* he's seen something," so I said, "Nancy, why don't you go down?"

Mr. LeBel did take two members of his family down to see the object.

Allan LeBel: He took me up first, and [when] we went up the road, he wouldn't go any further. You see, I can see good at night. My problem in the daytime is there was snow on the ground. With the light and reflection, I can't see distances. This was distant, against the sun, and he kept saying, "Can't you see it?" And I said "no" because it just looked like a big rock.

Ray Fowler: You didn't go any closer?

Allan LeBel: I wanted to but—no.

Joe LeBel: I didn't dare to go any closer.

Ray Fowler: How big was it compared to an automobile, say?

Joe LeBel: Oh, it was bigger than that. I'd say the length of this house. This house is fifty feet. It was long, and it tapered to the back and rounded off, just like an egg, on each end.

Ray Fowler: When you were closer, did you notice anything else on it other than the windows? Any seams or—?

Joe LeBel: No, no, it's just rough. It looked almost like—

Nancy LeBel: Old metal was all I could think of.

Joe LeBel: It looked almost like the surface of the brick on the fireplace there, rough, not shiny at all. Everything dull-like, just like a rock with moss on it. That's what it looked like, almost. Dark, dark gray.

Later in the afternoon, Joe took Nancy down to see the strange interloper in the woods.

Nancy LeBel: It was almost dark. It was about four-thirty, quarter of five, in January, whenever it was getting dark. We were about one hundred and fifty feet from it. He wouldn't let me get any closer, and I couldn't see it at first because it was just starting to get dark. He showed me where to look. And all of a sudden I could see the bubble windows in it. They seemed to be about in the middle of it. I couldn't see the whole ship, because it was in between trees, but I could see a portion of it.

Ray Fowler: If you were to guess—what would the shape of the whole ship be? You didn't see all of it, but you must have had an impression.

Nancy LeBel: Well, it was rounded, the part that I saw. The top was rounded and the part I was looking at seemed to be rounded, because the windows seemed to come out a little. They were definitely round. I could see about seven windows, right next to each other, lined up just like bubbles. All I could think of was a false eye.

Dave Webb: Does that mean that they stuck out at the sides?

Nancy LeBel: They seemed to, but I wasn't really close.

Ray Fowler: So they weren't *real* bubbles, but were sort of curved.

Nancy LeBel: Just curved, yeah.

Ray Fowler: OK. Were there any lights on this object?

Nancy LeBel: No. No movement, no nothing. That's why I wanted to get closer to it, but he wouldn't let me. He had got closer to it before he took me down.

Darkness set in and they returned home. The object left no imprint behind and it has not been seen there again. David Webb visited the site in April and, with Joe's assistance, took measurements indicating that the UFO was about 40 feet long by 13½ feet wide across its nearer or wider end, and possibly 10 feet high. Further measurements indicated that the white-suited, helmeted figure that had watched Joe cutting wood was standing about 300 feet west of the UFO. There was no evidence of environmental damage except for broken limbs on the two tallest trees in what would have been the path of the UFO's vertical descent.

On the following day, about 10 o'clock in the morning, Allan was glancing idly out the bathroom window. The rest of the family was away. Suddenly an object with a smooth, dull, steel-gray or silver surface rose up from behind the tree line. Four long legs or struts extended from its underside. The object rose slowly and deliberately out of his line of sight. He rushed outside, but saw nothing more of it. Later he found "pod marks" in the claylike soil where the object had apparently rested.

Only one of these marks was still visible when we visited the site. Dave Webb measured the imprint to be six inches wide at the top and about 4½ inches deep. He had Allan stand where he had remembered the other imprints to have been. The result was a roughly rectangular area. Allan felt that this represented the spacing between the four legs of the craft.

His sighting was still not the end of the matter. In February 1978, a month after Joe's encounter in the woods, Jerry and Marilyn were again visiting with Joanne's mother.

Joanne LeBel: We were sitting in the living room and for some reason we were all uneasy that night. Marilyn said, "What's that sound? It sounds like *bees?*" Jerry said, "Yes, I hear it." Then he looked around and said, "Oh, it's getting louder and louder." Though I couldn't hear it and Marilyn didn't hear it anymore. He had his two hands over his ears. He said the noise was terrible, just like a babbling it was going so fast. He was bent over and almost collapsed in the chair.

Then the strange noise stopped. It had been a painful and bewildering experience for Jerry. On another night in February, a wave of poltergeistlike activity broke out. In both Joanne's and her mother's homes, locked doors flew open. When knives were inserted in the jambs to prevent this disturbing phenomenon, the doors still would pop open, dislodging the knives!

April brought more terrifying events, and the desperate LeBel family decided to allow an investigation, providing their names were kept confidential. On the 8th, Nancy LeBel sat in her bedroom sewing. The rest of the family was watching television in the living room.

Nancy LeBel: About nine o'clock, Saturday night, I was sitting in my bedroom sewing and I had my record player going, singing along with the music. My door was open just about an inch, when I happened to look up. I knew somebody was standing there looking in 'cause the light from the head up shone in, but there was no light from there down. I could see the contour of a head looking in, but I couldn't tell who it was.

Ray Fowler: Could you give a basic description?

Nancy LeBel: He was about five-seven and slim. It looked like he had on an unzipped jacket. It just looked gray, but different. I couldn't see anything on the face. Figured it was just my father, so I said, "Cut it out" and went back to sewing. I looked up again, and it was still looking in, so I reached over and swung the door open. What I saw was some kind of a form fleeting away, really, really fast.

Joanne LeBel: My husband and my boy were on the rug in front of the fireplace, and I was on the couch. They were watching television. There was no one else in the house.

April 12, when David Webb and I first arrived for an initial interview with the LeBel family, we asked when the latest incident had taken place.

Joanne LeBel: That would be Sunday [April 9. Involved were] Douglas and my older son Allan, and two of my nieces.

Douglas LeBel: My cousin and me were minibike riding. We went down in the back woods and right past the piggery house. It's like a cement platform and we pulled in there. She sat down on the ground to have a cigarette and I waited until she was done. When we were getting up, I turned around and two large white heads stuck up out of the brush; it looked like someone was lying down or kneeling there. And the eyes were very large. They were like a dark bluish-black navy blue and it looked like they were moving back and forth. We didn't stay. I said, "Let's go!"

Ray Fowler: How far away were they?

Joanne LeBel: Well, from what Douglas told me, thirty, thirty-five feet. In that vicinity, because we went down and looked.

Ray Fowler: Were there any movements other than the eyes? You couldn't see any part of the body or anything like that?

Douglas: No. It was a head with no hair on it. It was like the eyes were covered all up through here. The face came down to here, but you really couldn't see anything because of the brush.

Ray Fowler: When you came back later, you didn't see any signs of broken bushes?

Joanne LeBel: No. Then the four of them went down later and saw them again.

Douglas LeBel: My brother Allan and my two cousins, Rose and Dot. We went further down where the line ends at my grandfather's land, and we really kind of got a weird *feeling* that we were being watched. My cousin was sitting beside my brother, and she said, "Hey, look!" She went running, and stuff started falling out of her pockets. I started to follow her and I really didn't get to see it. She said it was completely white and had black bands around its arms all the way up.

Ray Fowler: How many of these did you see?

Douglas LeBel: There was only one with black bands. It was really hard to see them because when you look at them, they've gone, just like that. All you can see is like a shadow of white, just moving fast.

Ray Fowler: How many individual entities did you see at the time?

Douglas LeBel: When my other cousin lit up a cigarette, the flame or something brought them closer. Every time you'd turn around there would be something there, but it would just be gone like a flash.

Ray Fowler: How long did this go on?

Douglas LeBel: Well, most of the time that we were down there. It eased up, but we still had the feeling that there was something still there. . . . There was a definite odor.

Joanne LeBel: All they could think of was sulfur, almost like a hot smell, like it had heat.

Douglas was digging near the woods on May 2, 1978, and had a feeling that he was being watched. Glancing up, he saw two figures in white suits watching him from behind adjoining bushes. He left the shovel and ran home.

David Webb continued his investigation into September of 1978. The final reported incident took place on either September 17 or 18, at about 2 in the morning. Allan glanced out the front window and observed six figures standing beside the road past their home. At first he thought there had been an automobile accident because of fog and because one figure was pointing in an odd way down the road. Peculiarly, the fog formed a sharply defined bank about 15 feet high in just that immediate area. Looking closer, Allan realized that five of these persons seemed to be wearing white suits, and the one who was pointing had on a black or dark suit. Their clothing was outlined by the light from a nearby street lamp. No UFO was seen and no other details concerning the entities were noticed because of the viewing distance of 250 feet. After about ten minutes, the strangely dressed figure walked into the woods. Allan woke up his mother, but by the time she got to the window, the strange persons had disappeared.

Shortly after our investigation began, the LeBel family put their house up for sale. Though they claimed they weren't doing so because of the many bizarre happenings, Mrs. LeBel did ask me if I thought she should tell prospective buyers of the things that had happened on the property: to be fair, perhaps people should be warned. I sincerely doubt that a future owner will have similar problems: for some unknown reason, the powers behind the UFOs seem to have singled out the LeBels for some type of specialized study.

Even the prowler with the white shirt and dark slacks seemed to be part of this specialized surveillance. It had all the characteristics of a robotlike device made to look human, but its peculiar ambulatory characteristics were a dead giveaway: Its walking speed was very slow, with the body held very erect and its arms rigidly by its side. These arms were never observed to bend at the elbow, nor were knee movements ever noted. When this entity turned, its whole body would rotate in a way the witnesses found hard to describe. No footsteps were ever found, even when there was snow on the ground. My own opinion is that it was a surveillance device operated by the helmeted figures seen in association with the landed UFO.

The LeBels have moved to Maine. We have had no further contact with them, but on record are many other similar cases of haunted witnesses. The UFO investigator finds their irrational experiences hard to accept, but the implications are mind boggling. If UFO entities are able to place witnesses in suspended animation and control their actions, might whole societies also be vulnerable to control by unknown powers? It is a frightening thought, especially when one considers that some witnesses have been physically and mentally impaired for life because of a close encounter with a UFO.

One can understand why the military is so determined to keep us from the answers.

CHAPTER NOTES

1. Raymond E. Fowler, *The Andreasson Affair* (New Jersey: Prentice-Hall, Inc., 1979), p. 9.

PRESSURE FROM THE PENTAGON

As a young teenager, I often listened to Frank Edwards to hear the latest on UFOs. One of the earliest radio broadcasters, he was the first network commentator to take UFO reports seriously. He publicized over 100 sightings by pilots, control-tower operators, and other trained observers on his nationwide newscasts and went out of his way to expose the Air Force's official secrecy and debunking of UFOs. But eventually Edwards's attacks on Air Force policy had such a wide effect that the government brought pressure on him through his sponsor, the American Federation of Labor.[1] Refusing to be censored, he quit the network and continued his battle on independent stations, syndicated programs, guest radio appearances and lectures. He also published two very popular books: the first, *Flying Saucers: Serious Business*, appeared in 1966. Frank died on June 23, 1967, having faithfully served on NICAP's board of governors from its inception in 1956. His *Flying Saucers—Here and Now!* was published posthumously in 1967.

I have come across several cases where investigating Air Force officers specifically told police, airline pilots, and government employees not to talk about their UFO sightings—and threatened investigators for releasing data to the public. Take, for example, Robert Todd, who searches out data on military UFO incidents and then demands it under the Freedom of Information Act. Once he apparently went too far, which resulted in FBI agents coming to his house to silence him.

The central figure in that event was an Air Force security specialist who requested that his name be kept confidential. He was assigned to the

6947th Security Squadron of the U.S. Air Force Security Service (AFSS) centered at Homestead AFB near Miami, Florida. He discussed his story with UFO lecturer Stanton Friedman, and eventually it became widely disseminated as a UPI dispatch of January 12 or 13, 1978.

One day in March of 1967, this particular squadron was located at Key West Naval Station on Boca Chica Key, only 97 miles from the Cuban coastline. Several such squadrons are scattered geographically to enable direction-finding equipment to locate land-based radar sites and communication centers and to plot aircraft movements via their flight transmissions. (I am personally familiar with these operations, as I served on a similar base in England during a tour with the AFSS.)

This particular day, Cuban air-defense radar controllers were overheard reporting a UFO approaching from the northeast. As soon as it violated Cuban airspace, two MIG jet fighters scrambled to meet it. The UFO was moving at 660 mph at 33,000 feet. Guided by ground radar to within three miles of it, the pilots described the object as a bright metallic sphere with no markings or appendages. When the Cuban interceptors' radio-contact attempts proved fruitless, Cuban Air Defense headquarters radioed the jet to destroy the intruding object. The jet flight leader reported back that his radar was locked on the UFO and his missiles were armed.

Within seconds the wingman was heard screaming to Cuban ground controllers that his flight leader's jet had suddenly exploded! Regaining his composure, he reported that there was no smoke or flame; that the MIG-21 had disintegrated. The Cuban ground-radar operators informed the lone pilot that the UFO had rapidly accelerated to about 100,000 feet and was heading south-southeast toward South America.

The United States Air Force Security Service unit was under the operational control of the National Security Agency. An intelligence report was quickly relayed to NSA about the bizarre incident. Strangely enough, NSA did not send the customary mandatory receipt for this report, so they sent it again. This time they received orders to ship all tapes and pertinent data on the incident to NSA and were told to list the cause of the Cuban jet's destruction in their own files as "equipment malfunction."

As many as fifteen to twenty people were said to have been aware of the incident. Presumably the AFSS data forwarded to NSA included direction-finding measurements that could be used to triangulate the Cuban jets' positions. If the AFSS radar-tracking equipment was sensitive enough, the UFO itself could have been tracked by its reflection of Cuban radar waves, but it was not known if our own radar tracked the jets and the UFO.

Eleven years after this episode UFO researcher Robert Todd heard about it, and from February to July 1978 sent FOIA requests for information to the Air Force, CIA, NSA, and Navy. None of these efforts proved successful, so he told the Air Force and NSA that he was going to query the Cuban government directly. Concerned that some of this information might be classified, he gave them twenty days to "provide advice as to what information in the attached statement should not be transmitted to the Cuban government."

This time Robert received a response! Around six o'clock on July 28, two FBI agents appeared at his door and interrogated him about his letter to NSA for an hour. Both men showed him FBI identification; but he never got their names. Robert signed a paper acknowledging that he had been read his rights; he waived his right to silence and told the FBI that he had nothing to hide.

The FBI agents proceeded to intimidate him by reading the espionage laws. He interrupted, saying he was familiar with them. One agent continued, saying that the laws carry a penalty of life in prison or death. Both hinted at the possibility of indictments. Had he ever written to a foreign government? Saying that the information he had was "secret or above," they pressed him for the name of his source of information.

The officials asked him if he knew Todd Zechel. Having recently interviewed Zechel by phone, he asked if they had tapped his phone. The men only smiled. Robert told them that he would demand the FBI file on this investigation of him through FOIA. Ironically, the agents said that the information he had given them couldn't be released in that fashion "because it was classified." They told him that this particular investigation would be filed under Counterespionage. Robert was pretty upset, but on the way out of the house, the FBI agents assured his mother that her son wasn't in any trouble: They described him as the "man on the end of a string."

The following week, on August 4, Robert received a phone call from Major Gordon Finley, chief of the Torts and Freedom of Information Branch, Air Force judge advocate general's office. The major told him that his data on the Cuban incident, if true, included classified information. He asked Robert how many copies he had concerning the incident, and then asked him to put them in a sealed envelope for someone to pick up. Robert refused to do this and demanded to know what classification was concerned. The major agreed with the FBI that it was secret or above.

Allan Hendry of CUFOS investigated this invasion of privacy by the FBI and the Air Force. On August 8 he phoned Major Finley, who confirmed that he had talked with Robert, but would not be pinned down on the nature of the data's classification. Investigators for the Citizens Against UFO Secrecy also queried the FBI about their investigation of Robert Todd. In response, Paul B. Lorenzetti, spokesman for the Philadelphia FBI Field Division, stated, "I'm not cleared to gain information in such an investigation." John Perks, FBI headquarters, Washington, D.C., said that he would check. Later his counterpart phoned back to state that: "We never confirm who we've talked to or who we haven't talked to. . . . We never do that." When queried, NSA spokesman Charles Sullivan retorted, "I'm not going to be responsive to you at all. You are not going to get anything from any government agency about another government agency. . . ." Robert stood fast in the midst of such threats—and has not been bothered since.

The military does not treat UFOs lightly, especially when disruption or destruction of military weapons is involved. I understand there are some few cases on record where private citizens were also advised not to publicize their sightings, but it came as quite a surprise when the Air Force pressured *me* not to publish data about certain UFO sightings.

When I was interviewed about UFOs by Stephen Webbe, a staff writer for *The Christian Science Monitor,* I mentioned being acquainted with a number of UFOs sighted over Minuteman installations. Showing great interest, Stephen asked me to document a specific incident for use in his article.

I chose one for which there were two highly reliable sources. One was Dr. J. Allen Hynek, who had assisted in investigating the incident for the Air Force. My second was the Air Force officer in charge of the Minuteman Launch Control Facility over which the UFO hovered. Stephen summarized the incident well:

AIR FORCE DENIES UFO INCIDENT

A United States missile program supervisor claims that mysterious unidentified flying objects have seriously imperiled national security. The Air Force denies it.

Raymond E. Fowler, project supervisor on a Minuteman missile program near Boston, asserts that [UFOs] have penetrated the restricted air space above America's Minuteman missile sites, jamming vital electronic equipment. He also says the objects eluded fighter aircraft scrambled to intercept them. . . .

Specifically, Mr. Fowler says he talked with an Air Force officer who had been in one of the subterranean Launch Control Facilities (LCFs) of a North Dakota Minuteman site on August 25, 1966, when radar operators picked up a UFO maneuvering over the base at 100,000 feet. . . . The officer declared that the LCF's sophisticated radio equipment, which enables it to receive firing instructions from coordinating centers and transmit them to the silo Launch Facilities (LFs) was blocked out by static when the UFO hovered directly over it. . . . Mr. Fowler recalls the officer saying that he could conceive of "nothing on earth" that could cause the equipment to malfunction from such an altitude, emphasizing that it was working perfectly before the object appeared overhead and after it left.

Asked to comment on Mr. Fowler's allegations, an Air Force spokesman in Washington declared that SAC, which operates the site, "could find nothing in its unit histories to confirm the presence of unidentified flying objects over it or indeed malfunctions in its equipment on the date mentioned."

Despite the Air Force's denial ... Dr. Hynek insists that the base was buzzed by a UFO. "I went there as the Air Force representative and talked to the people concerned after it happened," he says. Dr. Hynek was at that time acting as scientific consultant to Project Blue Book. Mr. Fowler says he was told that communications between land strike-teams (armed jeep patrols) dispatched to a spot where the first UFO appeared to land and intercepting aircraft were completely jammed by strong radio interference. Moreover, he says, missile site control found intense static disrupting communications with its strike-teams.

After UFOs had streaked away, Mr. Fowler claims that Air Force Intelligence teams descended on the base telling those who had seen or heard anything to keep quiet. ... He cites a Joint Chiefs of Staff regulation, last updated in 1966, which establishes a system for reporting UFO sightings to the Aerospace Defense Command at Colorado Springs ... and imposes penalties for the unauthorized disclosure of UFO information. But says an Air Force spokesman: "We're out of the UFO business."[2]

Wednesday morning, December 5, 1973, the eastern, midwestern and western editions of *The Christian Science Monitor* had just hit the newsstands. Shortly before 11 A.M., one puzzled Minuteman program manager burst into my office at work to warn me that a Captain Rick Fuller had just phoned from SAC headquarters at Offutt AFB, Nebraska, inquiring about me and the revealing newspaper article that had just been brought to his attention. Told that my boss's boss had just been notified, I became very concerned. The rest of the day passed quietly, however. I assumed that all was well.

The following day another coworker told me that while he was in the industrial-relations manager's office, a colonel had phoned from the Pentagon, and the coworker had inadvertently overheard a discussion concerning "SAC, Ray Fowler, and a newspaper article"! This hearsay was intriguing, to say the least, because no one had contacted me personally.

On Monday morning, another fellow employee retrieved from the trash a page from a telephone note pad from the industrial relations office. The cryptic remarks scrawled on the discarded page confirmed what I had been hearing secondhand:

Col. Coleman
Christian Science Monitor
Ray Fowler
Proj Supr-Minuteman

Displeasure at public discussion of operational readiness of systems. UFO sighting that rendered Minuteman system inoperative briefly.[3]

Recognizing Colonel Coleman as chief of the Public Information Division for the Air Force at the Pentagon, I called the industrial relations manager, who expressed surprise that I had found out about the calls and assured me the whole matter was just a tempest in a teapot. Nonetheless, I was annoyed by Colonel Coleman's covert interference. He should have called me, not my employer. It all seemed peculiar because much of the information had already been made public in one form or another. I now realize that their reaction was probably over *where* the information was published. One of the most respected international newspapers in the world had indicated that UFOs could easily disrupt the cornerstone of America's defense system.

On the following day, about midmorning, I was called into the department manager's office, who told me we both had an appointment with the branch manager. The Pentagon was threatening to send an official letter of complaint to my employer because of the article I had instigated, and he demanded an explanation for my actions.

I explained to them that Dr. Hynek had already published an article containing much of what I had heard independently from the Air Force captain, and that others had leaked data to the public concerning UFO visitations to Minuteman installations. To make a long story short, I was asked to produce evidence that such data had already been published before, in some public form.

On my request, Dr. Hynek sent me copies of his published material and called the Air Force's action "deplorable." Stephen Webbe felt that their threat was "preposterous," and asked to be kept informed. In any event, I presented Xerox copies of the appropriate material to my boss, who passed them on up the chain of command, and nothing more was said.

I sent my company a letter of apology for any inconvenience or embarrassment that the article caused. In it, I expressed my displeasure at the Air Force for threatening me through my employer, which act could very well have affected my reputation and livelihood. I pointed out that the article did not mention either the company's name or the identities of my informants, other than Dr. Hynek.

Stephen Webbe, of course, had wanted the Air Force's comments before the publication of his article, and had phoned the Pentagon. Initially he was told that the matter would be looked into and that someone would get back to him. No one ever did call back, so he continued phoning. Then he was told that no such incident had ever occurred. He reminded them that Dr. Hynek had already admitted to investigating the incident on their behalf! Again, Stephen was told that they would "look into it."

Surprisingly enough, Stephen was contacted and told that such an incident *had* occurred, but that the disruption at the missile site was caused by a local power failure! I laughed when Stephen told me this. First of all, no power blackout had occurred during the incident; the disruption was with the missile's communications system. Second, all major weapons systems have electrical power backups in case of power failure just as do hospitals and radio or TV stations. In the case of Minuteman, an external power cut would immediately have been picked up by special sensors that would start electrical generators in motion. In event of generator failure, backup batteries would still keep Minuteman under power.

Colonel Coleman's face must have turned red when Stephen got back to him with this information. Stephen did not wait for the Air Force to "get back to him" again; he went ahead and published the article. This gives some insight into how the Pentagon deals with sensitive UFO data. But much more hanky-panky may be going on behind the scenes: Certain UFO investigators seem to be under direct surveillance by one or more intelligence agencies.

CHAPTER NOTES

1. NICAP, *UFO Investigator,* October 1967, p. 8.
2. Stephen Webbe, "Air Force denies UFO incident," *Christian Science Monitor,* December 5, 1973, p. 1.
3. Personal files.

GOVERNMENT SURVEILLANCE

One of the Robertson Panel's major recommendations was that civilian UFO research organizations "be watched because of their potentially great influence on mass thinking if widespread sightings should occur."[1]

In their book *UFOs Over the Americas,* Jim and Coral Lorenzen relate how, even in the early days of the Aerial Phenomena Research Group (APRO), they may have been under surveillance. A letter from a zealous volunteer reflected the light in such a way that Mrs. Lorenzen could see her name faintly embossed or blind stamped on the top of the paper. Curious, she retrieved the letter and examined it closely. Apparently the writer had used the letter as a backing sheet for a memo or report.

Carefully shading the faint impressions left by the typewriter keys, Mrs. Lorenzen was astonished to discover the report contained a short history of her residences, a list of her habits, and an evaluation of her character. When confronted with her findings, the volunteer worker explained that this was his personal method of formalizing his feelings about people he met!

On another occasion, two men came to her rented house and told her they were painting contractors. She referred them to the landlord, but they showed no interest in obtaining his name and tried to engage her in conversation. Coral excused herself, and they left. Later she was surprised to see them sitting in their car parked down the street in a position where they could view her house easily. Still later she learned that APRO's treasurer and secretary had received similar calls from the same two painting contractors. This was curious—the treasurer's home had been newly painted, and the secretary lived in what was obviously an apartment building.

Shortly after the Lorenzens moved from Alamogordo to Tucson, another odd visitor told them he was an exterminator and was willing to examine their house free of charge. When the Lorenzens explained that they were renting the house, the man showed no interest in finding out who their landlord was but instead wanted to know why they had moved, where Coral's husband, Jim, would be employed, and asked questions about UFOs.

Coral had an associate whose husband was employed in the local military Office of Special Investigation (OSI). He confided with her that OSI had a large file on APRO and the Lorenzen family! A second, substantial bit of evidence concerned the Lorenzens' relationship with Dr. Hynek.

Brazilian medical scholar and surgeon Dr. Olavo Fontes worked closely with the Brazilian defense community and was one of APRO's leading UFO research consultants. While visiting the United States, he became friends with Dr. Hynek, and upon his return home, Dr. Fontes asked the Brazilian Air Force to send Dr. Hynek copies of official UFO reports. Brazil—enlisting the aid of an unnamed U. S. intelligence agency—promptly put Hynek, Fontes, and the Lorenzens under special surveillance. Later, from a friend who worked for the Brazilian government, Dr. Fontes covertly received a copy of an official Brazilian intelligence surveillance report, describing in great detail the movements and activities of Hynek, Fontes, and the Lorenzens. Later, when I met with Hynek at a Boston hotel, prior to his leaving Bluebook, the question of the Brazilian report came up. He informed me that both of us were probably being watched that day!

Even witnesses reporting UFO sightings to APRO are not exempt from such surveillance. On March 28, 1967, at about 2:25 A.M., a young man was driving home from his job to Munroe Falls, Ohio, when he spotted a luminous object hovering off the left side of the road. Four or five small creatures, "like midgets," were moving back and forth across the pavement. He braked immediately, but not in time—his car hit one of the entities! His first inclination was to get out and help, but the glowing object and little men seemed so unearthly that he sped away in great fright. When the witness talked with APRO *by phone,* he mentioned that he had physical evidence of this encounter.

Strangely enough, a total of four persons then attempted to gain access to this evidence! Two of them drove a car with unissued Ohio license plate numbers. When he refused to request the evidence back from APRO and give it to them, the other two then threatened his family. Mrs. Lorenzen, then director of APRO, wonders how these strangers knew about the alleged physical evidence, short of tapping the phones. I too have asked myself this same question a number of times.

On December 14, 1974, at about 7:30 A.M., Mr. and Mrs. Herbert

Lower of Townshend, Vermont, discovered a strange circular impression in the snow on their property. At about 8:00, the Lowers informed the widow of a deceased APRO investigator about the strange marking, and also phoned the local newspaper, the *Brattleboro Reformer,* about it. Reporter Greg Wordon responded to the call, arriving about 10:00 A.M. He interviewed the Lowers, photographed the landing area, and during the following week wrote up a front-page story on the incident.[2] The APRO investigator's widow called the *Keene Evening Sentinel* (New Hampshire), but they showed no interest whatsoever. Undaunted, she phoned a local real estate broker interested in UFOs, who referred her to Field Investigator Bob Jackson, who phoned me. I in turn informed the MUFON New Hampshire director. John Meloney was assigned to investigate the case. Around 1:00 P.M., I personally phoned the Lowers to inform them of our investigation plans, and asked them briefly to relate to me what had happened.

During that night, they said, their 14-year-old daughter Colleen awoke when a pinkish glow shone through a window. She did not get up to investigate. Then at 4:00 A.M. Mrs. Lower woke up. The dogs were barking, as they had for the last few nights, and she too saw a pink glow coming through her window. Too tired to get up, she dismissed the glow as probably the sunrise and assumed the dogs were barking at deer.

Later that morning, at about 7:30 A.M., Mrs. Lower got up from bed, put on the teakettle, then went to the living room. Drawing the drapes, she was startled to see a round, thawed marking in the snow only 15 feet away. There were 2 to 3 inches of snow on the ground, and it was still snowing. She watched, fascinated, as the flakes melted instantaneously upon contact with the bare oval.

Mrs. Lower quickly put on her coat and went outside. She noticed that the soil was "puffed up," the way a plowed field gets when it thaws in the spring. There were no footprints or any other markings around the mysterious thawed area. However, she did note a little lobe of melted snow about six inches long, protruding from the circle toward the house.

John arrived at the Lowers' home at 2:30 P.M. He photographed the area, secured soil samples, and took temperature readings at various soil depths. Later a radiological check was made, with negative results. Mr. Lower casually told John that he had put up a Keep Out sign, as instructed by *the man on the telephone.* Assuming that Mr. Lower meant me, John continued his tasks without questions until Mr. Lower mentioned that on the following day, the man would be sending a helicopter to examine the site.

John half wondered where I had secured helicopter services and puzzled about why others would be investigating after he'd been assigned to the case. About 4:00 P.M. John left for home. Shortly afterward his car skidded on ice and hit a tree. John wound up in Townshend's Grace Cottage Hospital with multiple fractures.

Two days later Colleen Lower was admitted to the same hospital with a neck injury; in the meantime, Bob Jackson took over the investigation. One day when both Bob and the Lowers were visiting John at the hospital, Mr. Lower said that the helicopter had come, but never landed as planned. John and Bob asked what he was talking about.

Mr. Lower said that on Saturday, the day he had reported the incident, several minutes after I had initially talked with him, the phone rang again. An authoritarian male voice identified himself as representing a government agency in Washington, claimed that he had heard about the incident, questioned Mr. Lower about it, and asked if it would be permissible—and possible—to land a small helicopter on his property. Assuming I had notified this agency, Mr. Lower told him where a helicopter could set down. Since it was still snowing, Mr. Lower suggested that the helicopter be sent the following day.

At about noon on Sunday Mr. Lower and his son were emptying rubbish not far from their home. Suddenly a whirring sound made them glance up, and they saw an unmarked helicopter flying low toward their home. It circled for about ten minutes, as if seeking a good place to land, then—as if the pilot had changed his mind—the helicopter left. Later I talked to others who had seen this mysterious helicopter, including Mrs. Lower's mother and the editor of the *Brattleboro Reformer.*

The known observers' general description was of a small craft, dark brown or tan in color, with an enclosed tail assembly. It had only one rotor blade and a glassed-in nose. I thoroughly checked military and commercial bases, but was unable to ascertain its origin. As far as we could find out, no one had phoned any government agency. Also, Mr. Lower had an unlisted number. A government agency could secure such a number easily, but this curious phone call had been received within minutes after I had talked to Mr. Lower. A strange coincidence—or was my phone tapped?

The following Tuesday, another mystery man called Mr. Lower's mother, saying he was a reporter for the *Brattleboro Reformer,* and asked for Mr. Lower's unlisted number. He then interrogated Mr. Lower by phone, but oddly enough did not mention his name. A check indicated that no one from that newspaper had been involved. But the Townshend thawed mark seems to have a conventional explanation. The people who owned the house before the Lowers revealed that the circle of melted snow lay directly over a dry well. Apparently hot laundry water seeping into it had caused the snow to melt. But the coincidental pink glow shining through the window, the "government" telephone call, and the helicopter were never explained.

On February 20, 1975, at 9:00 P.M. two female students, Hope and Nancy, both 17 years of age, were sitting on a stone wall facing a large green quadrangle containing a number of the dormitories of Phillips Academy in Andover. All of a sudden, directly in front of them, a group of lights fell from the western sky. The girls watched what seemed to be a plane descending straight down over the far end of the campus soccer field. At a point just above tree level, however, the lights stopped abruptly in midair.

They hung there for a moment, ascended straight up a short way, then hovered once again. Now curious, the witnesses hopped off the wall and hurried across the soccer field. In the meantime, the lighted object had begun moving very slowly toward the academy infirmary. When the girls reached the other side of the field, the object was directly over the infirmary, just a few hundred feet away.

Hope and Nancy stopped by a large oak tree. The strange object did not appear to be a plane or helicopter. It carried a large blue light on top and a circle of multiple red lights below. While they watched, the object turned slowly about and headed toward them. Before they could react, it was hovering about 75 feet directly over their heads. They described it as an oval object about 10 to 12 feet in diameter, its lights reflecting off a dull gray surface. Both stated that its bottom was round and convex in shape. It emanated a very soft hum, much like a small electric motor. Exhibiting a strange rocking motion, it remained overhead for only about 30 seconds before moving off on a semicircular track toward a bell tower, then disappeared behind trees to the south.

Just as soon as the object moved from overhead, the girls broke into a run. They alerted a total of thirteen other students, who saw the departing blue and red lights. One student phoned the Andover police, who called me at about 9:25 P.M. Then, about a half hour *after the police had phoned me,* a helicopter was heard approaching the darkened campus. The witnesses and other students spotted a very low-flying helicopter performing crisscross maneuvers over the quadrangle. None of them could see any markings on the craft.

When told this, I recalled that at Townshend, the unnamed man had told Mr. Lower that their agency had special helicopters "ready to go anywhere." A number of special UFO investigating teams could be stationed at strategically located military bases; perhaps the Andover copter was from Hanscom AFB at nearby Bedford. In any event, the police had phoned no one except me. A tap on my line could explain the helicopter's instant response. Why else would a strange copter fly a search pattern over the Phillips Academy campus?

Such helicopters have been seen many times during and after UFO activity. Two other local Massachusetts cases occurred during the huge UFO wave of 1966. On April 19, witnesses in a Bellingham neighborhood watched a humming cigar-shaped craft descend into a wooded area. Shortly afterward a helicopter and two aircraft appeared and circled this same area. The classic Beverly incident took place just a few days later. Investigating police told me that the police station had phoned Hanscom AFB about the incident. Again, shortly after the object had departed, a helicopter and two aircraft arrived and circled the sighting area.

Other curious telephone episodes come to mind. Once Dr. Menzel was on a local radio call-in show, making absurd remarks about UFOs. I decided to phone the station for a rebuttal, but could not. My phone went dead, and remained dead until the program was over. Even more thought provoking was the time John Fuller phoned me. Researching material for *Incident at Exeter,* he had just returned from the Air Force Office of Information at the Pentagon, where he confronted Lieutenant Colonel John P. Spaulding with the overwhelming UFO evidence that he had been obtaining from New Hampshire citizens. The Air Force officer listened for a while, John told me, then jumped up and angrily informed him, "I am an officer of the United States Air Force." With that, he saluted and stormed out, leaving John alone in the office.

We laughed about this and chatted about UFOs in general. After hanging up, I left my study and was entering the kitchen when the phone rang. A very polite but commanding voice said, "Who was that man you were talking to?" For some reason, I simply replied, "John Fuller." Whoever it was hung up. On two occasions (one answered by my daughter, the other by myself) puzzled telephone callers claimed that they had dialed Hanscom Air Force Base. I was even more puzzled how they could have reached my private home instead: The base is over twenty miles away, on a different exchange, and our telephone numbers bear no resemblance to each other!

One New England woman, well known because of her alleged UFO abduction, was hosting members of a BBC film crew at her home. Her husband placed an order for lunch to a quick-food establishment. One of the crew, who wanted his order changed, picked up the phone to call back. There was no dial tone; instead, a voice clearly said, "Pease Intelligence." The crewman quickly motioned to the film-crew director to come to the phone. The director picked up the phone and said, "Hello." A voice again said, "Pease Intelligence."

"You'll get promoted for this, sergeant!" the quick-witted film director replied. There was silence, then a *click!* Could it be that such phone taps originate from the Air Force Base located nearest their homes? In the case just cited, that would be Pease AFB at Portsmouth, New Hampshire. In my case, it would be Hanscom AFB in Bedford, Massachusetts.

Merlyn Sheehan, currently the MUFON section director for Norfolk County in Massachusetts, has had a long-standing interest in UFOs. At the time of her experience with this well-known abductee, she belonged to a small organization called the New England UFO Study Group. When the abductee and her husband addressed this group about their UFO experience, Merlyn decided to visit them at their house to ask some questions. From Merlyn's report to me:

Impulsively I called a friend who lived a few miles from me to ask her if she would use my car and drive us. . . . Being adventuresome, she agreed, even though we had no way of knowing if they would open their home to two strangers. So on a lovely morning in early Fall, 1963, we drove down the Maine turnpike towards our destination. We arrived there around 11:30 A.M. and knocked on the door. Our fears of rejection were unfounded as [the couple] welcomed us, invited us to sit down and proceeded to tell us the most exciting first-hand account.

At the time, they felt that they were being watched—by whom, they had no idea—and that visitors to their home were also being monitored. After about three hours, we thanked them for their hospitality and headed for our homes in Braintree and Weymouth. On the return trip, one particular station wagon seemed to pass us, go out of sight, then repeatedly turned up either beside us or in back of us. It finally vanished for good and we didn't think about it again.

After dropping my friend off in Weymouth, I drove home by a very circuitous route in order to avoid home-going traffic. I turned down my street just in time to see our friendly station wagon!

Months later, a neighbor who lives on a street in back of me, but from which my house can be seen, asked about a car which was quite often sitting near her home. Throughout the rest of the winter and into early spring, other neighbors reported strange cars, sometimes the station wagon, parked at various spots on the same street—but always with my house in view, and with the usual lone occupant.

One woman called and asked me if she should casually walk by and ask the man if she could direct him somewhere. I said perhaps it would be a good idea, but when she looked out the window, the car was gone. She felt he must have heard our conversation. Another friend at the foot of the street announced she had never remembered seeing so many men climbing telephone poles.

The last straw was when a conversation which my friend in Weymouth had engaged in one morning was *somehow played back that evening* when she was talking on the phone to someone else! Then, I decided to try to get a license number. Finally, a car came and parked near my house. It wasn't the station wagon, but the second time the same car returned, I used my binoculars, copied down the number, and called the Registry of Motor Vehicles. The girl said, "This is a military number."[3]

The same UFO abductee whom Merlyn had visited in 1963 continued to complain about apparent surveillance and harassment. Thus, a number of years later, she filed a complaint with John Meloney, one of our top investigators in New Hampshire, who at one time was an intelligence-report editor for the United States Office of Strategic Services. She told him of a number of strange incidents that indicated an ongoing surveillance and apparent attempts to frighten her, and John asked me for advice. I appointed Bob Jackson, then working as a professional detective, to assist in investigating her complaint. I held a debriefing with John after his investigation:

She thought she was being followed. . . . Then one day she said she thought someone had tried to run her over. When she got partway

around to her front door, a car started up suddenly and came zooming around the corner, went up in the yard, and headed right for her. She had to jump in the bushes. He was heading right for a tree stump in her yard, but was astute enough to just miss it. He wasn't drunk and out of control. She thought it must have been done on purpose. That really scared her. She contacted me and said she didn't know what to do.

I was afraid her phone was tapped, so I went to a pay phone and called her at work, not giving my last name. She knew my voice. I said that we could discuss "things" in the lobby of the Carpenter Hotel in Manchester at one o'clock. Then we hung up. . . . I thought if there was a phone tap, they wouldn't know that much. . . . Then I arranged with Bob Jackson to meet me at twelve-thirty at the same lobby. She didn't know he was coming. The Carpenter Hotel is across the street from a large parking lot. My wife and I parked our car at the south end of the lot. We walked into the hotel and I immediately spotted Bob Jackson standing in the lobby. I didn't see anyone else except somebody behind the desk. We shook hands and then walked into the cocktail lounge and picked a table off to one side.

I explained that the abductee didn't know that he was here, but that she was coming in half an hour. I asked him to interview her directly so that he could get his own impressions.

She showed up at one o'clock and was kind of surprised to see Bob. I explained that Bob was a detective who had experience with UFO investigation and that she could be very open with him.

He had her draw a diagram of her house, her neighborhood street and all of the surrounding houses. Then they talked about the car and the time she came home and saw someone run from the house; how she found things messed up on her desk and all the various things that had been happening.

After we'd been there a while, we felt we should go in the dining room. So we walked across a little hallway. We got a pretty good table around the corner so that if anyone came in the dining room, they would have to pass us. It came out that she felt she was being followed: She had seen this man several times—once in the parking lot behind her office, once pulling up to a stoplight in Portsmouth. One time she actually saw him inside the building where she worked, where the public was never supposed to go. Once or twice she thought she had seen him in the rearview mirror of her car, so Bob asked her to describe the man in detail.

Then Bob asked to be excused. He went out into the lobby, came back in about two minutes, and said, "The man that has been following you is in the lobby." That didn't seem possible because we covered our tracks in my call from the phone booth. That would imply that her office phone would have to be tapped.

In a few minutes, Virginia and the abductee started out to the rest rooms. Sure enough, they saw this man. Apparently he recognized them, because he immediately ducked into one of the phone booths as if he were going to make a phone call. Virginia turned and looked over her shoulder. He was just sitting there, making no effort to use the telephone.

When they got back, the abductee said, "Yes, that is the man—I don't know how he got here." She was not aware of being followed to the hotel.

We finished dinner and again Bob pulled a very clever stunt. He said, "We'll go out in the lobby, say good-bye, and shake hands. She will go out through the main door and go out to her car, and we'll see what happens." We just stood by the front door talking, not leaving, while she went out and got in her car in the middle of the parking lot. She started her motor but didn't go anywhere; she just let it run. The man in question walked out the exit and around to the south end of the parking lot, and started his car. But of course he didn't know where to go. We were standing there talking, and pretty soon it began to get embarrassing! He realized that he had been caught because he couldn't just sit there and run his car forever!

Bob said, "This guy knows he's been had now!" So the man got out and put on a little act, feeling in all of his pockets, pretending he had forgotten something. Finally he turned the engine off, put his hat back on, and went back into the hotel. In the meantime, the abductee was just sitting there with her engine running.

The minute the man went in the building, Bob signaled to her to drive off. "Look," he told us, "you get in your car now, and I'll phone you when I find out what's happening." We didn't want the man to find out who we were or which car we had. He didn't know Bob Jackson's car either, and Bob was going to make sure that he left after the other guy did. . . .

We circled around to make sure that we weren't being followed. Then we went home. A couple of days later, Bob phoned and said he had watched the man walk down the hall and into a phone booth. Bob got into the booth right next to him, put his ear to the wall and heard him say: "But, I've got to have help. I can't do this alone."[4]

Bob traced the man's license number to a businessman from Nashua. Was the businessman a covert agent assigned to watch this famous UFO abductee?

I remember a call from a man who had heard that I had investigated a crashed UFO incident, insisting that he'd like to see the witness's sketch. I'd mentioned this case during my lectures, but told him I'd rather not release any sketches. Several weeks later our family had sat down for supper when a sharp knock came at the front door. I opened the door and in stepped this same man. He was such a smooth talker that before I knew it, I had him seated in the living room. In the meantime, my wife reminded me that dinner was on the table. Again, he asked to see the sketches of the crashed UFO. Just to get rid of him, I guess—I showed him the sketch. He looked a bit disappointed and asked if there were sketches of the craft's interior. When I answered that the witness hadn't sketched the interior, he quickly excused himself and headed for the door.

Suddenly it dawned upon me that I couldn't remember the name he had given me on the phone. When I asked to see his credentials, he laughed and said that he did work for a government agency, but that it had nothing to do with UFOs. He muttered something to the effect that this particular agency would make a poor cover, and he was gone. I was so completely flabbergasted that I didn't even get the license number on his car. Whoever it was had managed to keep me off guard until he left the house.

One day my wife returned to our new car to find a police officer photographing it from different angles. When asked what he was doing, he replied that he was testing a new camera. Up until 1966, our phone was a two-party line with separate rings for each party. Then in 1966 the other party disappeared, but we were still classified and charged for a two-party line. One day as I was pondering about the curious things happening with my telephone it dawned upon me that I had become a national figure in ufology during the UFO wave of 1966. Was there a connection? Curiosity got the better of me, and I asked a friend who worked for the telephone company to check out my line for anything suspicious. He did, and told me that my phone line was connected to a tee or tap-off which the telephone company refers to as a bridging circuit. This would enable the telephone company—or any party it authorized—to listen in on my telephone line without detection. Unfortunately, my friend could not trace the other side of my line to its source. An engineer told me that with such a hookup, whenever my phone rang or whenever I lifted up my receiver another party could be alerted and monitor the call without detection. This would explain the strange clicks, why our phone inexplicably goes dead, and why friends tell me that my line was busy when no one is using my phone.

Is UFO information so vital that it requires such an operation?

CHAPTER NOTES

1. Robertson Panel (now declassified), pp. 18–24, Tab. A (As quoted in: E. U. Condon, *Scientific Study of Unidentified Flying Objects,* p. 525).
2. Greg Worden, "A UFO in Townshend? Something was there," *Brattleboro Reformer,* December 21, 1974, p. 1.
3. Personal files.
4. Personal files.

THE GOVERNMENT'S OWN INVESTIGATIONS

I have a copy of Pentagon correspondence dated May 26, 1970—a full five months after the Air Force allegedly ceased investigating UFO reports—signed by the then-chief USAF information officer on UFOs, Colonel William T. Coleman, Jr. It reads, in part:

The Aerospace Defense Command (ADC)... is responsible for unknown aerial phenomena reports in any manner, and the provisions of Joint Army-Navy-Air Force publication (JANAP)-146 provide for the processing of reports received from non-military sources.

"Non-military sources" include, among others, civilian airline pilots. JANAP-146E, Paragraph 101b, states, "The procedures contained in this publication are provided for: (1) U.S. and Canadian civil and commercial aircraft." These procedures were initially imposed upon airline pilots at a conference held in Los Angeles on February 17, 1954, between representatives of major airlines and Military Air Transport Service (MATS) intelligence officers. Severe restrictive procedures were levied upon airline pilots who reported UFO sightings through an official communication called a CIRVIS (Communications Instructions for Reporting Vital Intelligence Sightings) report. Regarding security, JANAP-146 issues the following warning:

SECTION III—Security
210. Military and Civilian
a. All persons aware of the contents of a CIRVIS report are governed by the Communications Act of 1934 and amendments thereto, and Espionage Laws. CIRVIS reports contain information affecting the National Defense of the United States within the meaning of the Espionage Laws, 18 U.S. Code, 793 and 794. The unauthorized transmission or revelation of the contents of CIRVIS reports in any manner is prohibited.

In lay terms, any airline pilot who talks about his UFO sighting after filing a CIRVIS report is liable to a 10-year jail sentence and/or a $10,000 fine!

After four years of this security procedure, 450 airline pilots signed a protest petition for the *Newark Star Ledger* datelined December 22, 1958. One disgruntled pilot termed the Air Force policy "a lesson in lying, intrigue and the 'Big Brother' attitude carried to the ultimate extreme." Fifty of the pilots who signed this petition had each sighted at least one UFO; the majority, several! They stated, "We are ordered to report all UFO sightings, but when we do, we are treated like incompetents and told to keep quiet."

Needless to say, very little is now heard about UFOs from American pilots. Most abide by the rules, others refuse to report UFOs at all, and still others file confidential reports to civilian organizations. A few defy JANAP-146-E and make their reports public. As far as I know, such pilots have never been prosecuted for not filing a CIRVIS report. I doubt the Air Force would carry out such a threat because of the undoubted publicity that would surround the case. Some airline pilots, because of Air Force pressure, are threatened by their companies.

Of several airline pilot UFO reports I have been involved with, only one crew reported their experience to the Air force. This particular report involved a spectacular *Type A* CE-III by a captain and copilot on February 14, 1973. Names have been changed to protect the witnesses' identities; the name of the airline must remain confidential.

Captain Jim Wheeler and copilot Jerry Maria were flying an unscheduled DC-8 charter cargo flight from St. Louis to Dallas. At about 2:30 A.M., the DC-8 was on a heading of 195 degrees about 40 miles east of McAlester, Oklahoma. Its airspeed was 510 mph and Captain Wheeler had just eased the big jet into a gradual descent from 21,000 feet. A near-full moon illuminated the sky about them.

Then Jerry pointed out the right cockpit window. There, just below the leading edge of their right wing, about 5,000 feet away, was what first appeared to be another commercial aircraft traveling on the same course and speed. Its steady amber lighting appeared unconventional, however. Suddenly, without warning, the craft rose straight up like an elevator! It performed a flat, right-angle turn directly toward the DC-8 and took up a position about 300 yards away, slightly above them.

The thing was disc shaped, with a central Plexiglas-like dome on top. Fearing a collision, the captain grabbed his mike and radioed the uninvited interloper to keep away. There was no answer. It just hung out there, paralleling their course.

Moonlight reflected off the unearthly oval object, making it appear like "a flounder lying on its side." About 75 feet long and 40 feet wide, it seemed to be constructed of a silvery, highly polished metal. The object was completely smooth, with no markings, wheel or maintenance hatches. Two very stubby finlike protrusions jutted out on each side, and two upright fins stood erect on either side of a rocketlike pod mounted on the object's trailing edge. Neither set of fins appeared to have moving parts such as ailerons. No glow or exhaust emanated from the pod.

The transparent dome crowning the top of the eerie object shimmered in the moonlight. "This thing just could not be," thought Captain Wheeler. He switched on the aircraft's weather radar system. A blip appeared on the edge of the phosphorescent scope. It really *was* there! As the radar waves hit its silvery surface, the flying nightmare reacted almost instantaneously, ascending straight up, retaining its forward speed, and then slid sideways 90 degrees, directly over the DC-8 and out of their sight. Both pilots glanced nervously about, wondering whether to report this bizarre incident to ground control. Perhaps it had gone away. It had not! They watched the flying nightmare descend straight down and take up a new position just below the leading edge of their left wing. Then it instantly dropped below and behind the jet airliner and out of sight again. Captain Wheeler gripped the controls to take evasive action, when the object abruptly appeared only 300 feet below them!

They looked down and into the dimly lit transparent dome on top of the UFO. Two, perhaps three shadowy entities could be seen moving within the hemispherical canopy. Then the alien vehicle suddenly moved out from under them and sped in front of the DC-8. They watched the object perform several smooth sine-wavelike up-and-down maneuvers before executing another right-angle turn, without curve radius, and speed away and out of sight.

The two pilots stared at the radarscope until the glowing blip disappeared off the screen at a distance of 50 miles. Approximately 18 minutes had elapsed since the intruder had first appeared. No electrical disturbances upon instruments were noted during that time. Captain Wheeler and copilot Maria realized that they should report their unbelievable encounter to ground control, so they attempted radio contact, but without success. Rather than try again, both agreed it might be best to keep the whole episode to themselves. But the experience weighed heavily upon their minds, so a month later they reported it to their supervisor, who in turn coordinated the report with the USAF. Soon after, both witnesses were questioned by Air Force Intelligence officers seriously interested in the sighting. Forms were filled out and signed.

Later more forms were filled out. Still later they were interviewed again. This time, however, USAF investigators seemed to deliberately attempt to persuade them that they hadn't really seen what had been originally described. Still later on, both were met at the airport by a government official (the witnesses will not identify the agency involved) who warned them not to talk further about the UFO sighting with anyone except authorized personnel. He stressed that even though the demand would not be put in writing, they must obey his order. Nonetheless, one pilot gave me a confidential report.

If the two pilots had followed the prescribed procedure of JANAP-146-E, their radio message would have been given high priority. Copies of the CIRVIS report would have been rapidly relayed to a very impressive distribution list, including the commanders of the Aerospace Defense Command and to the Air Force Chief of Staff. Why does the USAF disclaim interest in UFOs publicly, and yet show deadly covert interest?

The USAF is not acting unilaterally; it takes orders from the Joint Chiefs of Staff. Its intelligence activities are coordinated by high-level interests such as the National Security Council and the CIA, who are in turn controlled by the President of the United States. Because of its very makeup, however, the USAF must function as an integral, sometimes visible agency in collecting intelligence on unknown craft whose origin and purpose can only be speculated upon. To defend our country's airspace and to retaliate offensively in the event of enemy attack, the USAF employs the finest aircraft, missiles, and support systems in the world. Time and time again, however, these weapon systems have proved no match for UFOs. This is very serious business. The public at large who sight UFOs see only the tip of the problem.

Associate Len Stringfield once worked closely with the Air Defense Command, acting as civil defense coordinator between civilians reporting UFOs and fighter aircraft sent to intercept the objects. He has stated that during the 1950s General Benjamin Chidlaw, former head of U.S. continental air defense, admitted that "We have lost many men and planes trying to intercept them." One case that came to Len's attention involved an Air Force interceptor that the base operations vectored into the vicinity of UFOs recorded on radar. It literally fell out of the sky. I personally have talked with men involved both directly and indirectly with the loss of planes and/or men during UFO-intercept missions.

Retired Air Force Master Sergeant C.D., who was chief investigator of one of these bizarre events in June of 1953, waited twenty years before telling of the F-94C jet that attempted to intercept unknown objects near Otis AFB, Massachusetts, when they failed to respond to radar identification.

According to the pilot's sworn testimony . . . at an altitude of 1,500 feet over the Base Rifle Range, the engine quit functioning, and the entire electrical system failed. . . . The pilot yelled to the radar operator [over the battery-operated intercom] to bail out [and] jettisoned the canopy

because the aircraft . . . was seconds from impact. . . . He landed. . . . The crippled plane should have crashed . . . but it wasn't there. . . . The radar operator could not be found.

Sergeant C.D. stated that "this incident caused one of the most extensive and intensive searches I have ever seen . . . for three months. . . . The aircraft and the radar operator were never found." To add to the mystery, the jettisoned canopy *was* found within the confines of the rifle range. Other examples have been derived from confiscated memoranda and data released through the Freedom of Information Act during UFO researchers' ongoing lawsuits against the CIA. Names have been changed to protect the informants.

During the early spring of 1966, cold biting winds whipped around a low-lying building on the still-icy plains of Great Falls, Montana. The many identical structures protruding above the flatlands of Missouri, Montana, Wyoming, and the Dakotas are launch control support buildings—visible, above-ground evidence of America's deterrent to nuclear war.

Missile Combat Crew Commander Jack Davis and his fellow operator had routinely entered one of these buildings and had descended sixty feet into the underground launch control center, one of two heavily reinforced capsules that contain equipment necessary for the control of 10 missiles in separate underground launch facilities.

Upon relieving their counterparts, Jack and his seasoned associate sat down before the softly humming command and status consoles. This night, however, the usual monotony was shattered as abruptly, one by one, ten lights blinked on in perfect sequence across the status console. They indicated that a fault existed in *every one* of the 10 assigned missiles simultaneously!

Quickly the missile crew responded and electronically queried each launch facility to determine the seriousness of the situation. In each case, the answer that automatically flashed back on the status console indicated a no-go fault condition, signifying that not one of their assigned missiles could be launched. Nothing had ever happened like this before! Each fault was traced to the guidance and control system, the most sophisticated and *protected* component of the Minuteman missile! Hurried telephone communication revealed a frightening coincidence: Above-ground personnel had reported UFOs precisely during the failure of the ten missiles!

During the following spring of 1967, I received further data directly from acquaintances assigned to Minuteman bases. During the week of March 20, a full flight of ten missiles again became inoperative; radar confirmed a coincident UFO, and armed jet fighters attempted an intercept. Through my contacts, I was able to identify the exact flight of affected missiles. One of my acquaintances was a highly respected in-plant representative of the aerospace firm involved with Minuteman operations at Malmstrom AFB, where the incident had occurred. Not telling him what I knew, I asked him to phone his good friend, the assistant to the Air Force base manager, on behalf of his company, to ask what had gone wrong with those particular missiles.

When he did so, I watched his face go very grim. "Why did you ask me to do that?" he exclaimed when he hung up. "The reason for that flight going down is highly classified. I was told I shouldn't even be asking about it!"

When I grinned and told him what had happened, he said that the matter was a hot potato and that I had better drop any investigation completely. The Air Force was really uptight about such startling incidents.

Another civilian representative assigned to Grand Forks AFB, North Dakota, told me that an Air Force major friend of his got a good close look at a completely unconventional craft maneuvering in the area between the air base and missile site. As he got out of his car and approached it, it took off at tremendous speed. Superiors ordered him not to talk about the incident.

On March 5, 1967, just 15 days prior to the Malmstrom AFB incident, the 91st Strategic Missile Wing at a sister base also had an unwelcome visitor. Aerospace Defense Command radar tracked an unknown target descending over the Minuteman missile installations at Minot AFB, North Dakota. Strike teams were alerted and sighted a metallic disc-shaped craft ringed with bright flashing lights moving slowly over the supersensitive area.

Three armed teams in fast trucks pursued the alien vehicle as it maneuvered and finally stopped and hovered 500 feet off the ground. The strike teams held their fire. They had orders to capture it undamaged if it should land. Then abruptly it began moving once again and circling directly over a launch control facility. Back at Minot, F-106 fighter planes were awaiting orders from the North American Air Defense Command to launch an attack. Base operations became impatient and had just decided to scramble the jets without confirmation. Suddenly the UFO climbed straight up and streaked away at incredible speed.

A civilian employee at Malmstrom told me a bright, round, white object circled the missile site for prolonged periods on April 10 and 11, 1967. Apparently its altitude was beyond the operational capabilities of Air Force interceptors. Personnel who had sighted the strange object were told that it was a highly secret government test vehicle and not to be discussed. The local radio station was told to keep quiet about it.

Very rarely do such UFO sightings come to the attention of the general public. The following is one of these exceptions.

The leak came from personnel assigned to the U.S Army's Ballistic Missile Defense Systems Command in Huntsville, Alabama. *New York Times* science writer Barry J. Casebolt is to be credited for documenting this astounding incident. Dr. Hynek also informed me about the event. The following is excerpted from Casebolt's fine report published June 17, 1974, by *The New York Times*.

Last August [1973], the Air Force launched a Minuteman ICBM from

Vandenberg AFB . . . targeted for a point near . . . Kwajalein Missile Range. . . . The nosecone had separated from the third stage of the missile and it was coming in at about 22,000 feet-per-second. . . . At about 400,000 feet, radar picked up an inverted saucer-shaped object to the right and above the descending nosecone. . . . The object was described as being 10 feet high and about 40 feet long.

Army missile experts, who asked not to be identified, confided to Casebolt that *two* completely independent radar systems had simultaneously tracked the UFO. The object appeared (from photographs and other information, much of it classified) to have flown "under its own power." They assured him that the object was neither a natural phenomenon such as ionized particles, gases, or temperature inversion, nor was it pieces of the missile's stages. The Ballistic Missile Division community was at a complete loss to explain the object, which was tracked and photographed by precision instruments.

Casebolt then queried the Army's public-information office about the incident. Surprisingly, perhaps because of his excellent documentation of the incident, the Army office released the following statement to him:

Some unexplained aerial phenomena were observed by radar during a tracking mission at Kwajalein Missile Range last August . . . at an altitude of 400,000 feet and observed down to sea level where they disappeared. We can neither confirm nor deny the dimensions.

Amazingly enough, the Army spokesman also admitted that "Unexplained aerial phenomena *are not uncommon* [italics mine] in aerospace testing programs." Similar documented UFO-missile incidents date all the way back to 1948, when the United States first began flight tests of captured German V-2s at White Sands, New Mexico. During one launch, two small discs flew around the rapidly ascending V-2, maneuvering precisely in and out of its exhaust trail. Commander R. B. McLaughlin, U.S. Navy, made this report public and told the press and NICAP that he and his missile crew had made several good UFO sightings at the White Sands proving ground. In one particular case, on April 24, 1949, the UFO was tracked and photographed through a special telescope called a theodolite. Recorded data indicated that the object was about 40 feet wide and 100 feet long. It traveled over the missile range at an altitude of about 56 miles and at a speed of 7 miles per second!

I was able to gain firsthand information about an incident when UFOs interrupted a key missile test firing at Kwajalein Atoll, in August of 1974. A civilian meteorologist I'll call Jack, employed by the Air Force, was responsible for monitoring the weather in the missile's impact area prior to Minuteman's launch from Vandenberg. He sat scanning a radar screen that provided him 360-degree coverage of weather conditions around the atoll. This particular area was restricted; no known aircraft were in the area. As the launch countdown was nearing a close, Jack was about to pronounce the impact area satisfactory when suddenly a cluster of hard targets appeared on the radarscope! Quickly he tried using alternate frequencies to test for false targets. This made no difference: The targets remained.

When Jack reported the targets to mission control, he was informed that other radar systems were tracking the mysterious objects. Vandenberg was notified, and the missile countdown was put on hold until the objects left the impact area. It was feared that Kwajalein's automatic radar-controlled tracking devices would lock onto and track the UFOs, rather than the Minuteman. (This actually happened at Cape Canaveral when radar-controlled tracking equipment began tracking a UFO rather than a launched missile.)

During October and November 1975, several major Air Force bases were easily penetrated by UFOs. Through a leak by a Pentagon source, enough specific data was learned about the incidents to demand and receive *edited* government documents about them via the Freedom of Information Act. The reader will note the sometime use of the terms *unidentified, helicopters, aircraft,* and *targets* by the reporting Air Force bases. It's quite apparent that such terminology was the product of ignorance concerning the objects' identity. In reality, the USAF was dealing with the unknown! The following summaries are directly from the logs of NORAD which I have on file. (I have added local time in parentheses beside the military use of Zulu or international time. F-106s are high-performance interceptor aircraft. Italics are mine for emphasis.)

29 October/0630Z (1:30 A.M.): Command Director called by Air Force Operations Center concerning an *unknown helicopter* landing in the *munitions storage area* at Loring Air Force Base, Maine. Apparently this was the second night in a row for the occurrence. There was also an indication, but not confirmed, that Canadian bases had been overflown by a helicopter.

31 October/0445Z (11:45 P.M.): Report from Wurtsmith Air Force Base through Ops Center—incident at 0355Z (10:55 P.M.). *Helicopter* hovered over SAC *Weapons storage area,* then departed area. Tanker flying at 2,700 feet made both visual sighting and radar skin paint. Tracked *object* 35 nautical miles southeast over Lake Huron where contact was lost.

01 November/0920Z (4:20 A.M.): Received as info message from Loring Air Force Base, Maine, citing *probable helicopter* overflight of base.

08 November/0753Z (2:53 A.M.): 24th NORAD Region *unknown track* J330, heading SSW, 12,000 feet. 1 to 7 *objects,* 46.46N 109.23W. Two F-106 scrambled out of Great Falls at 0745Z (2:45 A.M.) SAC reported *visual* sighting from Sabotage Alert Teams (SAT) K1, K3, L1 and L6 (lights and jet sounds). Weather section states no anomalous propagation or northern lights. 0835Z (3:35 A.M.) SAC SAT Teams K3 and L4 report *target at 300 feet altitude* and L4 reports *target* at 5 miles. Contact lost at 0820Z

(3:20 A.M.) F-106s returned to base at 0850Z (3:50 A.M.) with negative results. 0905Z (4:05 A.M.) Great Falls radar search and height had intermittent contact. 0910Z (4:10 A.M.) SAC teams again had *visual* (Site C-1, 10 miles SE Stanford, Montana). 0920Z (4:20 A.M.) SAC CP reported that when F-106s were in area, *targets would turn out lights, and when F-106s left, targets would turn lights on.* . . . This same type of activity has been reported in the Malmstrom area for several days. . . . The track will be carried as a remaining *unknown*.

All of these Air Force bases belonged to the Strategic Air Command (SAC). The Malmstrom and Grand Forks bases house Minuteman missile sites. K1, K3, L1, etc., are missile locations. These visitations become more intriguing as we now turn to the 24th NORAD Region senior director's log (Malmstrom AFB, Montana).

07 November/1035Z (5:35 A.M.): Received a call from the 341st Strategic Air Command Post (SAC CP) saying that the following *missile locations* reported seeing *a large red to orange to yellow* object: M1, L-3, LIMA and L-6. The general object location would be 10 miles south of Moore, Montana, and 20 miles east of Buffalo, Montana. Commander and Deputy for Operations (DO) informed.

07 November/1203Z (7:03 A.M.): SAC advised that the Launch Control Facility at Harlowton, Montana, *observed an object* which emitted a light which illuminated the site driveway.

07 November/1319Z (8:19 A.M.): SAC advised K-1 says *very bright object* to their east is now southeast of them and they are looking at it with 10 x 50 binoculars. *Object* seems to have lights (several) on it, but no distinct pattern. The orange/gold object overhead also has small lights on it. SAC also advises female civilian reports having seen an object bearing south from her position six miles west of Lewistown.

07 November 1327Z (8:27 A.M.): L-1 reports that *the object to their northeast seems to be issuing a black object* from *it, tubular in shape.* In all this time, surveillance has not been able to detect any sort of track except for known traffic.

08 November/0635Z (1:35 A.M.): A security camper team at K-4 *reported UFO* with white lights, one red light 50 yards behind white light. Personnel at K-1 seeing same object.

08 November/0645Z (1:45 A.M.): Height personnel [i.e., radar] picked up *objects* 10–13,000 feet. . . . Objects as many as seven.

08 November/0753Z (2:53 A.M.): *Unknown* . . . Stationary/seven knots/12,000 . . . Two F-106 . . . notified.

08 November/0820Z (3:20 A.M.): Lost radar contact, fighters broken off.

08 November/0905Z (4:05 A.M.): L-sites had fighters and *objects* (in view); fighters did not get down to *objects*.

08 November/0915Z (4:15 A.M.): From SAC Command Post: *From four different points: Observed objects and fighters;* When fighters arrived in the area, the lights went out; when fighters departed, the lights came back on.

09 November/0305Z (10:05 P.M.): SAC Command Post called and advised SAC crews at Sites L-1, L-6 and M-1 *observing UFO.* Object yellowish bright round light 20 miles north of Harlowton, 2 to 4000 feet.

09 November/0348Z (10:48 A.M.): SAC Command Post confirms L-1, sees *object*, a mobile security team has been directed to get closer and report.

10 November/1125Z (6:25 P.M.): *UFO* sighting reported by Minot Air Force Station . . . moving east, about the size of a car . . . the *object* passed over the radar station, 1,000 feet to 2,000 feet high, no noise heard. Three people from the site or local area saw the *object*.

The above excerpts from official Air Force logs make a mockery of our government's insistence that UFOs do not exist! The Air Force also refused to declassify some of the documents requested, saying that the contents of such were "exempt from disclosure" under the FOIA. What else happened at these SAC bases on those eventful nights?

Canadian Air Force bases were also experiencing intrusions by UFOs. On November 11, 1975, for example, the Falconbridge radar station near Sudbury, Ontario, sighted UFOs visually and on radar. Other witnesses included civilians and a local policeman. A formerly classified report from NORAD in my files describes the incident:

Falconbridge reported search and height finder paints on an object 25 to 20 nautical miles south of the site ranging in altitude from 26,000 feet to 72,000 feet. The site commander and other personnel say the object appeared as a bright star but much closer.

With binoculars, the object appeared as a 100-ft. diameter sphere and appeared to have craters around the outside. Be assured that this command is doing everything possible to identify and provide solid factual information on these sightings.

I have also expressed my concern to SAFOI (Air Force Public Information) that we come up soon with a proposed answer to queries from the press to prevent overreaction by the public to reports by the media that may be blown out of proportion. To date, efforts by Air Guard helicopters, SAC helicopters and NORAD F-106's have failed to produce positive identification.

And what did SAFOI propose? Thanks to the Freedom of Information Act, we have the following memorandum to base commanders:

We believe . . . that unless there is evidence which links sightings or unless media queries link sightings, queries can be best handled *individually* at the source and as questions arise. Responses should ... emphasize that the action taken was in response to an *isolated* or specific incident.... Information Officers should keep all levels and appropriate MAJCOMS informed of questions asked, media affiliations and responses given.

Particular concern was shown that the incidents be treated as *local* occurrences. Officialdom did not want the public to know that UFOs were violating SAC bases at many different locations on the same nights—and that the objects easily eluded a variety of aircraft sent to pursue them. The *Bangor Daily News* joked that *Hogan's Heroes,* of TV fame, could have identified the intruder by turning on a searchlight! The wing commander at Loring Air Force Base retorted that his men were just as prepared as Hogan's Heroes would have been. Colonel Robert E. Chapman said that Loring's searchlights were "manned and ready to go" but were not turned on because they did not want to "blind" the pilot of the unidentified *helicopter* and jeopardize his safety. I hope the good Colonel is not as kind to the pilots of enemy aircraft! The best efforts of the United States and Canadian Air Forces, the Air National Guard, and the Maine State Police to capture the *helicopter* were all in vain.

Data in my files indicate that other countries are experiencing the same kind of events. A Belgian Army officer reported the following incident to U.S. UFO researcher, Major (Ret.) Colman VonKeviczky.

One of our NATO missile bases in the Mediterranean had a regular fire duel with a UFO hovering stationary far above sea level. The base observed that the missiles, once launched toward certain coordinates, were instantly annihilated; in fact, by repeating launching coordinates in the same direction, it appeared as if the missiles were hitting an invisible barrier in the sky. When we later developed film from the movie camera trajectory control, we found a distinct disc shaped object with a dome at its top hovering near the path of the missiles. As soon as the missiles drew near, a laserlike ray shot out of the craft and literally disintegrated the missiles. Incidentally, a control launch to the inverted direction (110 degrees) was unharmed.

The missile launches were part of a routine series of tests over a NATO base near Italy. The film was sent to Brussels and was also to be sent to the United States for computer evaluation.

In Iran, a UFO displayed complete control over the weapons systems of the modern jet fighter that attempted to shoot it down. I quote directly from the classified message sent from Iran to our government, recently declassified through the Freedom of Information Act. The incident is one of the most spectacular on record.

A. At about 1230 AM on 19 September 1976, the Imperial Iranian Air Force [IIAF] Command Post received four telephone calls from citizens living in the Shemiran area of Tehran saying that they had seen strange objects in the sky. Some reported kind of a bird-like object while others reported a helicopter with a light on. There were no helicopters airborne at that time. The Command Post called BG Yousefi, Assistant Deputy Commander of Operations. After he told the citizen it was only stars and had talked to Mehrabad tower, he decided to look for himself. He noticed an object in the sky similar to a star, bigger and brighter. He decided to scramble an F-4 [jet fighter] from Shahrokhi Air Force Base to investigate.

B. At 0130 hrs on the 19th, the F-4 tok off and proceeded to a point about 40 nautical miles north of Tehran. Due to its brilliance, the object was easily visible from 70 miles away. As the F-4 approached a range of 25 nautical miles, he lost all instrumentation and communications [UHF and Intercom]. He broke off the intercept and headed back to Shahrokhi. When the F-4 turned away from the object and apparently was no longer a threat to it, the aircraft regained all instrumentation and communications. At 0140 hrs, a second F-4 was launched. The backseater [radar operator] acquired a radar lock on at 27 nautical miles, 12 o'clock high position, with the VC [rate of closure] at 150 nautical miles-per-hour. As the range decreased to 25 nautical miles, the object moved away at a speed that was visible on the radar scope and stayed at 25 nautical miles.

C. The size of the radar return was comparable to that of a 707 tanker. The visual size of the object was difficult to discern because of its intense brilliance. The light that it gave off was that of flashing strobe lights arranged in a rectangular pattern and alternating blue, green, red and orange in color. The sequence of the lights was so fast that all the colors could be seen at once. The object and the pursuing F-4 continued on a course to the south of Tehran when another brightly-lighted object, estimated to be one half to one third the apparent size of the moon, came out of the original object. This second object headed straight toward the F-4 at a very fast rate of speed. *The pilot attempted to fire an AIM-9 Missile at the object but at that instant his weapons control panel went off* and he lost all communications [UHF and Interphone]. At this point, the pilot initiated a turn and negative G dive to get away. As he turned, the object fell in trail at what appeared to be about 3–4 nautical miles. As he continued in his turn away from the primary object, the second object went to the inside of his turn then returned to the primary object for a perfect rejoin.

D. Shortly after the second object joined up with the primary object, another object appeared to come out of the other side of the primary object going straight down at a great rate of speed. The F-4 crew had regained communication and the weapons control panel and watched the object approach the ground anticipating a large explosion. This object appeared to come to rest gently on the earth and cast a very bright light over an area of about 2–3 kilometers.

The crew descended from their altitude of 26M to 15M and continued to observe and mark the object's position. They had some difficulty in adjusting their night visibility for landing so after orbiting Mehrabad a few times, they went out for a straight in landing. There was a lot of interference on the UHF and each time they passed through a magnetic bearing of 150 degrees from Mehrabad, they lost their communications [UHF and interphone] and the INS fluctuated from 30 degrees–50 degrees.

The one civil airliner that was approaching Mehrabad during this time experienced communications failure in the same vicinity (KILO ZULU) but did not report seeing anything. While the F-4 was on a long final approach, the crew noticed another cylinder-shaped object (about the size of a T-bird at 10M) with bright steady lights on each end and a flasher in the middle. When queried, the tower stated there was no other known traffic in the area. During the time that the object passed over the F-4, the tower did not have a visual on it but picked it up after the pilot told them to look between the mountains and the refinery.

E. During daylight, the F-4 crew was taken out to the area in a helicopter where the object apparently had landed. Nothing was noticed at the spot where they thought the object landed (a dry lake bed) but as they circled off to the west of the area, they picked up a very noticeable beeper signal. At the point where the return was the loudest was a small house with a garden. They landed and asked the people within if they had noticed anything strange last night. The people talked about a loud noise and a very bright light like lightning. The aircraft and area where the object is believed to have landed are being checked for possible radiation. ... More information will be forwarded when it becomes available.[1]

This formerly classified teletype message was sent by Frank B. McKenzie, Colonel, USAF, to a number of highly placed individuals and organizations in the United States, including the White House, Secretary of Defense, CIA, and National Security Agency.

If Russian aircraft had performed such acts over *our* airspace, it could lead to a nuclear war. No wonder that significant UFO reports are classified and handled at the highest government levels. Additional information leaks amply demonstrate to me that our relatively young civilization is utterly defenseless against UFOs. One recent input, for example, demonstrates that UFO occupants must have an intimate knowledge of our technology.

An active Air Force colonel in SAC *knows* that UFOs have landed within remote Minuteman sites. Their presence has set off both outside and inside security alarms. When responding strike teams arrived at a given unmanned launch facility, they found that entry hatches to the deployed

Minuteman missiles had been entered! Even more disturbing, the huge, heavy steel hatches *had not been forced open*. Whoever or whatever entered was able to open a number of heavy secured doors, each of which had an individual classified combination to its lock!

No major military power could afford to admit that superior machines of unknown origin and purpose are flagrantly violating our planet's airspace. And remember that no one—I repeat, no one—knows *for sure* what their purpose is! Our government would not intentionally expose its people to uncontrollable social and political repercussions. Rather, it would initiate a top-priority effort to understand all aspects of the UFOs *and* achieve a similar space-travel capability. All hard scientific and technical UFO data would be classified and jealously guarded from foreign countries—especially potential enemies. Let's face it, the same security regulations and secrecy apply to *known* threats such as the intrusion of our country's airspace by Russian aircraft. Government secrecy on UFOs should not be compared with the Watergate cover-up; it has to do with legitimate, vital intelligence.

What kind of a defense have we against such things? Some might take consolation in those reports indicating that UFOs are not infallible. Their machines reportedly crash; their occupants die.

CHAPTER NOTES

1 Copy in personal files.

"RETRIEVALS OF THE THIRD KIND"

Not only did Frank Scully's book, published in 1950, strongly influence the contactee movement, but it also spawned the rumor of crashed UFOs and dead occupants. Later, *True* and the *Saturday Review* exposed the book's contents as a hoax played upon Scully by Newton. A few years later, the latter was charged with fraud for peddling a $4.50 piece of war surplus equipment as an oil detector for the price of $800,000.[1]

Tales of government retrieved UFOs and dead occupants persist to this day. Short of official admission, it's obviously impossible to prove such reports, but some of these rumors are highly placed. Several years ago, when appearing on the *Merv Griffin Show,* astronaut Gordon Cooper said he had heard the government was actually able to keep a few UFO occupant crash victims alive for several days!

I have personally investigated several interesting reports of this category. On Wednesday evening, March 6, 1968, while lecturing at the First Congregational Church in Braintree, Massachusetts, I briefly alluded to some retrieved fragments from a UFO crash at Ubatuba, São Paulo, Brazil, in September 1957. APRO was one of several organizations that had the material analyzed. The fragments were magnesium of an extremely high purity. A high content of strontium was particularly interesting, as were other features not associated with usual earthly production methods.

Just before I left, the minister, Dr. David E. Moore, told me that he and a very good friend had served together in Naval Intelligence. His friend, a lieutenant, told Moore that while on assignment in Mexico he had received an urgent message concerning the crash of a strange vehicle outside of Mexico City. When he arrived, the crash area had been roped off, and personnel were loading remains of an oval object and its occupants into trucks. He described the material being collected as looking like magnesium. As he drove up to the cordoned-off area, he was waved away. When he remained and tried to ask some questions a superior officer walked over, ordered him out of the area, and told him not to mention what he had witnessed to anyone.

I obtained the lieutenant's name and last known address, and finally traced him to Portland, Maine. I phoned him, used Dr. Moore as my reference, and identified myself as an early-warning coordinator for the USAF-sponsored University of Colorado UFO Study. He did confirm that he had known Dr. Moore. When I brought up the UFO incident, however, he was very quick to deny ever having been involved, and stated that they had probably talked about something that appeared in the newspapers. When I told him that Dr. Moore said he had actually described UFO fragments, he replied that he had probably told him about sketches in a newspaper account. He did state that he wished he could help me, but couldn't. He was in a big hurry to terminate the call, so I thanked him for his time and reluctantly hung up.

I then immediately placed a call to the minister and asked him to repeat the facts about the incident. He again told me exactly what his friend had told him. I then explained what the former Navy lieutenant had just said. Dr. Moore insisted that he remembered the details of his conversations with the lieutenant very well because of his great interest in this extraordinary event. He seriously doubted that his friend had concocted the story and felt that the retired intelligence officer did not want to become involved, since the lieutenant was receiving a Navy pension. My own feeling was that the incident was highly sensitive and that the lieutenant was bound to secrecy.

In 1967 one of our investigators, Nathan Gold, a senior scientist with a major company, told me how at a father-son Cub Scout banquet, a Mr. Bill Marsden had told Nat that back in the early 1950s both he and his wife had seen what appeared to be a crashed flying saucer.

When I asked Nathan to investigate this matter, he found that both Mr. and Mrs. Marsden were well educated and held a degree in law from the University of Breslav in Germany; she also had served in the German army. Mr. Marsden held a degree in physics and was manager of information services at a major electronics company. A check of their personal records indicated that the incident had occurred sometime between October 1953 and May 1954 at Mattydale, New York, a suburb of Syracuse. The following are excerpts from a written and taped interview with the Marsdens.

About 3 A.M. on a Sunday morning, my wife and I were returning home by car from visiting friends. We had not been drinking. As I crossed the thruway towards the airport [Hancock Field] going uphill, I noticed flashing red lights at the intersection. There seemed to be at least four or five police cars. I thought there was an accident and slowed to avoid trouble, but there was no accident I could see. After turning left to Mattydale, I looked over my right shoulder and saw an object that appeared to be 20 feet in diameter and possibly 15 feet high at the center; phosphorescent lights of several colors were spaced over the surface. The light from these light sources was strong enough to [illumine] quite a few men walking around the object and examining it. Some were uniformed, some not. One had what appeared to be a large press camera with a strap and was taking pictures. My wife remarked that it must be the Canadian AVRO disc that she had read about.

On Monday morning, I didn't find any news on it, so I called the city editor. He said he didn't know anything about it but would send a man to the sheriff's office to find out. I decided to call the sheriff myself and described the scene to the officer who answered. "Yes," he said, "we know about that, but it's a military secret and we cannot discuss it." I hung up and called the editor back. When I told him what the police officer said, he was very interested and said he'd look into it immediately.

On the way home from work, I purposely went by the area to examine the field. The weeds were freshly trampled down around a light ravine. The walls of this ravine were packed down in two spots where the object had apparently rested. Tire tracks indicated that a vehicle had entered the area from one street and left toward the other.

Both the police and the Air Force at Hancock Field told the city editor that no such incident had occurred. The sheriff also denied that anyone in his department had told Mr. Marsden that the incident was a military secret. Not wanting to be branded as some kind of a nut, Mr. Marsden dropped the whole matter.

I sent Nathan's report to NICAP. Local investigators attempted to locate the sheriff for questioning. Unfortunately the sheriff had since died, so I made a personal effort to locate men who had served on the Syracuse police force in 1953. I finally located several including the deputy sheriff, who had resigned from law-enforcement and was selling real estate. He denied any knowledge of the episode, but was very curious as to why I was inquiring about something that had occurred so long ago.

Only two men currently working for the Syracuse police force remembered incidents similar to Bill Marsden's report. A former dispatcher told me that he remembered a weather balloon falling to earth, a wing tank falling off a plane, and an aircraft crashing in the woods, all within the general time frame of the alleged UFO crash. A police captain said that when he joined the department back in 1957 there was talk about a so-called bomb report. Apparently some citizen had reported a bomb lying in a field in the vicinity of the Marsden sighting area. Police officers were dispatched and radioed back that the object certainly did not look like a bomb. The Air Force was contacted at Hancock Field. Investigating officers arrived on the scene, told the police it was a dummy bomb that had accidentally dropped from an aircraft approaching Hancock Field, and said that they would take care of it.

After my probe, I contacted Mr. Marsden again. Since I had just restudied his report in detail, I was impressed with the matter-of-fact description he gave of the event. Then I suggested he might have seen a balloon, wing tank, or bomb reflecting the police cruiser's flashing lights. He merely replied that this theory didn't explain why the object he and his wife had seen stood *much higher* than the men who encircled it. In addition, he stressed that the craft, carrying *individual* multicolor lights, was shaped like a bowl inverted upon a bowl, and there was a clearly defined edge where the rims of the bowllike segments touched.

In 1973 I came even closer to documenting the reality of crashed UFOs, with a signed affidavit from an alleged member of the USAF investigating team! He must remain anonymous; I've dubbed him Fritz Werner.

I, Fritz Werner, do solemnly swear that during a special assignment with the U. S. Air Force, on May 21, 1953, I assisted in the investigation of a crashed unknown object in the vicinity of Kingman, Arizona.

The object was constructed of an unfamiliar metal which resembled brushed aluminum. It had impacted twenty inches into the sand without any sign of structural damage. It was oval and about 30 feet in diameter. An entranceway hatch had been vertically lowered and opened. It was about 3½ feet high and 1½ feet wide. I was able to talk briefly with someone on the team who did look inside only briefly. He saw two swivel seats, an oval cabin, and a lot of instruments and displays.

A tent pitched near the object sheltered the dead remains of the only occupant of the craft. It was about 4 feet tall, dark brown complexion and had 2 eyes, 2 nostrils, 2 ears, and a small round mouth. It was clothed in a silvery, metallic suit and wore a skull cap of the same type material. It wore no face covering or helmet.

I certify that the above statement is true by affixing my signature to this document this day of June 7, 1973.

> Signature: Fritz Werner
> Date Signed: June 7, 1973
> Witnessed By: Raymond E. Fowler
> Date Signed: June 7, 1973

I watched as Mr. Werner carefully read and signed the final piece of documentation to a 65-page report I had prepared for NICAP. My attempts to substantiate Fritz Werner's incredible story had put me in contact with the AEC, Stanford Research Institute, Wright-Patterson AFB, former Project Bluebook personnel, and a number of persons within the military-industrial complex. Although no additional witnesses could be found, the peripheral names, positions, tests, dates, and places mentioned within Mr. Werner's personal account all check out exceptionally well.

Mr. Werner had kept his bizarre experience a closely guarded secret for almost exactly twenty years. If true, his story indicates that the physical recovery of manned UFOs had been kept secret for over two decades.

Between June 1949 and January 1960 Fritz held several engineering and management positions at Wright-Patterson AFB near Dayton, Ohio. During the period in which the incident took place, he worked within what was known as the Air Material Command Installations Division, within the Office of Special Studies headed by Dr. Eric Wang. His specialties at that particular time included the engineering design of Air Force engine test cells, development techniques for determining blast effects on buildings and structures, and the designing of aircraft landing gear. Fritz worked his way up to become chief of alighting devices within the aircraft laboratory, Wright Air Development Center; which position led him up to management positions at Wright-Patterson, and later at a variety of civilian companies involved with defense contracts. At the time of his reported experience, he was on special assignment to the AEC at the atomic proving ground in Nevada.

I was project engineer on an Air Force contract with the Atomic Energy Commission for "Operation Upshot-Knothole." My job involved the measuring of blast effects on various types of buildings especially erected for the tests.

On May 20, 1953, I worked most of the day at Frenchman Flat. In the evening, I received a phone call from the test director, Dr. Ed Doll, informing me that I was to go on a special job the next day. On the following day, around 4:30 P.M., I reported for special duty and was driven to Indian Springs Air Force Base near the proving ground where I joined about fifteen other specialists.

We were told to leave all valuables in the custody of the military police. I gave them my wallet, watch, pen and other things I don't remember. We were then put on a military airplane and flown to Phoenix. We were not allowed to fraternize.

There, we were put on a bus with other personnel who were already there. The bus windows were all blacked out, so that we couldn't see where we were going. We rode for an estimated four hours. I think we were in the area of Kingman, Arizona, which is northwest of Phoenix and not too far from the Atomic Proving Ground in Nevada. During the bus trip, we were told by an Air Force full-Colonel, that a super-secret

Air Force Vehicle had crashed and that since we were all specialists in certain fields, we were to investigate the crash in terms of our own specialty and nothing more.

Finally, the bus stopped and we disembarked one at a time as our names were called, and escorted by military police to the area that we were to inspect. Two spotlights were centered on the crashed object, which was ringed with guards. The lights were so bright that it was impossible to see the surrounding area. The object was oval and looked like two deep saucers, one inverted upon the other. It was about thirty feet in diameter with convex surfaces, top and bottom. These surfaces were about twenty feet in diameter. Part of the object had sunk into the ground. It was constructed of a dull silver metal like brushed aluminum. The metal was darker where the saucer "lips" formed a rim, around which were what looked like slots. A curved open hatch door was located on the leading end and was vertically lowered. There was a light coming from inside, but it could have been installed by the Air Force.

My particular job was to determine from the angle and the depth of impact into the sand, how fast the vehicle's forward and vertical velocities were at the time of impact. The impact had forced the vehicle approximately twenty inches into the sand. There were no landing gear. There also were no marks or dents, that I can remember, on the surface—not even scratches. Questions asked, having nothing to do with our own special areas, were not answered.

An armed military policeman guarded a tent pitched nearby. I managed to glance inside at one point and saw the dead body of a four-foot human-like creature in a silver metallic-looking suit. The skin on its face was dark brown. This may have been caused by exposure to our atmosphere. It had a metallic skullcap device on its head.

As soon as each person finished his task, he was interviewed over a tape recorder and escorted back to the bus. On the way, I managed to talk briefly with someone else who told me that he had glanced inside the object and saw two swivel-like seats as well as instruments and displays. An airman, noticing us talking together, separated us and warned us not to talk with each other.

After we all returned to the bus, the Air Force Colonel in charge had us raise our right hands and take an oath not to reveal what we had experienced. I was instructed to write my report in longhand and not to type or reproduce it. A telephone number was given me to call when the report was complete. I called the number and an airman picked up the report. I had never met nor talked with any of the investigating party. They were not known to me, although I think I recognized two officers' faces. One was from Griffiss Air Force Base at Rome, New York, and the other was involved with an Air Force Special Weapons Group based at Albuquerque. I later saw and recognized the Colonel-in-charge in a movie concerning Project Bluebook.

Mr. Werner confided that a year after his experience he was assigned to serve Bluebook as a official consultant. He sympathized with the Air Force's secret handling of the UFO problem: It did not have an answer regarding where UFOs originated. He felt that they probably still don't know. He said, however, that the Air Force did believe that UFOs were interplanetary vehicles and did not want to create national panic. In response to my questions relating to UFO propulsion systems, he said:

Well, we all had our guesses as to what it was. At the time, I happened to have contact with a professor in Germany from a very famous university. The Air Force had a contract with them to study antigravity. We didn't call it that exactly, but that's what the popular term was in which you would use the earth's magnetic fields as a form of propulsion. They were able to—with a lot of power, by the way—produce an antigravity machine. It was very impractical and as far as I know, still is impractical, but someday it will be perfected.

Fritz Werner's credentials are impressive. I checked out his professional resumé by calling former employers during a careful character check. Neither of the two former Bluebook officials that I talked with would confirm the incident. One asked, "Where is the object now?" The other got very nervous when I mentioned Dr. Eric Wang's Office of Special Studies. He asked me to leave him alone, as he wanted to live out his life in privacy.

The AEC in Washington and in Nevada both confirmed the dates and names of the tests that Fritz mentioned. They also confirmed the name of the test director, Dr. Ed Doll, and the chief of the Office of Special Studies as the technical and scientific monitor for the project. Further investigation revealed that Dr. Wang had died. I did manage to track Dr. Doll to Stanford Research Institute, but their personnel department did not know his whereabouts. They felt he had died.

Through correspondence with the Mohave County historian I found that Kingman was an unlikely place for the incident to have occurred. A four-hour drive at night in a bus with blacked-out windows could have conveyed the investigating team to any number of places. The historian felt that the vast range controlled by Luke AFB, southwest of Phoenix, was a more likely spot for the crash site. He stated that it is a real desert area with packed sand just as Fritz Werner described.

There were some inconsistencies associated with Fritz's story, but most appeared to be memory lapses. Former employers and professional acquaintances held Mr. Werner in high esteem. Everyone described him as a highly competent, technical, and moral individual. I found that he holds two bachelor's degrees, in mathematics and physics, and a master's degree in engineering. He is also a member of a number of professional organizations such as the American Association for the Advancement of Science, and is involved in a variety of civic groups. The only out-of-the-ordinary activities in his personal record are a keen interest in parapsychology, and past involvement—with other professional people—in psychic experiments. In my final report, I discussed the possible explanations of his account. There seemed to be no motive for a hoax, and no apparent evidence for a psychosis. His associates felt strongly that he was not the type to perpetrate practical jokes.

To pin down the exact date of the crash, Fritz mentioned that he may have written something in his diary at that time. After a search, he found the penciled diary that he kept meticulously in those days. When I examined its pages, there was no doubt as to its authenticity. The obviously aged page for May 20, 1953, read:

Spent most of the day on Frenchman's Flat surveying cubicles and supervising welding of plate girder bridge sensor which cracked after last shot. Drank brew in eve. Read. Got funny call from Dr. Doll about 1000. I'm to go on a special job tomorrow.

My eyes then skipped over to the entry on May 21.

Up at 7:00. Worked most of day on Frenchman with cubicles. Letter from Bet. She's feeling better now—thank goodness. *Got picked up at Indian Springs AFB for a job I can't write or talk about.* [italics mine]

Tantalizing as the Werner story might be, we still have no proof that such incidents have occurred. (How many would believe the government were it to state that studies had been made of crashed UFO vehicles and occupants? Some still believe our manned trips to the moon were simulated in Hollywood studios.) But in early 1977 one UFO nearly did crash in my relative backyard—less than 100 miles away.

I hastily plugged in my tape recorder to monitor the 6:30 A.M. newscast datelined Thursday, January 13, 1977. Three days earlier,

An object [had fallen] from the sky . . . but at the moment, no one is talking. Something with a highly unusual amount of radiation plunged into a small pond. The National Guard is going to start draining the . . . pond this morning. . . . The federal government is going to be there. . . . The townspeople say they've been told to be quiet.

Phone calls to state and federal authorities were met with a curt "No comment." My assigned investigator was handicapped by threats to arrest trespassers at the crash site. Nonetheless, in several days he was on-site conducting an inquiry. The following is a classic example of how officials react when suddenly confronted with a crashed, highly radioactive unidentified object.

Monday, January 10, 1977, blizzard conditions prevailed in the remote New Hampshire village of Wakefield, population 1,400. At noon the thermometer read 5 degrees F. William McCarthy stood idly looking out the window at the persistent snow blanketing his horse farm. Glancing toward his 105- by 75-foot farm pond, he saw what appeared to be a hole in the ice. Finding this hard to believe—just yesterday his horses had frolicked over its frozen surface—he flung on a coat and trudged down for a closer look. Astonished, he found a perfectly round hole whose smooth, sheer sides extended straight down through fourteen inches of solid ice! There were no signs of cutting or fracture. An eight-inch collar of slush around its perimeter gave the impression that something had melted its way through.

Cautiously he peered down into the hole, through several feet of crystal-clear water, and sighted a twelve-inch-square box on the pond's bottom! He looked long and hard. It was not an illusion. He quickly ran back to the house to get members of the family to come down and see it. Then he struggled through the snow to the barn for a rake, a hoe, and a pole to retrieve the strange artifact. Hurrying back to the pond, he poked at where the box had been. Now there was a dark square hole that extended 3 feet downward. McCarthy poked the pole into the pond's hard-packed bottom to mark the spot.

Puzzled and excited, the family summoned longtime friend Bob Palmer to examine the mysterious hole. Bob arrived around 2:30 P.M. He felt that the situation might be dangerous and phoned the police, who soon arrived with the local Civil Defense radiological monitor. His Geiger counter registered a frightening 3 roentgens per hour! Normal background radiation for that area was only rated at thousandths of a roentgen per hour. The radiological monitor warned the McCarthy family to stay away from the pond; the officials sped off to report their startling findings to superior officers.

Within a half hour the police phoned and arranged for a follow-up radiation check by State Deputy Civil Defense Director Wesley Williams. In the meantime, long fingers of slush began to creep outward from the melted hole. By 4:00 P.M. a 10-foot circle of slush encompassed the original opening!

Strangely enough, no one arrived to perform the follow-up check that afternoon or evening. The confused McCarthy family finally gave up waiting and went to bed. At 2:00 A.M. the family's dog began barking frantically. William wearily got out of bed and glanced outside. There was Deputy CD Director Williams and two other unknown men down at the pond. They had brought two Geiger counters. When the first one was turned on, it malfunctioned with a loud ping. It may have been set for a lower reading and the needle may have gone wildly off scale. Undaunted, Williams secured the second instrument, whose needle read 2 to 3 roentgens per hour of gamma radiation. This was alarming, as was the fact that the pond's entire surface had melted. The water on the ice was so deep that he could only get within 10 feet of the hole marked by McCarthy's pole. The Geiger counter continued to give a high reading for the whole general area around the pond. Greatly concerned, the party left to file a report with the New Hampshire Civil Defense Director, George McAvoy, who in turn issued an urgent communication to Governor Meldrim Thomson, Jr.

McCarthy got up the next morning and went outside to look at the pond. In spite of a near-zero temperature, the top of the entire pond had melted. And about fifty feet from the original hole was another opening. It appeared as if something else had entered the pond—or the initial object had *left* the pond! Shortly afterward a representative of the attorney general's office arrived and officially warned them not to let the horses or dog drink from the pond. He came back later in the day and showed great concern that some water might be seeping out. He also ordered them to keep the incident secret because an official inquiry was in process.

On the following day, Wednesday, the pond froze over again. Disregarding the order to keep away from the pond, McCarthy walked out on the ice to the now-rigid outline where the hole had been. The ice was so clear that he could see the bottom of the pond. He was amazed to see what appeared to be a freshly cut, six-inch-wide trench on the pond bottom connecting the square hole to where the second hole was! One might theorize that the object descended several feet into the bottom of the pond, and then burrowed along the bottom before leaving through the second hole.

The attorney general's office called McCarthy to say that a trained team of investigators would arrive on the following morning to retrieve any object that might be in the pond. In the meantime, the police department had proclaimed the area off limits and warned the townspeople not to talk about the incident to anyone.

Early Thursday morning a veritable army of news-media people, curiosity seekers, and officials arrived. The state police escorted all but official investigators off the property. Sensitive radiological monitoring equipment was set up. Futile attempts were made to drain the pond. As an alternative measure, a 6- by 3-foot hole was sawed in the ice where the original hole had been. Distant onlookers, including neighbors and reporters, stated that they saw a black *thing* placed in a van that abruptly left the area. The official team of investigators packed up their equipment quickly and followed suit. Within the hour a statement was released from the governor's office that read in part:

The entire report is false.... [It] was caused by false preliminary instrument readings. ... More sophisticated readings revealed negative findings.... There was no object.... [It] was ... shadows of cracked ice.[2]

Both local and state officials were well aware that there had been no cracks in the ice. When queried, the adjutant general's office explained to us that a plastic bag seen being carried away from the pond contained instruments. On the other hand, the governor's office told us that the bag contained water and sediment samples. To further compound the mystery, officials denied that any foreign object had been removed from the pond—in spite of the fact that it was seen by responsible persons. Hank Nichols, a reporter for the *New Hampshire Times,* stated that:

All attention was focused on the plastic bag of mud—well, almost all attention. Some students from nearby Brewster Academy had come over to the farm, and, after being shooed away from the pond by the police, had ended up down the road from the house. Looking out at the pond across the field near where the road into the pond had been plowed, they saw and photographed two men walking away from the pond toward a parked car. The photograph shows the first man carrying a long pole which McCarthy says is a long-handled fish net. It could be. The second man is slightly hunched over, carrying a small but apparently heavy object. McCarthy estimates it weighed 40 to 50 pounds.[3]

Mrs. McCarthy said that a second plastic bag was also taken into a *federal* vehicle.

Later, after my investigator finally began his inquiry without police interference, I phoned Civil Defense Director George McAvoy. He offered no concrete explanation for the initial high radiation readings and tried to explain them away as peculiar "electrostatic conditions" generated by the snowstorm! Pressed further, however, he admitted to me that the Geiger counter used by his deputy was in good condition. He said that it had been tested afterwards at a state laboratory in Concord, New Hampshire, at zero temperatures, but nothing was found to be wrong with it. He also told me that the state of New Hampshire had sent the instrument to Washington, D.C., for further testing. McAvoy was very careful to come to the defense of the McCarthy family, and said, "It's not a hoax. There was some phenomenon."

Physicist Bill Morrison of Brewster Academy, Wolfboro, New Hampshire, sent me a signed statement that he had taken Geiger counter readings of pond sediment shortly after the official investigators had left the scene. His instrument registered .05 to 1.5 milliroentgens, considerably higher than normal background radiation of .02 milliroentgens per hour.

What about the melted ice? One person suggested that the farmer had placed a heated cylinder block on the ice to perpetrate a hoax. Some guessed that a snowmobile had fallen through; others said that fishermen had cut the hole. A state official proposed that perhaps "water currents from springs" were the cause. McCarthy retorted that he had had the pond dug by a backhoe himself. There were no springs, no fish, and the pond was fed exclusively by runoff water from rain and melting snow. McCarthy added that his pond dries up completely in the summer. *He* had no trouble understanding what had happened: An object landed on his pond, melted down through the ice, and ended up on the bottom.

About a week and a half after the hole had appeared in the pond, one of McCarthy's dogs vomited and began to pine away. This particular animal had gone outside at 7:00 A.M. on the day the hole was discovered. (The second dog stayed inside, as it did not want to go outside in the stormy weather.) McCarthy took it to a local veterinarian, who operated on the dog in an attempt to relieve its pain. McCarthy said, "The [internal] organs were a mess—he'd never seen anything like it." The symptoms were those of arsenic or strychnine poisoning, yet there were no traces of these poisons found in the dog's body. The symptoms also fit those of radiation poisoning! Interestingly enough, later on, when spring arrived, a maple tree near the pond also died; it was the tree closest to the spot where the hole had appeared in the ice.

Reporter Hank Nichols learned that several months after the incident the McCarthys had traveled to Massachusetts to buy a horse. When the horse's seller discovered who this family was, he told them that he had watched the news coverage of the event on television and seen one of his relatives among the investigating officials. He was surprised because this particular relative was working for a West German research company at the time, and never mentioned that he had been back in the States on that day. Also, when a friend's relative who worked in the New Hampshire state laboratory at Concord asked about the mud samples taken from the pond, he was told, "The less you know about it, the better." I was told by an anonymous source that the strange object had been whisked to Pease AFB and flown to an unknown destination. The route over which it was carried was monitored by a special instrumented van to assure that no dangerous radiation was being left behind in the carrier vehicle's wake.

Reporter Hank Nichols summed up his thoughts quite nicely:

The problem with the official resolution of the McCarthy Pond enigma is that it takes a long time to find nothing—some people spend days and weeks finding nothing. But the people who came to McCarthy's pond found nothing in just a few hours. Since the departure of the last individual on that Thursday morning, McCarthy has not had any official inquiries into what happened at his pond. . . . The pond was never fully drained and studied.

The solution is unavoidable. The people who visited McCarthy's pond knew what they were looking for, found it, and left. . . . McCarthy says today . . . "How could they be so sure there was no need to come back and take another look?"[4]

During our investigation, a USAF security officer told me that he could not comment directly on the official inquiry, but was nonetheless sympathetic with our efforts to investigate the incident. However, he was also quick to add that we would "never really find out what happened." I reluctantly have to agree.

Len Stringfield, a fellow board member of MUFON who specializes in investigating cases of this nature, has dubbed them Retrievals of the Third Kind. Len has had a long background in UFO research. Between 1953 and 1957 he screened and reported UFO activity in Ohio for the Air Force Air Defense Command. Currently he is director of public relations and marketing services of DuBois Chemicals in Cincinnati. The following data has been culled from extensive case histories compiled by Len.

The first incident may concern an additional witness to the UFO crash in Mexico that I tried to pin down. Dr. Moore estimated that his Naval Intelligence friend had witnessed the retrieval of the object and its occupants in 1950. Len stated that the crash occurred in 1948. This is probably correct, because his informant, an Air Force technician, told Len that his uncle had been assigned to cordon off the crash site. At the time, the uncle was Provost Marshal at Carswell AFB, near Fort Worth. UFO researcher Todd Zechel recently tracked the man down. Now a retired Air Force colonel residing in Florida, he told Zechel that the UFO crashed about 30 miles across the Mexican border from Laredo, Texas. It was recovered by U.S. troops who were sworn to secrecy and told that if they said a word about the incident, they would be the "sorriest people around." The colonel also stated that aboard the craft was found one dead alien about 4½ feet tall, completely hairless, with hands that had no thumbs. On March 15, 1978, Zechel phoned Len that the colonel had signed an affidavit pertaining to these and other details of the Mexican incident.

Another report stems from 1952, the year of the great UFO wave. Concerning this particular event, Len has contact with four different informants. One highly reliable person holds a technical position at a large General Electric plant. His brother, a former Air Force radar operator, confided in him that he had tracked a crashing UFO in 1952 from Edwards AFB, California. Rumors spread among base personnel that within the UFO had been found dead humanoids approximately 4½ feet tall. The craft was reportedly held temporarily in a hanger there before being shipped to Wright-Patterson AFB. Len tried to discuss the episode firsthand with the informant's brother. Alarmed, the former serviceman stated that information concerning the occurrence was classified; he would not discuss it.

Another apparent source is a former USAF quartermaster who in 1952 was stationed at Godman Field, Kentucky. Late one night a large military flatbed truck under heavy guard made a stop at the base. Rumors soon spread over the base that its hidden cargo was a UFO. And a man and wife who resided in Circleville, Ohio, in 1952 claimed that they had been in a traffic jam near Wright-Patterson AFB, caused by a similar truck and an armed motorcade.

Further support for this case comes from John Schuessler, deputy director of MUFON and an engineer for the McDonnell Douglas Company at NASA. He has held many top assignments, including group design engineer responsible for the development of the life-support and thermal-control system equipment for Skylab. John's parents have a close friend and neighbor who served as a guard at a receiving gate for internal security at Wright-Patterson in 1952. While on duty he saw a similar vehicle arrive on base, carrying a tarpaulin-covered craft. He stated that deceased bodies of little humanoids, packed in crates, also passed through this security area. John tried to arrange a meeting with this man, but he refused to talk about it to anyone anymore.

Len's last lead concerning the 1952 UFO crash involves an experience by a Mr. T., who today holds a high technical position in civilian life. In the spring of 1953, he was 20 and a radar specialist with Secret security clearance.

While stationed in Ft. Monmouth, New Jersey, in 1953, he and a small select number of radar specialists were summoned to view a special film at the base theater. Without any briefing, the 16mm movie projector was flicked on, and the film began to roll on the screen, showing the usual flaws and scratches found in combat photography film. Suddenly... there appeared a desert scene dominated by a silver disc-shaped object imbedded in the sand with a domed section at the top. At the bottom was a hatch or door that was open.

In the next scene, Mr. T. recalls seeing 10 to 15 military personnel all dressed in fatigues and all without identification patches, standing around what appeared to be a disabled craft. By judging their height against the UFO, Mr. T. determined that its width was approximately 15 to 20 feet in diameter and that an open hatch or door at the bottom was about 2-½ feet wide and perhaps 3 feet high. At this point Mr. T. had no idea of the movie's purpose. I asked about the activity of the personnel. "They were just looking at the object," he said.

Then the movie switched to what appeared to be the interior of the craft. A panel with a few simple levers was shown, and he remembers being impressed by the muted pastel colors and sudden glares of white—the sign of poor photography. Again there was a change of scenes. Now in view were two tables, probably taken inside a tent, on which, to his surprise, were dead bodies. Two were on one table, and one on another. Mr. T. said the bodies appeared little by human standards and most notable were the heads, all looking alike, and all being large compared to their body sizes. They looked mongoloid, he thought, with small noses, mouths, and eyes that were shut. He didn't recall seeing ears or hair. The skin, he said, was leathery and ashen in color. Each wore a tight-fitting suit in a pastel color.

The sight of the dead bodies was the end of the movie. Most military movies credit the Signal Corps or some other source. This one "stopped cold," said Mr. T. When the lights came on in the theater, the officer in charge stood up and instructed the viewers to "think about the movie," and added firmly, "Don't relate its contents to anyone." Mr. T. said that in good faith, he didn't even tell his wife, who lived near the base. To Mr. T.'s surprise, two weeks later, he was approached by an Intelligence Officer on the base and told, "Forget the movie you saw; it was a hoax." Shortly after, he heard from a couple of top security officers on the base that a UFO had crashed in New Mexico and had been recovered with its occupants. The date of the crash was 1952, said Mr. T. Commented my informant, "The 5-minute-long movie certainly was not a Walt Disney production. It was full of scratches, poor coloring, and texture." Years later, he met an old army acquaintance who also was a radar specialist. To Mr. T.'s surprise, he learned that this man too, had seen the same film at another base under the same similar hush-hush conditions. He believes that the crashed craft and the dead bodies were *bona fide*. It would have been difficult, even by a major Hollywood studio, to have made dummy bodies look so real for use in an otherwise so makeshift film. And for what morbid purpose?

The next case from Len's file may concern another witness to the 1953 UFO crash case that Fritz Werner witnessed somewhere in Arizona. Len received information about this event from Cincinnati-based researcher Charles Wilhelm. A friend of Charles's father is a metallurgist and was an Air Force major stationed at Wright-Patterson AFB in 1953. In April of that year he was flown to an unknown hot and sandy destination. He was blindfolded, and driven to a point about 30 minutes away from a base of operations. There, inside a tent, standing in soft sand, his blindfold was removed. From there, he was taken to a location where he saw a silvery metallic craft about 25 to 30 feet in diameter. The exterior of the craft was not damaged. However, his on-the-spot two-day analysis of the craft's metal showed it was not native to earth. The major observed that the alien craft's entrance seemed to be about 4 to 5 feet high and 2 to 3 feet wide. He was not permitted to enter.

In his own report, Stringfield made the following comparison to my case on Fritz Werner:

Major D.'s blindfolded trip to the crash site, similar to Fritz Werner's, indicates that it was common procedure for the military to use extreme security measures relative to UFO retrievals. It is to be noted that Major D.'s experience takes place in April, a month shy of Fritz Werner's . . . in May of the same year. Also to be noted is that Major D. did not see any dead bodies. . . . If both the reports of Werner and D. are describing the same event, it is possible that D. used the wrong month.

It would be beyond the scope of this chapter to deal with all of Len's fairly extensive retrieval cases, but the next excerpt may possibly concern the same incident mentioned by astronaut Cooper:

"I'm almost positive it happened in 1973," said my informant, a man with a long career as a military pilot who held the rank of Warrant Officer in the Army during the early 1950's. Now [in late summer 1977] serving in the Air National Guard, he stood facing a large wall map of the United States in a back room of the Administration Building at Lunken Airport in Cincinnati... as he tried to recall the exact time when he stood ... at a distance of about 12 feet, peering at five crates on a forklift inside a hanger at Wright-Patterson AFB. In each of three crates, he said, were the recovered dead bodies of small humanoids; the contents of the other two crates were not discernible.... He pointed vaguely to an area in Arizona on the map. "Here's where it approximately happened," he said. "It was in a desert area, but I don't have the name of the location."

He made certain there was no one else in the map room when he told me about the incident. "It's still a secret, and at the time I had to swear to it." he said. "I was in the right place at the right time when the crates arrived at night by DC-7." As we stood at the map, my informant described what appeared to be hastily prepared wooden crates. In these, little humanoids, appearing to be 4 feet tall, were lying unshrouded on a fabric which, he explained, prevented freeze burn from the dry ice packed beneath. As a number of Air Police stood silent guard nearby the crates, he managed to get a reasonably good but brief glimpse of the humanoid features.... Their heads were disproportionately larger than the bodies, with skin that looked brown under the hangar lights above. The head appeared to be hairless and narrow. The eyes seemed to be open, the mouth small, and nose, if any, was indistinct. The humanoids' arms were positioned down alongside their bodies, but the hands and feet, he said, were indistinct... they appeared to be wearing tight-fitting dark suits, and, because of the tight-fitting suit ... one of the humanoids appeared to him to be female. He said, "Either one of the aliens had an exceedingly muscular chest or the bumps were a female's breasts." Later, he learned from one of the crew members, with whom he bunked at the barracks, that the body of one of the aliens was, indeed, that of a female.

My informant also heard from the crew member that one of the little humanoids was *still alive* aboard the craft when the U.S. military team arrived. Attempts were made to save its life with oxygen, but were unsuccessful.... How did the military know about the crash and where to go? He said he heard from a crew member that the UFO was picked up by special tracking equipment at Mt. Palomar in California. They provided the coordinates to the military to determine the crash area. The retrieved craft was sent to Wright-Patterson.

Len comments further that his informant furnished other details concerning his encounter at Wright-Patterson and on other sensitive UFO issues. Upon his request, this data was not made available to others.

Crash rumors often center around Wright-Patterson AFB. A Mrs. G., who had known UFO researcher Charles Wilhelm very well as a teenager, developed cancer. Aware of her impending death, she decided to relate to him some startling information about what she had seen during the performance of her secret duties at Wright-Patterson.

In 1955, according to Wilhelm, she was assigned to a post to catalogue all incoming UFO material, during which time approximately *1,000 items* were processed! These included items from the interior of a recovered UFO brought to the air base. All items were photographed and tagged. In her cataloguing duties, Mrs. G. also was witness to the conveyance, by cart, of two dead humanoid bodies from one room to another. The bodies, preserved in chemicals, were 4 to 5 feet tall; they had generally human features except that the heads were large relative to their bodies, and their eyes were slanted. There was no word as to whether the bodies were brought in from a recent crash or had been at the base morgue for years. After telling Charles Wilhelm some of the barest facts she knew, she commented, "Uncle Sam can't do anything to me once I'm in my grave." Wilhelm saw Mrs. G.'s Wright-Patterson AFB identification badge prior to her death six months later.

The next source, like Mrs. G., made certain that his details would not be released until after his death.

"My information," Len states, "comes secondhand from a person who requests that his name not be used in any way concerning his knowledge of retrieved UFOs and the preserved alien bodies maintained in secret storage at Wright-Patterson."

This person, who has read my book, *Situation Red,* is aware of my position in research but refuses to discuss what he knows with me by phone or in person. My firsthand informant is his son, with whom he had shared some general information about UFOs a couple of years earlier. . . . The young man's father got his UFO input from his cousin, an Air Force major who was specifically assigned to a UFO project for about 5 years at Wright-Patterson. Formerly a pilot, the Major had also served at a missile site overseas and presently is assigned to a new technical duty. I do have these latter details, but was asked not to be specific.

So significant was the Major's information that the father felt compelled to write down some specific details about the retrieved UFO and the humanoids; which information, he sealed in an envelope and placed in his safety deposit box. His instructions were that the envelope was not to be opened until after his death. Some of the general information known to my informant concerns Wright-Patterson's storage of an intact UFO, and parts of damaged UFOs, and the preservation of dead alien bodies under glass in special refrigerated conditions. The Major also reportedly said, "We have the proof that UFOs are extra-terrestrial." My informant is not kidding about his father's UFO notes being stored in a safety deposit box. He also is not kidding about his father's staunch reluctance to discuss with me the contents of his notes. Personally, I must agree with the father's position of keeping a trust when it concerns the status and welfare of a close relative.

The next case was given to Len directly from a firsthand participant in a crash investigation.

On April 7, 1978, Steve Tom, NBC radio newsman, Chicago, and I were linked up by phone for an interview with a former Air Force Intelligence Officer, Major J. M., residing in Houma, Louisiana . . . to obtain firsthand the Major's role in the retrieval of an alleged crashed UFO northwest of Roswell, New Mexico, in the summer of 1947.

. . . A sheep rancher found fragments of metal and other material on his 8,000-acre property. When he informed the Air Force base in Roswell of his discovery, Major J. M. and aides were dispatched to the area for investigation. There he found many metal fragments and what appeared to be "parchment" strewn in a 1-square-mile area. "The metal fragments," said the Major, "varied in size up to 6 inches in length, but were of the thickness of tinfoil. The fragments were unusual," he continued, "because they were of great strength. They could not be bent or broken, no matter what pressure we applied by hand."

The area was thoroughly checked, he said, but no fresh impact depressions in the sand were found. The area was not radioactive. The fragments were transported by a military carry-all to the air base in Roswell and from that point he was instructed by General Ramey to deliver the "hardware" to Ft. Worth, to be forwarded to Wright-Patterson Field for analysis. When the press learned of this retrieval operation and wanted a story, Major J. M. stated, "To get them off my back, I told them we were recovering a downed weather balloon." When the Major was asked for his opinion as to the identification of the fragments, he was certain they were not from a balloon, aircraft, or rocket. He said because of his technical background, he was certain that the metal and "parchment" were not a part of any military aerial device known at that time.

Len commented that the year 1947 heralded the first great wave of UFO reports. The retrieval of unusual fragments in secrecy suggests that they were a part of an unknown aerial device or craft.

Some of Len's leads on UFO crashes come from attendees of his lectures. On April 6, 1978, he addressed the World Wings Association, an aircraft pilots' group. Afterward, a highly reputable member of the association gave him the name of a former Air Force sergeant stationed at Wright-Patterson, and Len promptly made an appointment with the source.

M. S., while serving at Wright-Patterson in 1977, made close acquaintance with a Major General T., who was assigned at Wright-Patterson for top security work in the Logistics Command. His rank and the nature of his work entitled him to a plane at his disposal at all times. The General's daughter (name known to me) and M. S. were seriously lovelorn, and on that basis were frequently together. This allowed M. S. to be the guest at the General's home where he and the General had private chats. Both being endowed with the highest security ratings, they discussed UFOs. From General T, my informant related, details were disclosed concerning a UFO that had crashed in the southwest . . . United States in 1957. At that time, General T. was Lt. Colonel T. According to the General, radar had confirmed that an alien craft had crossed the skies over the United States at great speed. It was tracked to the point of its crash. The area, as in most, was "roped off" and the National Guard summoned (with canines) for maximum security.

From the damaged craft, four humanoid bodies were recovered with great difficulty because of the inability to penetrate the craft's metal structure. The bodies were found badly burned, some parts so severely that certain features were indistinguishable. However, the suits they wore—appearing silver—were not damaged by the obvious intense heat endured inside the craft. Said the General, "The suits were fused to the flesh." M. S. said, according to the General, the four bodies, approximately 5 feet in height, were sent to Wright-Patterson AFB where General T. had seen them in a deep freeze morgue, kept at approximately 120 degrees below zero for preservation. . . . The heads of the aliens were, by human standards, larger proportionately than the bodies. Facial features were erased by the heat factor.

The craft? The General related that scientists assigned to the task of dismantling it ran into difficulty. To get inside, they concentrated in an area where a fissure or crack had resulted, probably from impact. Shipment to Wright-Patterson, said the General, "Was by rail, using two military conveyance rocket cars, properly camouflaged and classified as 'rockets.'"

On another occasion, M. S. was a guest of General T. at his home. He was shown a Top Secret document concerning a landed UFO. The incident occurred at Nellis AFB, Nevada, in 1968, and M.S. expressed disbelief when he read the report. Stamped TOP SECRET, it read in part: Large UFO hovered over Nellis AFB for 3 days. Three small alien craft were observed separating from parent craft. One landed on the air base grounds. Sent to greet the landed craft was a Colonel with security detachment properly armed. There was no mention of attempt to assault the craft. While waiting for a sign of intent, a humanoid was observed to disembark from the craft, who was described as "short and stocky." Then a beam of light was directed at the Colonel. The Colonel was instantly paralyzed, according to the report. Orders then came from the officer next in command for his troops of the security detachment to fire, but their weapons were mysteriously jammed. The Colonel was recovered and hospitalized. . . . The UFO was observed to retreat to its parent craft and then departed.

Len checked out the existence of General T. and his secret assignment at Wright-Patterson AFB through an Intelligence source, and obtained additional corroborative information concerning the Nellis AFB incident.

This time, Len's informant contacted him after reading his book.

"Situation Red, The UFO Siege, really did it," said A. K., calling me from California on June 19, 1978. "It convinced me that I should tell my story to you about a UFO that landed or had maybe crashed at Ft. Riley, Kansas." . . . He, of course, asked to keep his name confidential because he recalled a general who was on the scene of the landing, warning that he would have his "expletives" shot off if he talked.

The incident occurred on the crisp, cold night of December 10, 1964. At 2:00 A.M., A. K., a PFC on guard duty at the Motor Pool, and three other Army personnel of the 1st Division on regular guard duty, were summoned by the officer of the day, Lt. H., to join him by vehicle to a remote area on the base described as a training area in Camp Forsyte, which is part of the Ft. Riley complex. On departure to this area, he was issued an extra clip for his M-14 rifle. "I was scared," admitted A. K. "In fact, I'm trembling right now as I'm telling you this." . . . After driving a good distance, Lt. H. parked his vehicle along-side the road. He, A. K. and the other guards were ordered to hike about a half mile across an open flat field. Before him, A. K. watched the searchlight beam from an overhead Huey helicopter playing down on the field. It was focused on a large round object resting on the ground. PFC. A. K. and his comrades stood in shock. . . . Already on the scene were about 10 Army personnel of various ranks, including a Major General. Promptly, A. K. was asked for his ID and given a direct order by the General to patrol the grounded craft by circling around it and to "shoot anyone if they tried to force their way to the craft." At this time, PFC. A. K. was sharply admonished about keeping the incident secret. "When I was in the Army, when a General told you something, you obeyed!"

The lone Huey chopper continuously flew overhead while certain personnel on hand checked the object with instruments, and maintained communication by field radio with headphones. Nearby a 5-ton truck was parked with lights off. On two occasions the Huey chopper flew over (or someone?). When the Huey was away, a "deathly quiet" prevailed, he said. "It was eerie!" A. K. said that on several occasions during his 2½ hours of guard duty, he got close to the metallic craft. "The air was much warmer when I got close," he said. The grounded UFO, which had impacted into the soil and stood at a tilt, was approximately 35 to 48 feet in diameter and 12 to 18 feet in height. It was perfectly round, shaped like a hamburger bun. In the middle, or at the equator, of its smooth aluminum-like surface, was a black band made up of squares, each jutting out about 10 inches. A. K. could not determine if the squares were windows or what purpose they served. The only protruding part on the UFO, said A. K. was a fin-like device and beneath it an aperture which may have been an exhaust unit.

A. K. said the UFO was not lighted; he sensed no vibrations from its power system and smelled no odors. "It was dead," he said. Asked about recovery of occupants from the craft, he replied, "Sorry to disappoint you, but I was not aware of any life inside the craft, or if any bodies were taken out of it later."

A. K. was relieved of duty and returned to the base. He never did hear anything about the disposition of the alien craft. Prior to his bizarre nighttime experience, however, there were rumors of UFO sightings at the base.

The last case came to Len's attention via his son-in-law, Jeffrey, a professor of theater arts at a Florida college. Jeffrey informed Len that he had talked with a person who held a responsible position in a financial capacity with a private firm in Tampa and had formerly served in military intelligence. He gave Len this individual's name and where he could be reached. On July 5, 1978, Len talked with Mr. J. K. at length about his alleged observation of alien corpses, other aspects of crashed UFOs, and a certain computer bank or "dump file" that contained secret information on UFOs dating back to 1948. J. K., who served in NIKE Missile Air Intelligence (ADCAP), related the following data, which Len summarized as follows.

1. He observed nine deceased alien bodies preserved in deep-freeze conditions under well-lighted, thick glass enclosures. The bodies were short in stature, about 4 feet in height. Their skintone appeared, under the lighting, to be grayish in color. The research area where the bodies were preserved was under heavy guard, inside and out. While viewing the subjects, he was told that 30 bodies were held in preservation at that time at the air base.

2. He did not see, firsthand, alien craft stored at Wright-Patterson, but was told that such craft were on the base. He was also told that an alien craft was held at Langley AFB and another at McDill AFB in Florida.

3. He knew of three key areas in the 1960s where certain secret UFO operations were conducted other than at Wright-Patterson AFB. Bases

cited were Langley, Avon Bombing Range—a part of McDill AFB complex near Sebring, Florida, and at Seymour-Johnson, a Navy Training Center in Norfolk, Virginia.

    4. At certain military bases, highly trained mobilized units were in a constant "ready" state for dispatch to any area in the U.S.A. to recover downed or crashed UFOs.

    5. During the Vietnam crisis, during J. K.'s tenure of service (1966–1968), five crashes of UFOs occurred in the tri-state area of Ohio, Indiana and Kentucky. There was one known incident of a retrieval of three alien bodies. During this latter incident there occurred an alleged shooting of the alien forces by our military units. This was triggered by the uncertainty of the aliens' intent. Hostility was presumed, said J. K. The location or time of these incidents were not disclosed.

    6. Said J. K.: "Since 1948, secret information concerning UFO activity involving the U.S. military has been contained in a computer center at Wright-Patterson. At this base, a master file, written in computer language, is maintained, with duplicate support backup files secreted at other military installations." Said J. K.: "Get the complete 'file dump,' both the master and the support backup files, and you've got all the hidden UFO data."

    Len adds, as a postscript of J. K.'s testimony, that obviously the UFO files available to the public at the National Archives in Washington do not reveal the hard facts regarding UFO military cases. Concerning J. K.'s disclosure of military units subject to dispatch to retrieval areas, Len is aware of such groups:

These special forces, known as "Blue Berets," can operate secretly and effectively by using "diversionary tactics" to prevent public interference. Such diversions include creating power blackouts.

Len's files include a composite from many case histories concerning the alien creatures retrieved from these craft. According to Len, some of this information comes from firsthand sources actually involved in postmortem research. The names of the medical centers and the identity of the informants may not be disclosed at this time. Len has abstracted data to establish a general anatomical configuration of the alien beings. He states that the features of the alien are akin to earth's Homo sapiens; that is, the alien has a head, torso, arms, hands, and is bipedal.

    There the likeness ends.

    1. The approximate height of the alien humanoid is 3½ to 4½ feet tall. One source approximated 5 feet.

    2. The head, by human standards, is large when compared with the size of the torso and limbs.

    3. The facial features show a pair of eyes described variously as

large, sunken, or deep set; far apart or distended more than human; and slightly slanted, appearing "Oriental" or "Mongoloid."

4. No earlobes or flesh extending beyond apertures on each side of the head.

5. Nose is vague. Aperture or nares are indicated with slight protuberance. One and two nares have been mentioned.

6. Mouth indicated as a small "slit" or fissure. In some instances, no mouth described. Mouth appears not to function as a means for communication or as orifice for food ingestion.

7. Neck described as being thin; and in some instances, not visible because of garment in that section of body.

8. Hair: some observers described the humanoids as hairless, some say that the pate shows a slight fuzz. Bodies described as hairless.

9. Torso: small and thin fits the general description. In many instances the body was observed wearing a garment. From medical authorities, no comment. No abdominal navel indicated.

10. Arms are described as long and thin and reaching down to the knee section.

11. Hands: Four fingers, no thumb. Two fingers appear longer than others. Some observers had seen fingernails; others without. A webbing effect between fingers was noted by three authoritative observers.

12. No description available of legs or feet.

13. Skin description . . . is gray according to most observers. Some claim beige, tan, brown, or tannish or pinkish gray and one said it looked almost "bluish gray" under deep freeze lights. In one instance the bodies were charred to a dark brown.

14. Teeth unknown. No data from dental authorities.

15. Reproductive organs: This biological region is "sensitive," that is, to qualify a point, "secret." One observer claims no male or female organs were identified. No genitalia. In my nonprofessional judgment, the absence of sexual organs suggest some of the aliens, and perhaps all, do not reproduce as do *Homo sapiens,* or that some of the bodies studied are produced perhaps by a system of cloning or other unknown means.

16. In some incidents of retrieval, the humanoids appear to be "formed out of a mold," or sharing identical biological characteristics.

17. Brain capacity: Unknown.

18. Blood: Liquid is prevalent, but not blood as we know it.

19. Sustenance for existence. No food or water intake is known. No food found on craft in one known retrieval. No alimentary canal or rectal area described.

20. Humanoid *types.* Unknown. Descriptive variations of anatomy may be no more diverse than those known among Earth *Homo sapiens.* Other alien types, reportedly varying in range from human to more grotesque configurations, are unknown to me. Speculatively, if these types exist, they may have their origins in other solar systems or have roots on different planets within one solar system.

21. I know of the names of two major medical centers in the Eastern United States where continuing specialized intensive research is conducted on deceased alien bodies. Other hospitals where research reportedly has been conducted are in Indiana, Illinois, Texas, Southeastern and Western U.S.A.

Len qualifies the many reports that he has on file:

The information, while it may seem provocative to the media and to the average researcher, does not admittedly constitute the final proof that UFOs are of extraterrestrial origin. But, indeed, if my data from reliable and diverse sources are received with an objective and unbiased mind, then . . . it will be difficult to explain away the correlative physical similarities of the recovered humanoids. . . . As vital data continues to reach me from responsible sources. . . . As the pieces of the puzzle suddenly fall into place for me, each a corroborative clue, I realize . . . that our giant Intelligence community, both military and covert agencies, have been sitting atop a real Pandora's Box. . . .

This leads to the oft-asked question: Why *doesn't* our government tell us what is going on?

CHAPTER NOTES

1. Roland Gelatt, "Flying Saucer Hoax," *Saturday Review of Literature,* December 6, 1952, p. 31.
2. Meldrim Thomson, Jr., Governor, State of New Hampshire, *Official Press Release,* January 13, 1977 (copy in personal files).
3. H. Nichols, *New Hampshire Times,* October 12, 1977, p. 4.
4. *Ibid.*

18
WHERE DO WE GO FROM HERE?

By this time one would think that civilian UFO research would have provided definitive answers to the origin and purpose of UFOs. Unfortunately this is not the case, partly because the recognition of UFOs as a valid scientific problem has been a long time coming.

Remember Dr. Robert Low's infamous memo that John Fuller exposed in *Look* magazine? One damning paragraph concisely describes the firmly entrenched, dogmatic, fearful attitude of the old-line traditionalists in high academic and research circles. Before writing the memo Low had consulted informally with a number of such colleagues in the Boulder, Colorado, area.[1]

B. is very much against it. G. L. thinks it would be a disaster. G. D. likewise is negative. Their arguments, combined, run like this: In order to undertake such a project, one has to approach it *objectively* [italics mine]. That is, one has to admit the possibility that such things as UFOs exist. *It is not respectable to give serious consideration to such a possibility.* Believers, in other words, remain outcasts. B. suggested that one would have to go as far as to consider the possibility that *saucers, if some of the observations are verified, behave according to a set of physical laws unknown to us. The simple act of admitting these possibilities, just as possibilities, puts us beyond the pale,* and we could possibly lose more *prestige* in the scientific community than we could possibly gain by undertaking the investigation.[2]

Low is saying, quite clearly, that since UFOs cannot coexist with the current scientific model of the universe, science must not admit the possibility that such things exist.

To be fair, I must admit some have already dared speak out on UFOs, much to the chagrin of these elite. The late Dr. Margaret Mead, the world-renowned anthropologist who held the coveted post of president of the American Association for the Advancement of Science, committed an act of scientific blasphemy. This remarkable, courageous woman not only suggested UFOs' extraterrestrial origin, but criticized her colleagues' backward thinking in a September 1974 article in *Redbook*.

There is every indication that emotions, rather than research, account for the older generation's closed-minded attitude. A questionnaire was sent to the late Dr. Donald Menzel, former director of the Harvard Observatory, concerning a symposium being held by the American Psychological Association. One question asked, "What should be done with UFO reports that cannot be explained?" Dr. Menzel's answer was short and to the point: "Throw them in the wastebasket!"

Today that situation is changing radically. Organizations like APRO, CUFOS, and MUFON now bristle with board members at the Ph.D. level. No doubt younger members of the engineering and scientific communities appear more open-minded about the real scientific challenge of UFOs. A recent opinion poll by a highly respected research and development journal bears this out.

GOOD CHANCE UFOS EXIST IN SOME FORM
Do applied scientists and engineers laugh at people who believe in Unidentified Flying Objects? . . . No way. A large number of them believe in UFOs themselves. And only a few of them believe that most UFOs are reported to authorities.

These statements are drawn from results of a recent Opinion Poll survey of more than 1200 scientists and engineers in all fields of research and development. When asked, "Do you believe that UFOs exist?" 61% of the respondents said that they believe UFOs probably or definitely exist. Only 28% of the scientists and engineers in the pool said they believe that UFOs probably do not or definitely do not exist. . . . The poll showed *a strong correlation between age and belief in UFO existence.*

The respondent researchers younger than 26 were more than twice as likely to believe in the existence of UFOs than were those older than 65. And the degree of belief declined at a steady rate from youngest to oldest. . . . Even after allowing for the high level of sampling error . . . inherent in our survey, the correlation was striking.

Do these scientists believe in UFO existence because they have seen one? Eight percent of the respondents said they have. Another 10% say *perhaps* they have seen a UFO. That's more than one out of every six R & D scientists and engineers, if these results can be projected to the industry.

Perhaps because they are insiders to high technology . . . more than 40% believe UFOs originate in "outer space," while only 2% believe they originate in the U.S.A. As for originating in Communist countries, less than 1% believe that. More than a fourth . . . say they believe that UFOs are natural phenomena.[3]

In the early 1970s, certain individuals chose to specialize in some particular aspect of ufology's ever-more-complex field. A brief chapter cannot do justice to these dedicated researchers' contributions, but it is most important for the serious student to know who these specialists are and what their specialty is. Some key personalities are summarized below, in alphabetical order.

Irving Anderson has studied the periodicity of UFO waves. Ted Bloecher has conducted an in-depth study of the 1947 wave, and is cochairman of a group studying close encounters of the third kind; this group has computer-coded about 2,000 such cases. About 200 of these involve alleged abductions of witnesses. Reverend Barry Downing is a MUFON consultant in theology. Tom Gates has worked in the area of UFOs and public awareness. Loren Gross has done specialized studies of the UFO waves of 1896 and 1947. Dr. Richard F. Haines is concentrating his studies in two areas: airplane-pilot reports and the psychophysical and biological aspects of viewing very bright objects. Dr. James Harder specializes in the use of hypnotic regression. Dr. Harold I. Heaton specializes in the study of animal reaction to UFOs. Dr. David Jacobs is a specialist in the history of the UFO problem. Dr. Alvin H. Lawson is closely studying the value of using hypnotic-regression techniques with UFO abductees. Dr. Bruce S. Maccabbee has conducted research into FBI files on UFOs and photo analysis. James McCampbell is involved with studies of interference with automobile electrical systems and other UFO effects. He has written a book summarizing some of his studies.[4] Fred Merritt studies the shape and dimensions of UFO imprint patterns. Vincente-Juan Ballester Olmos of Spain has made a study of the relation of UFO sightings to population. Dr. Ted Peters's specialty is theology and UFOs. Ted Phillips specializes in documented close encounters of the second kind, physical-trace cases. Dr. David R. Saunders is the original author of UFOCAT, a computerized listing of over 60,000 UFO cases. He, like Irving Anderson, is interested in the periodicity of UFO waves. William Spaulding, director of Ground Saucer Watch, is heavily involved in using the digital computer in UFO photo analysis. He also is part of a team that has sued the CIA for UFO information through the FOIA. Dr. Leo R. Sprinkle is probably this nation's foremost expert in the hypnotic and psychic aspects of UFO research. Ray Stanford has helped provide a fully instrumented UFO detection and tracking station as a functional model for UFO research. Called Project Argus, it is located near Austin, Texas. Len Stringfield researches rumors concerning crashed UFOs and government confiscation of the craft and alien bodies. David Webb works with Ted Bloecher as a specialist on the sightings of humanoids associated with UFOs. He has a special interest in UFO abduction cases. Dr. Ron Westrum's area of special interest is the effects of UFOs on society.

Many of these gentlemen have earned doctorates and are working as professionals within the scientific community. Examples of their work may be found within the pages of CUFOS and MUFON proceedings, copies of which are available from these organizations for a nominal fee.

Most scientists believe that intelligent creatures probably exist elsewhere in the universe. It's the suggestion that such creatures are visiting us *now,* via UFOs, that's anathema. Usually the scientific ufologist and the scientific theoretician aren't on speaking terms, but on August 29 and 30, 1974, Dr. Peter A. Sturrock, a ufologist and plasma physicist at Stanford University, organized a workshop on extraterrestrial civilization (ETC). For the first time, highly qualified groups of both persuasions met together.

Coverage of this meeting in the June 1975 edition of the *Astronautics and Aeronautics* journal was written by astronomer John B. Carlson, University of Maryland, and Dr. Sturrock, both scientists who are actively studying UFOs. In the article they discuss the differences between the two opposing, yet overlapping, groups (italics mine):

Group A comprised primarily of scientists who study the problem theoretically, on the basis of our understanding of the physical universe—its composition and laws. . . . Excellent collections of articles from Group A have been presented in the volumes *Interstellar Communication* and *Interstellar Communications: Scientific Perspectives.* Both books point to searching for radio signals which appear to carry intelligent information as a plausible investigative approach to the possibility of ETC. . . . Group A contains *both* theorists and observers—or would-be observers.

Group B comprises another association of scientists . . . trying to understand the phenomenon called "UFO." . . . Very few of these scientists have made any firsthand observations relevant to this study, . . . Almost all of their activity comprises "data analysis": an attempt to collect, evaluate, systematize, and analyze observations made by other people. Very few scientists, if any, would *definitely* assert that the UFO phenomenon *is* a manifestation of ETC, *but most scientists* involved in this study consider this to be an open hypothesis. . . .

. . . *There has been no previous meeting involving both groups.* The Stanford ETC Workshop resulted from the view that this lack of professional contact was a serious omission.[5]

How can scientists studying the same basic problem ignore each other for so many years?

We would guess that members of Group A tended to believe . . . the

"UFO Data" to be useless from a scientific point of view; that . . . *the theoretical case against interstellar travel overwhelms any claim of observational evidence that it occurs.*[6]

To put it rather simply, the informed ufologist cannot be bothered with theorizing. He is investigating hundreds of UFO reports that give strong indication that ETCs exist and are now visiting us. Why spend huge amounts of money and time listening for ETCs when there's every indication that they're already here?

This, however, is foolhardy to the theorist. Current scientific understanding tells him that such things can't be, so why bother to study UFO reports? Carlson and Sturrock comment that:

Although some members of Group A opted for "the bias to remain skeptical" . . . the group showed an obvious interest and expressed the willingness to "sit and listen" to Group B. . . . *This was taken by all to be a sign of progress.* . . . Group A is still waiting for "unimpeachable results" from Group B, but mutual scientific support and respect will contribute greatly toward opening up opportunities for research. . . .[7]

Scientists in other countries are finally grappling with UFOs. France, for one example, is by far the most open in this respect: For years its national police force has been trained in the investigation of UFO reports as standard operating procedure. The gendarmerie work hand in hand with military and civilian researchers, and in 1977 the French government created a fully funded, high-level civilian scientific UFO study called *Groupe d'Etudes des Phenomènes Aerospatiaux Non-Identifées* (GEPAN).

During 1977 GEPAN—a branch of the French equivalent of NASA—conducted a thorough study of selected, previously investigated UFO reports. During 1978 its operations expanded into the investigation of current cases. As part of this UFO project's functions, three special groups were created: rapid intervention, physical traces, and radar alert. Recently both MUFON and CUFOS received copies of a summation of GEPAN's initial 5-volume, 500-page report. The actual report has a very limited distribution confined to 140 copies. The following summation was prepared by one of the reviewers of the French UFO-study report, sociologist Dr. Ronald Westrum. Both the study and its report would have thoroughly shocked the likes of the University of Colorado's Dr. Robert Low. The French investigators tackled a number of close-encounter cases for special study (italics mine):

The bulk of the work was devoted to eleven cases of *high credibility* and *high strangeness* . . . [which] were studies in great detail; only two proved to have a conventional explanation. In the other nine, it appeared that the distance between the witnesses and the objects was less than 250 meters. Of the five volumes of the report, three were entirely devoted to analysis of these eleven cases, all except one of which was pre-1978. The earliest was 1966. Two of the cases were *humanoid sightings*.

The analysis and investigation was carried out by a four-person team in each case; the team included a psychologist, who separately carried out a psychological examination relevant to the evaluation of the testimony of the witnesses. The care with which distances, angles, and psychological factors were evaluated makes the bulk of the Condon Report seem very poor by comparison. In many cases, the investigations were textbook models of how such investigations should be carried out.[8]

The report's conclusion should have great influence upon the future of UFO research in other countries, including ours.

In nine of the eleven cases, the conclusion was that the witnesses had witnessed a material phenomenon that could not be explained as a natural phenomenon or a human device. One of the conclusions of the *total* report is that *behind the overall phenomenon there is a "flying machine whose modes of sustenance and propulsion are beyond our knowledge."*[9]

The report honestly admits that UFOs are flying machines that we do not presently understand. I am sure that our government and others came to this conclusion secretly back in the 1940s. Strangely enough, newspapers in the United States have ignored this highly significant report and its far-reaching conclusion.

It is very encouraging to see that former GEPAN director Dr. Claude Poher has become one of the board members of CUFOS. Dr. Alain Esterle, the current director, paid MUFON a visit in June of 1979. Arrangements have been made for data exchange between MUFON and GEPAN. In the past Russia has usually been close-mouthed concerning UFOs, studying the problem secretly and explaining them away publicly. Now the situation is changing radically: Russia is openly soliciting UFO information from MUFON, CUFOS, and many individual UFO researchers, including myself.

When NICAP received leaked classified information on the Iranian F–4 UFO encounter, who should come openly knocking on its door but the KGB! A contact at NASA recently sent me a Xerox copy of an official Air Force memorandum sent to the USAF Foreign Technology Division (FTD), home of the now defunct Project Bluebook. This particular memo, sub-titled *Soviet News Abstracts Publication* and dated January 31, 1979, alerts FTD of latest Russian UFO policy.

Title: UFO SIGHTINGS PROMPT STUDIES BY ACADEMY OF SCIENCE
Abstract: . . . Admitting that there have been reliably recorded cases of

phenomena that still cannot be attributed to any known physical process, the authors explain that these phenomena warrant scientific investigation without sensationalism. They say that organizations of the USSR Academy of Sciences have been conducting research for a number of years on anomalous phenomena in the atmosphere in order to obtain reliable, objective data concerning these processes and the physical conditions accompanying them. . . . And they give the address of the USSR Academy of Sciences Department of General Physics and Astronomy for reports of sightings of such phenomena.[10]

Ironically, civilian UFO researchers in the United States are being asked to cooperate with UFO studies being conducted by foreign governments! If members of the United States Academy of Sciences are doing UFO research, it is being done secretly under military contract. Thus far the influence of GEPAN and Russia's more open attitudes has only instigated FBI background checks of persons sharing UFO data with Russian scientists!

Regardless of the military, things seem to be looking up. The American Psychological and Sociological associations featured serious discussions on UFOs at their 1978 annual meetings. The Institute of Astronautics and Aeronautics has sponsored national and local UFO symposiums. A recent poll mailed to members of the American Astronomical Society elicited a positive response from 53% of those polled. Over 80% expressed a willingness to contribute to the resolution of the UFO problem if they could see a way to do so! In many quarters, scientific interest in UFOs is there, and funding would have occurred years ago if not for the strong influence of high-level military interests. The psychological warfare played through Project Bluebook has—intentionally—adversely affected both scientific and public opinion.

The military UFO interest, stung by adverse publicity and the inability to answer to thousands of UFO reports, has retreated into the shadows of classified operations. The Air Force, weary of being the whipping boy for higher-level interests, used the Condon Report to get them off the UFO hook. Now that Project Bluebook is closed, there is no one *officially* responsible to the public for the UFO problem. All attempts to force release of this data via major congressional investigations and hearings have failed. The CIA refuses to release certain hard data on national security grounds— but ironically, according to our government, UFOs present no threat to national security.

The state of Mississippi made the very latest attempt to instigate a major UFO investigation. Since Dr. Hynek was called to testify during preliminary hearings at the state level, I'll let him tell the typical, frustrating story (italics mine).

On January 25, 1979, I was one of three individuals invited to testify before the Mississippi House Rules subcommittee on the subject of

UFOs . . . because of a case I investigated. . . . The issue: a resolution to reopen a formal investigation of the UFO phenomenon. . . .

Readers will recall the CE-I that startled Deputy Sheriff Ken Dreel and Constable James Ray Luke as they sat in their car on a dark lonely road four miles west of Flora, Mississippi. A pale blue "dish" with 7 or 8 round windows rushed over their car, and the men drove away fast in fear. Many additional witnesses returned to the site to watch a light in the sky which they believed to have been associated with the officers' sighting.

One of those additional sighters was patrolman Herbert Roberts, who has since become the Chief of Police in Flora. Chief Roberts described his experience to Representative Horace Buckly, who was also impressed by news coverage of the newly-released Freedom of Information Act documents pertaining to UFOs. Thus, Buckly, along with Representatives O'Beirne, D. Anderson, R. Anderson and Owens, authored House Resolution No. 14, calling for a complete Senate investigation of UFO sightings.

I flew down to the state capital for the 1:30 meeting. Among the dozen members in attendance were the three people asked by Buckly to appear: Chief Roberts, for "local" interest, Todd Zechel on government information, and myself on behalf of civilian efforts. The chairman of the proceedings was Ed Perry. . . . When Zechel read a letter by Col. Charles Senn of the Air Force Office of Information to Lt. Gen. Crow (Ret.) of NASA, the sparks began to fly. The letter has Senn stating, "*I certainly hope you are successful in preventing a reopening of UFO investigations*" by NASA, which Zechel considered face value evidence of a *conspiracy*. [Representative H. L.] Meredith interrupted here, doubting that conspiracy was the only interpretation and stressed that he "*didn't want a fight*" with *the government*. Then he stated the prevailing attitude that would come to characterize the whole meeting: if military personnel are experiencing the kinds of UFO events described by Zechel's documents, then "*surely there is somebody in this government that knows what* [the UFO phenomenon] *is, and there is a purpose in the national interest for not disclosing it . . . and to find out just from a curiosity standpoint*—'we want to know about it'—*What if we told everybody we were developing the atomic bomb?*"

Zechel argued that the government has never asserted that the UFO subject is a national security matter or is classified information, which they *do* assert about "the atomic bomb." . . . Meredith tried to counter this with a claim made earlier by Chief Roberts that "*someone from the Air Force*" *contacted him about his sighting*, proving that "they" were *secretly* active. His allotted time now expired, Zechel could only state frustration with *the legislators' attitude that "if the government wants to cover up UFOs, that's fine with us."* . . .

Zechel argued in vain that similar trust in "national security" with Watergate and the Gulf of Tonkin affairs would have been a grave error.... One of the only statements made by someone other than Meredith was concern that *"the government needs national security and secrets....* I think the government has gone too far in letting out a lot." ... Some of the representatives up for reelection actually covered their faces when TV cameras came strolling into the room!

The outcome was obvious; the resolution was killed by a legislative deadline in February. Apparently there was not even a vote in the subcommittee on the resolution.[11]

In 1978 and 1979 a resolution was presented in the United Nations —by the tiny country of Grenada, who had nothing to lose as far as national security goes!—suggesting that it sponsor an international UFO investigation. Both the United States and Britain frowned upon the proposal because it concerned *their* national security. Nonetheless, a number of UFO experts and outstanding witnesses, including Dr. Hynek, testified of the urgent need for a UN study of UFOs.

I ask that there be devised a mechanism within the United Nations Organization whereby scientists in member nations can bring together and interchange their ideas and their investigative work.[12]

Former astronaut Gordon Cooper sent a written statement to be read at this important meeting (italics mine):

I believe that these extraterrestrial vehicles and their crews are visiting this planet from other planets, which obviously are a little more technically advanced than we are here on earth. I feel that we need to have a top level, coordinated program to scientifically collect and analyze data from all over the earth concerning any type of encounter ... interface with these visitors in a friendly fashion. ... This acceptance would have tremendous possibilities of advancing our world in all areas.... I did have occasion in 1951 to have two days of observation of many flights of them, of different sizes, flying in fighter formation, generally from east to west over Europe. They were at a higher altitude than we could reach with our jet fighters of that time. ...

Several of us [astronauts] ... have had occasion *to see a UFO on the ground, or from an airplane.* ... If the United Nations agrees to pursue this subject, and to lend their credibility to it, perhaps many more well-qualified people will agree to step forth and provide help and information.[13]

In my opinion, civilian UFO research is at a dead end. I must confess that after years and years, investigating and documenting the same types of unexplained events has become routine and frustrating. It is disheartening to realize that the detailed, concise, typewritten reports I mail to MUFON and CUFOS will be filed and lost in a mountain of other reports. But all unknowns do become a statistic in a computer program, retrievable for special study by interested scientists. Some are selected for study and a few are briefly summarized in UFO journals of very limited distribution.

Organizations such as MUFON and CUFOS can do little more than they are doing at present. For the most part, UFO research work is voluntary and part-time. Photographs, soil samples, and other alleged UFO evidence necessarily take a back seat to the routine work of earning a living. Such second-rade methodology does not impress members of the scientific community.

Over the years I have seen UFO reports progress to the amazing experiences of reliable witnesses who reported on-board contact with UFO occupants. But still another level looms ahead: what is commonly known among UFO researchers as cattle mutilation.

The first—and last!—nationally publicized incident of this kind was the famous "Snippy" case in Colorado in 1967. The strangely mutilated horse died under seemingly very strange circumstances during a local flap of UFO sightings. (At the time, a top NICAP official confided to me that other reports of this nature were arriving at headquarters, but that NICAP had decided not to publicize them lest they upset the public!)

Now, over a decade later, literally thousands of cattle throughout the western and midwestern states have been found mysteriously mutilated. Over and over again, animals have suffered precise surgical excision of their sexual and excretory organs, tails, udders, and other parts. In some incidents, only one or two parts or organs have been removed—for example, one or both ears, the eyes, tongue, or lips. Almost every month my news-clip service picks up new examples of these bizarre incidents.

Interestingly enough, a case of cattle mutilation coincided with the LeBel case. In October 1977 a farmer found the bodies of black and white spotted calves on a property adjoining the LeBel land, only half a mile from where Joe LeBel saw the landed UFO several months later. The animals' heads had been torn off, and their internal organs were missing. One calf's front leg was missing, and dried blood was found only near the bodies.

The owner's first thought was that wild dogs in the area were responsible, but no teeth marks were found on the calves. He decided to bury and forget them. Other than coincidence, there is no proof that UFOs were responsible for the mutilation. Local authorities and UFO researchers have tried unsuccessfully to explain such mutilations as the work of satanist groups, or as secret autopsies performed by U.S. Intelligence teams, but in reality there are no earthly explanations for the thousands of events of this type that have occurred.

On April 20, 1979, Senator Harrison Schmitt and R. E. Thompson, U.S. attorney for New Mexico, sponsored hearings on the problem, attended by UFO researchers, veterinarians, law enforcement personnel, and professional research scientists. Also prominent in the audience and witness stands were ranchers and Indian officials who had personal contact with the mutilations. Carl W. Whiteside of the Colorado Bureau of Investigation went statistically through some 30 cases officially investigated at the state level and concluded that more than just a significant number remained with no apparent solution.

The result of these New Mexico hearings was the official appointment of a state mutilation investigator—Ken Rommel, a recently retired agent from the Santa Fe FBI office. He stated that if UFO occupants were at fault, he would bring them in by their "little green ears." Lots of luck, pal!

Most UFO researchers probably do not want to believe that UFOs are involved—because of the fearful implications! Mice, dogs, cats, and chimpanzees are all subject to research in mankind's laboratories. If UFO occupants are indeed killing and dissecting our cattle, what's to stop them from performing experiments on some hapless human beings? Unpleasant and disturbing as the problem may be, a number of UFO researchers have launched special mutilation investigative groups, such as Project Stigmata, to work with cattlemen and state investigators conducting official inquiries. The results of their investigations will probably generate a new major controversy within ufology, whose resolution may very well deliver the physical proof of UFO reality to the Group B scientists. Meanwhile, the best we civilians can do is to supply well-documented UFO reports to individual scientists. But the UFO problem is too big and complex; one might just as well ask these groups to evaluate the performance of a secret foreign fighter that has repeatedly violated our airspace. Only the U.S. government with its military and intelligence branches, funded laboratories, and intragovernmental cooperation with other countries could carry out such a mission. Although I cannot prove it, I feel certain that this type of study has been underway for decades, that high-level investigations have obtained physical proof that UFOs are craft from another world—but that officialdom hasn't a clue as to the UFOs' exact origin or motivation. The elite GEPAN project could only confirm what we have known for years—that UFOs are flying machines of unknown origin which we do not understand.

It would seem that the higher the public interest, the more nervous the Pentagon becomes, misinterpreting curiosity and interest for panic. UFOs continue their intensive operations, barely interrupted by man's puny efforts to understand and cope with them. Perhaps this will always be the case, but I believe that over the last three decades these enigmatic craft have been engaged in a vast, tireless mission, which may now be reaching a point of fruition.

During the national tour to promote my book *The Andreasson Affair*, I heard the same question over and over again: "If UFOs are visitors from outer space, why don't they land openly and introduce themselves?" My retort was that UFOs may already be introducing themselves to our generation—slowly and meticulously conditioning us to accept their presence in our skies. Interestingly enough, a copy of the *International UFO Reporter* came just in time for me to include as part of this chapter Dr. Hynek's editorial on this very subject:

Suppose you were given the job of selling an idea... quite foreign to popular thinking, and one which runs against common sense, against scientific and military opinion, and against the learned opinions of the intelligentsia... to the majority of the population of the United States.... To attain the actual acceptance of this idea by more than 100 million people, the majority of our population, would be... a major accomplishment, and a very expensive one!

Yet this has been accomplished without the spending of one cent . . . and against a barrage of ridicule, of active opposition from science, the military, and the press! Of course, it took some thirty years to do it.

The Gallup Poll earlier this year indicated that 57% of the American population feels that UFOs are "for real." Yet thirty years ago, when the "campaign" started, the whole idea... would have been regarded as preposterous. Quite a successful advertising campaign!

But who put it on?... [Some think] *that the whole UFO phenomenon is indeed some sort of cosmic conditioning process perpetrated on the human race to raise our consciousness, to prepare us for the next stage of evolution,* ... almost subliminally, without causing panic or upsetting our economy or mental health. A mass landing of UFOs or any sort of direct confrontation... would almost *certainly have done this.*[14]

If we take certain CE-III cases seriously, we shall conclude that the UFO operators can project telepathic thoughts into human minds. During her study of UFO evidence, the late Dr. Margaret Mead noticed a peculiar coincidence:

Sightings seem to become more numerous at those times when we on earth are taking a forward step into space. In 1897, four years before the first dirigible was successfully flown in France, sightings of phantom airships—never satisfactorily explained—raised excitement to fever pitch in America in 20 states where they occurred. Late in World War II, crews of bomber squadrons in several war theaters described disturbing "blobs of light," which came to be known as "foo fighters." ... Again, there was a worldwide wave of sightings in 1957 when Russia and the United States launched the first satellites. And most recently, in the autumn of 1973, just before the unmanned U.S. spacecraft Pioneer Ten was to fly past Jupiter and out of our solar system, a new wave of sightings began.[15]

Air Force scientific consultant Dr. J. E. Lipp was also struck by such coincidences. The formerly secret files of Project Sign contain his memorandum to Brigadier General Putt, director of research and development for the United States Air Force, concerning the sudden appearances of flying discs in the 1940s, back when Mars and Venus were considered possible origins:

Various people have suggested that an advanced race may have been visiting Earth ... at intervals from decades to eons. Reports of objects in the sky seem to have been handed down through the generations. ... One ... hypothesis ... is that the Martians have kept a long-term routine watch on Earth and have been alarmed by the sight of our A-bomb shots. ... The first flying objects were sighted in the Spring of 1947, after a total ... 5 atomic bomb explosions. ... Of these, the first two were in positions to be seen from Mars.[16]

Another highly respected Air Force consultant to Project Sign, the nuclear physicist Dr. George E. Valley, was also impressed by the beginning of waves of UFO sightings and the atomic age. In 1948 he wrote:

Such a civilization might observe that on Earth we now have atomic bombs and are fast developing rockets. ... We should, therefore, expect at this time above all to behold such visitations.

Since the acts of mankind most easily observed from a distance are A-bomb explosions, we should expect some relation to obtain between the time of A-bomb explosions, the time at which the space ships are seen, and the time required for such ships to arrive from and return to home base.[17]

Both Lipp and Valley suggested that our atomic explosions attracted them; Margaret Mead has still another idea:

The simplest—and the most likely—explanation of the coincidence of sightings and events on earth is our own growing awareness. With each increase in expectation of what human beings could invent to lift themselves off the surface of the earth, more people accepted the evidence of their own eyes when they saw unidentifiable objects crossing the sky. ... And what one man saw, others could accept with their own eyes.

That there are waves of "visits" by UFOs seems uncontestable. But that sightings are much more massive just when we are entering some new phase of space exploration may be due to our own heightened interest in and greater sophistication about what is possible.

The late Carl Jung, in his book *Flying Saucers*, published in 1959 ... neither rejected nor accepted the reality of UFOs. What he suggested was that there is *also* a psychological component—what he called a living myth or a visionary rumor that is potentially shared by all human beings in a period of great change and deep anxiety about the future. UFOs, he speculated, might be a world-wide visualized projection of this uneasy psychic state. But he also speculated that the two unknowns—UFOs and our human visualized projections—may simply "coincide in a meaningful manner."[18]

Is it possible that superintelligent beings have nurtured man along his evolutionary way, influencing our technological developments and our space-travel plans? For example, were we to take CE-III cases like *The Andreasson Affair* at full face value, we would find that:

1. UFO occupants have watched mankind since man became man.
2. They love mankind.
3. Some previous historical contacts were recorded by Biblical writers within a religious context.
4. There seems to be a connection between UFOs and Judeo-Christian tradition.
5. Mankind is currently being programmed for large-scale overt UFO contact.

Mrs. Andreasson reports being told that other human beings, like herself, had been abducted. In their subconscious minds had been implanted important information that would be revealed only at the "appointed time." The large influx of UFO activity, she was allegedly told, was preparation for overt contact with peoples of the earth. Such accounts seem unbelievable, yet so are many other now-accepted facets of the UFOs.

Even our straying astronauts are still connected by a technological umbilical cord to Mother Earth. Trapped by the fences of gravitation and life-supporting atmosphere, we have no place to go, no defense. We can either expand our minds and emotions through serious UFO study, or we can choose to dismiss them and go back to grazing and chewing our cuds. Regardless, we seem to be the object of intense attention, perhaps as potential candidates in an intergalactic community of other created beings.

Are we ready?

CHAPTER NOTES

1. E. U. Condon, director, *Scientific Study of Unidentified Flying Objects* (New York: E. P. Dutton & Co., Inc., 1969), p. 548.
2. Personal files.
3. "Opinion Poll Results," *Industrial Research/Development,* July 1979, pp. 139, 140.
4. J. M. McCampbell, *UFOlogy, New Insights from Science and Common Sense* (Belmont, California: Jaymac Co., 12 Bryce Court, Belmont, CA 94002, 1973).
5. J. B. Carlson and P. A. Sturrock, "Stanford Workshop on Extrater-

restrial Civilization: Opening a New Scientific Dialog," *Astronautics and Aeronautics,* June 1975, p. 63.

    6. *Idem*

    7. *Ibid.,* pp. 63, 64.

    8. "First Summary of the Work of the French Government's 'GEPAN' UFO Organization," *International UFO Reporter,* Vol. 3, No. 10/11, October/November 1978, p. 22.

    9. *loc. cit.*

    10. Personal files.

    11. Allan Hendry, "UFOs and Government: Domestic," *International UFO Reporter,* Vol. 4, No. 2, August 1979, pp. 7–9.

    12. "U.N. Background," International UFO Reporter, Vol. 3, No. 10/11, October/November 1978, p. 9.

    13. UN Press Release GA/AH/1479, November 27, 1978.

    14. J. A. Hynek, "Editorial," *International UFO Reporter,* Vol. 4, No. 2, August 1979, pp. 1, 16.

    15. "UFOs: Visitors from Outer Space?—September 1974" from *Aspects of the Present* by Margaret Mead and Rhoda Metraux. Copyright © 1980 by Mary Catherine Bateson Kassarjian and Rhoda Metraux. By permission of William Morrow & Co.

    16. J. F. Lipp, *Project Sign Technical Report No. F-TR-2274-IA, Appendix "D"* (Wright-Patterson AFB, Dayton, Ohio: AAF Air Material Command, February 1949), p. 29.

    17. *Ibid.* (Appendix "C"), p. 25.

    18. Mead and Metraux, *op. cit.*

SELECTED BIBLIOGRAPHY

Angelucci, O., *The Secret of the Saucers,* Amherst, Wisconsin: Amherst Press, 1955.

Astronautics and Aeronautics (November 1970 and June 1975).

Ayres, William H. (R. Ohio), A letter in possession of NICAP dated January 28, 1958.

Bethurum, Truman, *Aboard a Flying Saucer,* Los Angeles: De Vors and Company, 1954.

Carpenter, Donald G., Major, USAF, ed., *Introductory Space Science,* Volume II, USAF Academy, 1968.

Condon, E. U., director, *Scientific Study of Unidentified Flying Objects,* ed. Daniel S. Gillmor, New York: E. P. Dutton and Co., Inc., 1969.

Craig, Roy, A letter in my possession to Raymond E. Fowler dated at Boulder, Colorado, October 16, 1968.

Fowler, Raymond E., "Angel Hair—Spider's Web or UFO's Wisp?" *UFOlogy* (Fall 1976) 25–28.

Fowler, Raymond E., Personal files, UFO Report No. 66-26 A/B.

Fowler, Raymond E., *The Andreasson Affair,* New Jersey: Prentice-Hall, Inc., 1979.

Fowler, Raymond E., ed., *The MUFON Field Investigator's Manual,* Seguin, Texas: MUFON, 1975.

Fowler, Raymond E., *UFOs: Interplanetary Visitors,* New York: Exposition Press, Inc., 1974; New Jersey: Prentice-Hall, Inc., 1979; New York: Bantam, 1979.

Fry, Daniel, *Steps to the Stars,* El Monte, California: Understanding Publishing Company, 1956.

Fry, Daniel, *The White Sands Incident,* Los Angeles: New Age Publishing Company, 1954.

Fuller, John G., "Flying Saucer Fiasco," *Look*, Vol. 32, No. 10 (May 14, 1968), 58–63.

Fuller, John G., *Incident at Exeter,* New York: G. P. Putnam's Sons, 1966.

Gallup, George H. Jr., and Tom Reinken, "Who Believes in UFOs?" *Fate* (August 1974), 55.

Gelatt, Roland, "Flying Saucer Hoax," *Saturday Review of Literature* (December 6, 1952), 31.

Graham, Billy, *Angels: God's Secret Agents,* New York: Doubleday & Co., Inc., 1975.

Hall, Richard A., ed. *The UFO Evidence,* Washington, D.C., NICAP, 1964.

Hendry, Allan, *The UFO Handbook,* New York: Doubleday and Co., Inc., 1979.

Hynek, J. Allen, A letter in my possession to Raymond E. Fowler, dated at Evanston, Illinois, June 2, 1969.

Hynek, J. Allen, "UFOs," *The Christian Science Monitor* (April 22, 1970).

Hynek, J. Allen and Jacques Vallee, *The Edge of Reality,* Chicago: Henry Regnery Co., 1975.

Hynek, J. Allen, *The UFO Experience,* Chicago: Henry Regnery Co., 1972.

Industrial Research/Development (July 1979), 139, 140.

International UFO Reporter, Vol. 3, No. 10/11 (October/November 1978), 22 and Vol. 4, No. 2 (August 1979), 7–9.

Jacobs, David, *The UFO Controversy,* Indiana: Indiana University Press, 1975.

Karth, Joseph E. (D. Minnesota), A letter in possession of NICAP dated August 24, 1960.

Keyhoe, Donald E., *Aliens from Space,* New York: Doubleday & Co., Inc., 1973.

Keyhoe, Donald E., *Flying Saucers: Top Secret*, New York: G. P. Putnam's Sons, 1960.

Keyhoe, Donald E., *The Flying Saucers are Real,* New York: Fawcett Publications, Inc., 1950.

McCampbell, J. M., *UFOlogy, New Insights from Science and Common Sense,* Belmont, California: Jaymac Co., 12 Bryce Court, Belmont, CA 94002, 1973.

McDonald, James E., *UFOs: An International Problem* (Pamphlet), Presented March 12, 1968, at the Canadian Aeronautics and Space Institute Astronautics Symposium, Montreal, Canada.

McLaughlin, R. B., Commander, U.S.N., "How Scientists Tracked a Flying Saucer," *True* (March 1950), 28.

Mead, Margaret and Rhoda Metraux, "UFOs—Visitors from Outer Space?" from *Aspects of the Present,* New York, William Morrow & Company, Inc., 1980.

Menzel, Donald and Lyle G. Boyd, *The World of Flying Saucers,* New York: Doubleday & Co., Inc., 1963.

Michel, Aimé, *Flying Saucers and the Straight-Line Mystery,* New York: Criterion Books, 1958.

Nichols, Hank, "McCarthy's Pond Revisited," *New Hampshire Times,* Vol. 7, No. 16 (October 12, 1977), pp. 2–5.

Powers, William T., "Letters," *Science,* CLVI (April 7, 1967).

Project Sign Technical Report No. F-TR-2274-IA, Appendices "C" and "D," February 1949.

Rayle, Warren D., "Ball Lightning Characteristics," *NASA Technical Note D-3188,* p. 13.

Ruppelt, Edward J., *The Report on Unidentified Flying Objects,* New York: Doubleday & Co., Inc., 1956.

Santorini, Paul, A letter in my possession to Raymond E. Fowler, dated at Athens, Greece, August 6, 1973.

Saunders, David R. and Roger R. Harkins, *UFOs? Yes! Where the Condon Committee went wrong,* New York: World Publishing Company, 1968.

Shepard, Roger N., "Tornadoes: Puzzling Phenomena and Photographs," *Science,* CLV (January 6, 1967), 27.

Shklovskii, I. S. & Carl Sagan, *Intelligent Life in the Universe,* San Francisco: Holden Day, Inc., 1966.

Stanford, Ray, *Socorro "Saucer" in a Pentagon Pantry,* Austin, Texas: Blueapple Books, P.O. Box 5694, Austin TX 78763, 1976.

Stringfield, Leonard H., *The UFO Crash/Retrieval Syndrome,* Seguin, Texas: MUFON, 103 Oldtowne Road, Seguin, TX 78155, 1980.

Tazieff, Haroun, *When the Earth Trembles,* New York: Harcourt, Brace & World, Inc., 1966.

The UFO Investigator, Washington, D.C., NICAP (October 1967), 8.

UFOs: The Credibility Factor, Columbia House L-P Record, Rising Sun Music, Inc., 1975.

U.S. Congress, House of Representatives Armed Services Committee, *Unidentified Flying Objects Hearing,* 89th Congress, Second Session, April 5, 1966.

U.S. Congress, House of Representatives, Committee on Appropriations, *Hearings, Civil Supersonic Aircraft Development (SST),* 92nd Congress, First Session, March 1–4, 1971, pp. 587, 592.

Vallee, Jacques, *Anatomy of a Phenomenon,* Chicago: Henry Regnery Company, 1965.

Vallee, Jacques, *Challenge to Science,* Chicago: Henry Regnery Company, 1966.

Vallee, Jacques, "The Conspiracy Theory," *EASTWEST Journal*, Vol. 9, No. 2 (February 1979), 40.

Vallee, Jacques, *Passport to Magonia,* Chicago: Henry Regnery Co., 1969.

Vallee, Jacques, *The Invisible College,* New York: E. P. Dutton & Co., Inc., 1975.

Van Tassal, G. W., *I Rode in a Flying Saucer,* Los Angeles: New Age Publishing Co., 1952.

Webbe, Stephen, "Air Force Denies UFO Incident," *The Christian Science Monitor,* (December 5, 1973), 1.

Webbe, Stephen, "Mystery Object Stirs New Hampshire Folks," *The Christian Science Monitor* (July 30, 1974), 48.

Worden, Greg, "A UFO in Townshend? Something was there," *Brattleboro Reformer* (December 21, 1974), 1.

Zechel, Todd, "NI-CIA-AP or NICAP?" *Just Cause* (January 1979), 5–8.

Amesbury News, Amesbury, Massachusetts (October 6, 1965).

Bangor Daily News, Bangor, Maine (March 26, 1966).

Boston Herald, Boston, Massachusetts (April 24, 1967).

Haverhill Gazette, Haverhill, Massachusetts (October 27, 1965).

Milford Daily News, Massachusetts (June 26, 1978).

National Enquirer, Lantana, Florida (June 28, 1978).

Newburyport Daily News, Massachusetts (February 14, 17, and 18, 1976).

The New York Times, New York City, New York (August 1, 1952).

Salem Evening News, Salem, Massachusetts (July 7, 1947).

San Diego Evening Tribune, California (November 30, 1973).

INDEX